Kamikaze Diaries

Kamikaze Diaries

Reflections of Japanese Student Soldiers

Emiko Ohnuki-Tierney

The University of Chicago Press
Chicago and London

Emiko Ohnuki-Tierney is the William F. Vilas Research Professor in the Department of Anthropology at the University of Wisconsin–Madison. She has written a number of books in English and Japanese, including *Kamikaze, Cherry Blossoms, and Nationalisms: The Militarization of Aesthetics in Japanese History* (2002), also published by the University of Chicago Press.

The University of Chicago Press, Chicago 60637
The University of Chicago Press, Ltd., London
© 2006 by The University of Chicago
All rights reserved. Published 2006
Printed in the United States of America

15 14 13 12 11 10 09 08 07 06   1 2 3 4 5

ISBN: 0-226-61950-8 (cloth)

Library of Congress Cataloging-in-Publication Data

Ohnuki-Tierney, Emiko.
   Kamikaze diaries : reflections of Japanese student soldiers.
      p.   cm.
   Includes index.
   ISBN 0-226-61950-8 (cloth)
      1. World War, 1939–1945—Aerial operations, Japanese. 2. Kamikaze pilots—Diaries. 3. Japan. Kaigun. Kamikaze Tokubetsu Kōgekitai.   I. Title.
   D792.J3O265   2006
   940.54′49520922—dc22
   [B]
                                                         2005035596

This book is printed on acid-free paper.

May the reflections of these young men
whose lives were cut short
provide us with strength to fight against all wars

Contents

Acknowledgments *ix*
Author's Note *xi*
Preamble *xiii*

Introduction   *1*

CHAPTER 1   Sasaki Hachirō   *39*
             *"What is patriotism? . . . the killing of millions of people and
             depriving billions of people of basic human freedom . . . ?"*

CHAPTER 2   Hayashi Tadao   *71*
             "All will crumble / Japan will meet its finale."

CHAPTER 3   Takushima Norimitsu   *103*
             *"Why must we fight? We no longer have any purpose for
             fighting."*

CHAPTER 4   Matsunaga Shigeo and Matsunaga Tatsuki   *135*
             "War is another name for murder."

CHAPTER 5   Hayashi Ichizō   *163*
             "We are assigned the location of our death."

CHAPTER 6   Nakao Takenori   *185*
             "Am I to simply die without any meaning to my life?"

Notes *213*
References *219*
Index *225*

Photographs follow page 142

Acknowledgments

The idea for this book was originally proposed by the University of Chicago Press, which published my book *Kamikaze, Cherry Blossoms, and Nationalisms: The Militarization of Aesthetics in Japanese History.* I found the diaries left by highly intelligent young men who perished in a meaningless war so painful to read that without the sustained encouragement of my colleagues I would not have been able to complete the task. I gratefully acknowledge moral support extended by Martin Dworkin, Henry Rosovsky, Peter Spear, Peter Stansky, and Halliman Winsborough. I thank Norma Field for her suggestion for the book title, *Kamikaze Diaries.* Stephen Vlastos, Keith Hart, and Bruce Cumings offered their advice and comments on my discussion of the kamikaze metaphor and 9/11, now included in the preamble. David Brent's prodding rescued me from a most superficial reading of Kant's aesthetics. H. Mack Horton translated the poems of Teika through which Matsunaga Tatsuki expressed his innermost thoughts and which now are available in Horton's exquisite translation. My discussions with Kishi Toshimitsu have been invaluable, and he also located invaluable photos of wartime propaganda for me. Grey Osterud was indeed more than an editor extraordinaire, as she is known; her scholarly commentaries and antiwar moral stance quickly created a bond between us. Richard C. Miller offered his expert knowledge of European publications and music, in addition to his collegiality. Critical commentaries on various aspects of this project were offered by Kenji Tierney, who also located important publications and the illustrations that are used in this book. Elizabeth Branch Dyson was most helpful in offering me advice and facilitating the review process in such an efficient and pleasant way.

The lectures I gave on this subject were important opportunities for me to think about this project, and I thank the following host institutions, as well as the comments from the audiences: the American Academy of Arts and Sciences (Midwest Center); the University of Chicago; Durham University; the École des Hautes Études en Sciences Sociales, Paris; the University of California, Berkeley and Los Angeles; Harvard University; the University of Hong Kong; the International House of Japan; the University of Iowa; the University of Kansas; the London School of Economics; Middlebury College; Oxford University; the University of Pennsylvania; Seijō University; the University of Wisconsin; and Yale University.

Above all, I thank the siblings of these fallen soldiers, who, despite the pain they felt every time their brothers' memories were evoked, encouraged me and supplied me with invaluable material, including photos from their family albums: They are Sasaki Taizō, professor of physics at the University of Tokyo, Nakao Yoshitaka, professor at Seinan Gakuin University, and Umezawa Shōzō. Their discussions with me strengthened my resolve to complete this project. I express my gratitude to Kasuga Takeo, who gave me permission on September 8, 2000, to use his letter describing the night before the pilots took off (quoted in the Introduction).

I am most grateful to the William F. Vilas Trust Fund of the University of Wisconsin–Madison, whose generous support enabled me to complete this project in a timely fashion.

E. O.-T.

Because each student wrote his diary differently, I chose the best way to introduce a particular student, without imposing a uniform format for all the chapters. Always trying to follow a somewhat chronological order, I also used the themes as an organizational principle. The balance between the two differs from student to student. For example, for Sasaki Hachirō (chapter 1), the thematic arrangement received priority, whereas for others, more emphasis was placed on chronological sequence.

When dates were noted, I have included the date of the diary entry with the month, the day, and the year. Not all entries were dated; for undated entries I have noted the numbers of the pages where they appeared. The years are given using the secular English system of dating, with B.C.E. for "before the common era" and C.E. for "during the common era," since the Latin Christian forms, the Japanese forms used after the Meiji Restoration, with the fictional date of the enthronement of the so-called first emperor counted as the first year, and another Japanese system using the years of the emperor's reign are all religious-cum-political.

The days of the month are usually given according to Japanese time, which is a day ahead of the United States. For example, World War II ended on August 14 in Japan. The dates given in the diaries and letters are those given in the original writings or publications.

Unless otherwise indicated, all translations from the Japanese are my own. Words in brackets are my editorial insertions. The student soldiers frequently used foreign languages, including the titles of books, articles, and works of music. When I was sure of spelling errors, I simply noted the correct spelling. Given that this book is addressed primarily to English-speaking readers, the titles appear first in standard English translation, when available, followed by the titles in the original language in brackets.

I follow the Japanese convention for names, with the last name followed by the first name without a comma in between.

"How lonely is the sound of the clock in the darkness of the night" is the first line of a poem titled "Stillness," composed by Nakao Teketoku, a *tokkōtai* (kamikaze) pilot, on September 20, 1942. He perished at the age of twenty-two (see chapter 6). Student soldiers in their late teens to early twenties often grabbed the clock to stop it, since with every tick the hand was advancing toward their death. Inconceivable as it is today, well before they were drafted into the military these young men had been living in the shadow of imminent death because the Japanese state had managed to promote and inculcate in the minds of the people the idea that all the Japanese, but especially the soldiers-to-be, must sacrifice their lives for the country.

We begin with the voices of tokkōtai pilots and other student soldiers, whose diaries and reflections make up this book.

> I don't know if I am supposed to win this war but I will fight as much as I can, leaving my fate in your hands. . . . I pray that we will see the day as soon as possible when we welcome a world in which we do not have to kill enemies whom we cannot hate. For this end, I would not mind my body being ripped apart innumerable times. (Miyazawa Kenji, quoted by Sasaki Hachirō, November 10, 1943)

> There is some sign of a new ethos for a new era. However, even though the material foundation for the new era is already being built, we cannot help but notice the legacy of old capitalism. If the power of old capitalism is something we cannot get rid of

easily but if it can be crushed by defeat in war, we are turning the disaster into a fortunate event. We are now searching for something like a phoenix which rises out of ashes. Even if Japan gets defeated once or twice, as long as the Japanese survive, Japan will not be destroyed. It looks as though we are "a carp on the cutting board [*sojō no koi*]." I am not being pessimistic, but we cannot deny reality. We have to move on, overcoming the times of difficulty. (Sasaki Hachirō, May 14, 1943)

I do not want to die! . . . I want to live. No, I don't want to die. . . . I feel lonely. I don't know why I feel so lonely. (Hayashi Tadao, November 26, 1940)

The End of Imperial Japan

Ruining and crumbling
Decadence
Nothing will be left
The end of all; All will crumble
Japan will meet its finale
That taboo
Catastrophe

Hayashi Tadao, 1945

A Beautiful Illusion

Illusions in the letters from my comrades
Many beautiful illusions
All beings are born of illusion
And they all die into illusion. . . .
I sleep intoxicated by the beauty of amber-colored wine
Illusion of peace—no, we must not laugh

Matsunaga Shigeo, February 12, 1938

I dreaded death so much. And yet, it is already decided for us. . . .
    Mother, I still want to be loved and spoiled by you. . . . I want to be held in your arms and sleep. (Hayashi Ichizō, April 12, 1945)

These passages from the diaries of tokkōtai pilots do not fit the image of the "kamikaze" held outside of Japan. Many historical facts are tossed into the "dustbin of history," to use Walter Benjamin's well-known expression. But it is dangerous when a caricature entirely replaces a historical fact. In the United States especially, tokkōtai are called "kamikaze" with exclamation points, as in the film *Tora! Tora!* "The Kamikaze!!" became synonymous with reckless people, fanatical chauvinists, the inscrutable and untrustworthy "Other," and even "suicide bombers."

The continuing power of this image was intensified after 9/11, when the U.S. government and the American mass media misleadingly but persuasively framed the event with the twin metaphors of Pearl Harbor and the kamikaze. The aerial destruction of the World Trade Center in New York City was dubbed the "Homeland Attack," analogous to the opening of the Pacific front in World War II,[1] which was initiated by the Japanese air attack on the U.S. naval base at Pearl Harbor. The kamikaze became the Ur-model for suicide bombers.

The surprise attack was an important element of the parallel constructed after September 11, 2001. The 1941 attack was known in advance, since by 1941 Japan's imperial ambitions and military aggression were clearly visible across Asia. The Roosevelt administration knew by means of intelligence intercepts that a Japanese attack in the Pacific was imminent. Some historians claim that President Roosevelt waited for Japan to strike first because he knew that a surprise attack on American territory would be a powerful weapon to stir up popular patriotism to justify the entry of the United States into World War II.[2] Although this is a familiar tactic used by many states at the onset of a war, evidence for Roosevelt's knowledge of the precise timing and location is not strong enough to support this conclusion.

Prior to 9/11, anti-Americanism was rising all over the world, especially in the Middle East, and the White House ignored warnings given in August 2001 that al Qaeda was planning a terrorist strike in the United States. Moreover, the warnings that preceded 9/11 were much less specific as to the certainty, place, time and means of attack than were the warnings given prior to the Pearl Harbor attack.

Thus, in 1941, there was an attempt by the American government to make the Pearl Harbor attack seem a sudden attack, whereas in 2001 it was more of a surprise for the government and for the people. President George W. Bush, echoing Roosevelt, declared that the event marked a "Day of Infamy," and this echoed through American political discourse after 2001. "A surprise attack on our homeland" became a powerful weapon with which to stoke patriotism, which was then translated into support for militarism, especially the occupation of Iraq as part of the "war on terror." The mass media played a major role in propagating the parallel, as exemplified in the two-column visual presentation of it in the *New York Times* on December 8, 2001.

Except for this quasi similarity, these two events are not parallel: on December 7, 1941, one nation's military forces attacked those of another, whereas on September 11, 2001, individuals who did not represent a nation-state hijacked civilian airplanes and turned them into inconceivably powerful weapons against twin office towers filled with civilians, as well as the U.S. military headquarters at the Pentagon. International warfare conducted between state-organized military forces should be clearly distinguished from "terrorism" carried out by individuals and social groups. The Japanese pilots were uniformed members of the armed forces of a nation at war who had been drafted into their country's armed forces, not volunteers. They targeted military objectives, not civilians.

December 7, 1941, was not an attack on the American homeland. Hawaii was valuable to the United States primarily as a military outpost in the Pacific. Annexed in 1898 and declared a territory in 1900, Hawaii was not admitted to the Union until 1959. It was a marginal place, geographically, ethnically, and politically. The U.S. military base at Pearl Harbor was far from the American homeland and a far cry from the World Trade Center, whose twin towers were the symbolic center of American global power in the world economy, situated in none other than New York, arguably the most important city in the United States.

The carefully staged photograph of six marines raising the flag on Iwo Jima came to symbolize the valor of all American soldiers in "recapturing the American homeland." The dramatic finale of 9/11—New York firefighters lifting this sacred national symbol over the crumbled ruins of incinerated buildings at "Ground Zero"—was juxtaposed to the Iwo Jima photo. Like the marines, the firefighters "regained America," transforming tragedy into triumph. The capture of Iwo Jima by the marines was militarily significant, providing an airfield for refueling and enabling the Americans to bomb the Japanese homeland far more effectively. It also prevented the Japanese from turning the tide for good. Yet that tiny, remote island was not the homeland for either the Japanese or the Americans.[3]

Another element of the false analogy between 9/11 and the events of World War II is the rhetorical parallel made between suicide bombers and kamikaze. *Suicide bombers* is a term used to refer to a wide variety of individuals around the globe about whom we have little information. I provide a more comprehensive comparison at the end of the introduction, but here let me briefly point to the basic differences between the two. First, the tokkōtai pilots did not commit suicide. In 1941, at the time of the Pearl Harbor attack, the missions were flown with planes fully equipped to return to waiting submarines. The pilots were killed when their planes were shot down. And those pilots flying in 1944 and 1945—the exclusive focus of this book—were not suicide bombers. They were sent on bombing missions in planes not equipped to return, but they did not volunteer in the same way the contemporary suicide bombers do. Thus, in both cases tokkōtai pilots did not commit suicide; they were killed in action. In sharp contrast, contemporary suicide bombers are civilians who consciously volunteer to die by turning themselves into weapons.

The purpose of my argument so far is not to condone or make excuses for Japanese military aggression, including the Pearl Harbor attack, which has been condemned not only by Americans but also by the Japanese. Its aim is to warn against the "staying power of this flawed and disturbing analogy," which has promoted "flawed thinking" for the interpretation of the 2001 incident (Cumings 2001).

As the lives and writings of tokkōtai pilots show, their desperate struggles to find meaning in a fate they could not avoid bear no resemblance to those of anyone seeking martyrdom. This is so despite the Japanese government's sustained propaganda campaign to apotheosize those fallen soldiers into symbols of martyrdom for the imperial nation. This book sets aside the nationalist myths that governments on both sides of the war have constructed and places the tokkōtai pilots in historical context and makes their voices and thoughts available to contemporary Americans, Japanese, and others in order to introduce the human beings and the anguished voices behind the caricature.

Before 2001, I undertook the translation and interpretation of the writings of tokkōtai pilots as part of a larger study of military ideology in imperial Japan. My 2002 book *Kamikaze, Cherry Blossoms, and Nationalisms: The Militarization of Aesthetics in Japanese History* traced the Meiji government's propagation of its imperial ideology and promotion of its aggressive militarism by means of the deployment—and manipulation—of key cultural symbols of the land and people of Japan. I use the term *ideology* to refer to ideas that are deployed for the exercise of power (compare Wolf 1999, 4). That work centered on the ways in which war and death were aestheticized by the uses of cherry blossoms in the state's attempt to persuade citizens to sacrifice their lives to nationalist and imperialist goals. Many readers responded to the chapter in which I introduced the diaries of four young tokkōtai pilots to show how different they were from the Western image of "kamikaze." Readers on several continents asked for more first-hand sources that would offer insight into the thoughts of these young men, and I produced this book in response to those requests. Using the diaries, letters, and essays they left behind, I tried to describe and understand their personal lives as well as their intellectual and political perspectives and to portray them as human beings in painful agony regarding the inevitable early death they faced because they had the ill fortune of being born and reaching adulthood at the darkest period in Japanese history. Given the deeply engraved and distorted image of kamikaze outside of Japan, I use the military term *tokkōtai*, or "special attack force."

The project for my 2002 book began as a study of symbolic communication using cherry-blossom viewing (*hanami*) in Japan as an example. For some time after I began that project, I did not know that Japan's successive military governments extensively used the beauty of the flower to make their operations acceptable to the people. The project became the most difficult one I had undertaken, not only because of its enormous scope, but also because it was psychologically taxing; I could hardly read the diaries without being deeply affected by the writers' cries of agony, on the one hand, and their minds, which sought the height of intellectual development, on the other. I was sustained by my admiration for these young men, and by the rage I felt against the forces that terminated their short lives. I began to feel compelled to introduce their voices in the hope that such a colossal tragedy would not happen again in Japan or elsewhere.

The writings left behind by tokkōtai pilots and other student soldiers who perished in the futile military operations conducted by the Japanese at the end of World War II yield stunning and profound insights into the position and consciousness of young soldiers under the extreme conditions of modern warfare. In order to understand their thoughts and dilemmas, we need to analyze the circumstances of the war in which the young men were placed and explore the broader intellectual currents that provided them with spiritual resources as they faced their deaths.

Toward the end of World War II, when an American invasion of Japan's homeland seemed imminent, Ōnishi Takijirō, a navy vice-admiral, invented the tokkōtai ("Special Attack Force") operation, which included airplanes, gliders, and submarine torpedoes (for details, see Ohnuki-Tierney 2002, 157–75). None of these manned weapons systems was equipped with any means of returning to base. Ōnishi and his right-hand men thought that the Japanese soul, which was believed to uniquely possess the strength to face death without hesitation, was the only means available for the Japanese to bring about a miracle and save their homeland, which was surrounded by American aircraft carriers whose sophisticated radar systems protected them from being destroyed by any other means. When the operation was instituted in October 1944, not a single officer who had been trained at the military academies volunteered to sortie as a pilot; all knew too well that it was a meaningless mission ending in death. Of the approximately four thousand tokkōtai pilots, about three thousand were so-called boy pilots, who were drawn from among newly conscripted and enlisted soldiers who were enrolled in a special program aimed at training very young boys. Roughly one thousand were "student soldiers," university students whom the government graduated early in order to include them in the draft.

The writings left behind by the student soldiers who died in the tokkōtai operation provide invaluable testimony to these young men's struggle to sustain their connections to the rest of humanity amid the wrenching conditions of war and to find meaning in a death they felt was decreed for them. Unfortunately, the boy pilots who faced the same fate left virtually no diaries or comparable records behind. The student soldiers who perished left a substantial body of handwritten documents expressing their thoughts and feelings: diaries, soliloquies, essays, poems, and letters. These extraordinarily well-educated youths were reflective and cosmopolitan. They drew on their knowledge of philosophy and world history as they tried to understand the situation in which they inadvertently but inescapably found themselves amid the global conflagration. Many of the student soldiers were political liberals, even radicals. They were most unlikely to volunteer as tokkōtai pilots and are therefore excellent test cases. I decided to examine their diaries in order to understand why even the most liberal of them replicated the military ideology *in action* by becoming tokkōtai pilots and to ascertain whether and to what degree they came to embrace the ideology of sacrifice for the imperial nation that was inculcated by the Japanese state.

The diaries of fallen student soldiers, including tokkōtai pilots and other student soldiers who perished in combat, were initially introduced to the general public in edited collections of their writings. The first volume (Tōkyō Daigaku Gakusei Jichikai and Senbotsu Gakusei Shuki Henshū Iinkai 1947) has a preface by Nanbara Shigeru, the president of the University of Tokyo, which lost the highest number of students in the war. Although such works made student soldiers' writings known beyond the small circle of their families and friends, they were not comprehensive or representative. They are extremely selective in their choices of material to include, with short excerpts from writings by many student soldiers, reflecting the biases of the editors, and they cannot readily be checked against the full corpus of the writings the authors left behind. Single volumes dedicated to the writings of individual students over a long period of time are the most reliable sources for their thoughts (for a critical assessment of sources, see Ohnuki-Tierney 2002, 187–91). I have focused on six such books: five devoted to a single student and the sixth to two brothers. They were edited by surviving family members or close friends.

Some diary entries have been left out of even these volumes, but when we have a large corpus of writing these omissions are not as problematic as when only a few entries have been selected for inclusion. Diaries spanning many years are important, since the years spent at higher schools and universities are crucial for understanding the gradual process whereby these young men struggled and came to terms with the path to death.

The amazingly lengthy diaries left by these young men evince the importance of writing as a mode of communication in Japanese life. In a culture in which verbal communication in the form of debates, dialogues, or oratory is not well developed, writing is the most serious mode of communication, and many individuals express their innermost thoughts and feelings in written form. Diary-keeping has been an important cultural practice in Japan ever since the Heian period, when the diary developed into a special genre of literature, and some diaries, including those written by women, became world classics.[1] The sheer quantity of writings left by these student soldiers is in part the result of this persistent cultural practice, which was extended to the "reading diary" required informally at the higher schools. These young men were exceptionally well educated, and reading and writing were their major daily activities. The particular situation these students faced in wartime, however, also made a difference: the diary became an important means by which they struggled to understand and come to terms with the imminent death they faced.

The seven diaries I have chosen to include in this book were kept by Sasaki Hachirō, Hayashi Tadao, Takushima Norimitsu, the brothers Matsunaga Shigeo and Matsunaga Tatsuki, Hayashi Ichizō, and Nakao Takenori. Sasaki, Hayashi Tadao, Hayashi Ichizō, and Nakao were briefly introduced in chapter 6 of my book *Kamikaze, Cherry Blossoms, and Nationalisms: The Militarization of Aesthetics in Japanese History* (2002). In that book I also introduced the diary of Wada Minoru, a tokkōtai torpedo pilot who died of suffocation when during a test operation his torpedo sank to the bottom of the sea because of a mechanical malfunction. For reasons of space I decided not to include his diary in this work.

THE TOKKŌTAI OPERATION:
RECRUITMENT OF STUDENT SOLDIERS

These university students were drafted after the Tōjō government, acting twice in quick succession, shortened the length of a university education. Once on the base, many were subjected to harsh corporal punishment on a daily basis. Some had been patriotic before they were drafted, but life on the base extinguished any enthusiasm for fighting—or for anything else, for that matter. They had already reached the point of no return. By the time they were drafted, Japan's defeat was imminent. They had been dropped onto a malfunctioning rollercoaster fast descending toward a fatal crash, as it were, without the ability to either stop or safely ascend and go around again.

The Japanese military tradition had a distinctive, almost unique element. Whereas German soldiers were told to *kill,* Japanese soldiers were told to *die.* The cruel character of the Japanese military is evident from the beginning of its modernization at the end of the nineteenth century. In the military code for the imperial navy and army (*Kairikugun Keiritsu*), issued in 1872, surrender, escape, and all other actions by which soldiers might save their lives in situations of unavoidable defeat were punishable by death (Yui, Fujiwara, and Yoshida 1989 [1996], 180–99). The system made no allowance for conscientious objectors. Any soldier who would not obey military rules and his commander's orders was shot on the spot, without a charge against the one who shot him. Furthermore, people feared that such an offense by a soldier would lead to the punishment of his immediate and extended family members, just as during the Edo period the government warned that "crime extends to five generations and punishment to five affinal relationships" (*tsumi godai ni oyobi batsu gozoku ni wataru*)—that is, the punishment of a large number of people related to him by blood and marriage (Irokawa 2003, 160–61; Oguma 2002, 33). These rules were intended to hold an entire kin group responsible for the actions of an individual and, thus, to reinforce the social pressure on soldiers to obey orders. In practice the system suppressed complaints by soldiers' parents and made soldiers fearful of committing any violation, let alone defection. As the military government turned Japan into a police state, all those who refused to comply with its orders were jailed. By the 1940s, many had been tortured to death, decimating the ranks of known dissidents and deterring others from expressing any opinions that might be considered hostile to the state. In Japan, the military government left no room for political or guerrilla resistance movements like those in Germany, France, and other countries ruled or occupied by fascists.[2]

Nowhere was the basic stance of the Japanese military more conspicuously played out than during World War II. Even when entire corps of Japanese soldiers faced utterly hopeless military situations, the soldiers were told to die happily. This policy led to the infamous mass suicides (*gyokusai*) on Attu, Saipan, and Okinawa Islands and elsewhere and culminated in the tokkōtai operation. Conditions on the military bases gave these young men little chance to opt for life in any case. According to

Irokawa Daikichi, an eminent historian who was drafted from the University of Tokyo as a student soldier and spent time at the Tsuchiura Naval Base, the first lesson a student soldier like him was taught was how to use his own rifle to kill himself rather than be captured alive. Each new conscript was trained to use his toe to pull the trigger while pointing the gun precisely at a certain point under his chin so that the bullet would kill him instantly. He was supposed to use this technique if he was trapped in a cave or in a trench surrounded by the enemy. If he did not kill himself but tried to escape, he might be shot from behind, because his superiors and some comrades believed in the state dictum that one must never be captured by the enemy. In sum, once a youth was drafted, he had reached a point of no return—a powerless position that many soldiers recognized for what it was (Irokawa, pers. comm., May 20, 1999).

Noma Hiroshi depicted Japanese military life in his 1972 novel *Zone of Emptiness*. Although some officers were kind to student soldiers, many acted harshly toward them. Some commanding officers believed in the idea that corporal punishment developed the soldiers' spirit, while others maltreated them only to inflict punishment. Student soldiers were often targeted by professional soldiers who had risen through the ranks and resented the privileged backgrounds that enabled them to study when others could not afford to receive a higher education.[3] Any minor action that irritated a superior could be a cause for corporal punishment, not only of the individual involved but also of his entire group. Irokawa (1993, 54; see also 48) offers a vivid description of the "living hell" that awaited the student soldiers:

After I passed the gate to the Tsuchiura Naval Air Base, "training" took place day after day. I was struck on the face so hard and frequently that my face was no longer recognizable. On January 2, 1945, Kaneko (Ensign) hit my face twenty times and the inside of my mouth was cut in many places by my teeth. I had been looking forward to eating *zōni* [a special dish with rice cakes for the New Year]. Instead, I was swallowing blood from the inside of my mouth. On February 14, all of us were punished because they suspected that we ate at farmers' homes near the base to ease our hunger. In the midst of the cold winter, we were forced to sit for seven hours on a cold concrete floor and they hit us on the buttocks with a club. Then each of us was called into the officer's room. When my turn came, as soon as I entered the room, I was hit so hard that I could no longer see and fell on the floor. The minute I got up, I was hit again by a club so that I would confess. A friend of mine was thrown with his head first to the floor, lost consciousness, and was sent to a hospital. He never returned. All this savagery was orchestrated by the corps commander named Tsutsui. I am still looking for this fellow.

Irokawa's experiences were all too common. The Tsuchiura Naval Air Base was especially notorious in this respect. Sasaki, Hayashi Tadao, and Nakao were stationed there, and their diaries record senseless punishments and mental and physical suffering inflicted on their fellow soldiers.

Hayashi Tadao and others reported that the strict enforcement of petty regulations, including extreme censorship and the taboo against almost any book, dampened young men's willingness to work for the causes advocated by the military, including sacrifice for the emperor. Irokawa Daikichi wrote:

> Memorizing and reciting the *Imperial Rescript to Soldiers* (*Gunjin Chokuyu*) of 1882, written in archaic language, were a daily exercise. If we failed in the accurate recitation of the *Rescript*, we were hit to the ground, as I experienced personally. It would be hard to estimate how many soldiers in fact became alienated from the emperor and imperial ideology by "lynching." (Pers. comm., May 13, 2003)

Irokawa's analogy to lynching is deliberate, highlighting the severe, possibly fatal punishment of any soldier who refused to comply with every demand of his superiors.

The rescript contained a now-infamous passage: "Do not be beguiled by popular opinions, do not get involved in political activities, but singularly devote yourself to your most important obligation of loyalty to the emperor, and realize that *the obligation is heavier than the mountains but death is lighter than a feather*" (Yui, Fujiwara, and Yoshida 1989 [1996], 174; emphasis added).

Their diaries show that almost all these young men, including those who had previously expressed their desire to protect their "ancestral land," became less patriotic while they trained on the base and as they approached their death.

BEING "VOLUNTEERED" TO BECOME TOKKŌTAI PILOTS

Because the tokkōtai operation was a guarantee of death, the top military officers, quite hypocritically, decided not to make this operation an official part of the imperial navy or army, where orders were issued in the name of the emperor (Morioka 1995, 6; Oguma 2002, 31–32). They preferred to make it appear that the corps was formed voluntarily and that men volunteered to be pilots.

In most instances, all the members of a military corps were summoned to a hall. After a lecture on the virtues of patriotism and sacrifice for the emperor and Japan, they were told to step forward if they were willing to volunteer to be tokkōtai pilots. Sometimes this process was done in reverse: men were told to step forward if they did *not* want to be pilots. It would have been extremely difficult, if not impossible, for any soldier to stay behind or to step forward when all or most of his comrades were "volunteering." Sometimes the officer in charge went through a ritual of blindfolding the young men—a gesture ostensibly intended to minimize peer pressure—and asking them to raise their hands to volunteer. But the rustling sounds made by the uniforms as the men raised their hands made it obvious that many did so, leaving those who hesitated without any choice (Hattori, pers. comm., May 18, 1999). For example, Yamada Ryū, who after the war belonged to the Anabaptist Church and devoted his life to its ministry in Kyūshū, was "forced to volunteer to be a pilot for the inhumane tokkōtai operation" (Yamada Ryū 1997).

Coercion from above was complemented by solidarity among soldiers. The writings that tokkōtai pilots left behind reveal that they did not resist volunteering simply because of peer pressure but because they could not bear to protect their own lives while seeing their comrades and friends offering theirs. Admiration of those who had already gone on the fatal missions frequently appears in pilots' writings. Ichijima Yasuo, who was born in 1922 and died as a navy ensign on April 29, 1945, was a graduate of Waseda University.[4] In a letter to a friend, he quotes a well-known poem by Ryōkan (1758–1831)—"Falling cherry blossoms, remaining cherry blossoms also be falling cherry blossoms" (Kaigun Hikō Yobi Gakusei Dai-14-kikai 1966a, 124), implying that as the other pilots had fallen, so would he. Ichijima's admiration for the pilots who had already perished contributed significantly to his thinking when he sought to rationalize his death as he contemplated his own mission. Ichijima was a devout Christian who belonged to the well-known "Cherry Blossom Church" (Morioka 1995, 72–73). He expressed his willingness to serve his country but did not mention the emperor (Morioka 1995, 67). It was extremely difficult for a soldier to seek to spare himself, to claim an exemption from the fate of his comrades. The determination to combat the egotism brought forth by capitalism and modernity was a major element of the students' idealism. The tactic of asking men to volunteer may very well have been based on a calculated appeal to young soldiers' moral principles and comradeship.

Furthermore, if a soldier had managed to be courageous enough not to volunteer, he would have been consigned to a living hell. Any soldier who refused would become persona non grata or be sent to the southern battlefield, where death was guaranteed. Some soldiers actually managed to say no, but their refusal was disregarded. Kuroda Kenjirō decided not to volunteer, only to be taken by surprise when he found his name on the list of volunteers for the Mitate Navy tokkōtai corps; his superior had reported proudly that all the members of his corps had volunteered (Kōdansha Sōgō Hensankyoku 1997, 5).

After the pilots were selected, the officer in charge of a particular corps decided who should go on the missions and in what order they would depart. Irokawa (pers. comm., May 20, 1999) and other former soldiers explain that family background and other forms of privilege kept some pilots from being chosen. Sons of important political or military officials and prominent businessmen, along with members of the royal family, would volunteer without ever being selected to fly to their deaths.[5] As a bow to the system of primogeniture, the oldest son or an only son was often spared so that he could take care of his parents. On the other hand, soldiers who had mechanical, navigational, and other skills essential for pilots were favored for selection. Someone who was seen to be physically fit was put under more pressure to volunteer. The editor of Sasaki's diary maintains that he was designated to fly because he was small but athletic (Fujishiro pers. comm., May 25, 2003). The criteria for selection were never disclosed publicly (Umezawa Shōzō, pers. comm., June 20, 1999).

Sometimes merely being disliked by the superior in charge of the corps was fatal. In the case of navy lieutenant Fujii Masaharu, a student soldier, the officer was irritated by Fujii's habit of sitting in a corner of the room staring into the void without saying a word. He "tapped" Fujii's shoulder and told him to lead the tokkōtai corps, despite the fact that no officers above the rank of lieutenant and lieutenant junior grade who were graduates of the Naval Academy were sent on tokkōtai missions. Fujii was speechless and thought it was an "act of murder under the disguise of a military order." Realizing that he had no choice, however, he sarcastically told the pilots in his corps: "Let's bite into the ground of Okinawa together" (Misa n.d., 29–31).

All along the way, but especially on the military base, student soldiers' minds and hearts were torn by agonizing conflict more intense than their or my words can express. For many student soldiers, it was psychologically easier to become tokkōtai pilots when they knew that, with Japan's defeat in sight, their lives were in extreme danger no matter what course of action they took (Irokawa 1993, 3). As some of them put it, if one was likely to die anyway, one might as well die a hero. Yet agony over their approaching death is evident throughout their writings and in their final diary entries. It also appears in their responses to psychological questionnaires administered in late May 1945, two months after the battle for Okinawa had started. In their answers, one-third of the members of the tokkōtai unit of the Sixth Army Air Force Corps remained undecided about the mission and felt conflicted about it despite its inevitability (Ikuta Makoto 1977, 210, cited in Ninagawa 1998, 130–31). Some pilots were so tormented by thoughts of their imminent death that they prayed that the time would come as soon as possible in order to terminate their agony, as we will see repeatedly below.

By June 1945, according to Irokawa (2003, 165), there was an atmosphere of defeat on the tokkōtai base during the last stage of the battle of Okinawa. No one sang patriotic songs such as "The Cherry Blossoms of the Same Year," the navy cadet song that was once enormously popular among soldiers. Instead, the song that was most frequently sung and that touched the hearts of the soldiers was a lullaby from Itsuki, in Kumamoto Prefecture, Kyūshū, called "Lullaby from Itsuki" ("Itsuki no Komoriuta"). The text, in the Kumamoto dialect, portrays the depth of the sadness of a small girl who was forced to take care of young children far from home. The verses that follow express a nostalgic longing for home and for death as an end to exile:

> I long for the day I can return to my beloved parents when my service is
>   over.
> I am here far away from home. Even when I die, no one will cry for me;
>   how lonely it is only to hear cicadas cry.
> No one will come to visit my tomb. Then, I am better off buried along the
>   road,
>   since someone might offer flowers.
> I don't care which flowers they offer. Perhaps camellia blooming in the wild
>   along
>   the road? No water is necessary, since it will rain.

The Night Before the Final Flight

Despite the numerous published testaments, photographs, and films that depict smiling pilots saluting or waving goodbye as they take off on their final mission, a rare description of the night before departure tells a very different story. It occurs in a letter written on June 21, 1995, by Kasuga Takeo, who was eighty-six years old at the time, addressed to Umezawa Shōzō. Kasuga was drafted and assigned to look after the meals, laundry, room cleaning, and other daily tasks for the tokkōtai pilots at the Tsuchiura Naval Air Base. He describes the night before their final flights:

> At the hall where their farewell parties were held, the young student officers drank cold sake the night before their flight. Some gulped the sake in

one swallow; others kept gulping down [a large amount]. The whole place turned to mayhem. Some broke hanging light bulbs with their swords. Some lifted chairs to break the windows and tore white tablecloths. A mixture of military songs and curses filled the air. While some shouted in rage, others cried aloud. It was their last night of life. They thought of their parents, their faces and images, lovers' faces and their smiles, a sad farewell to their fiancées—all went through their minds like a running-horse lantern [a rapidly revolving lantern with many pictures on it]. Although they were supposedly ready to sacrifice their precious youth the next morning for imperial Japan and for the emperor, they were torn beyond what words can express—some putting their heads on the table, some writing their wills, some folding their hands in meditation, some leaving the hall, and some dancing in a frenzy while breaking flower vases. They all took off wearing the rising sun headband the next morning. But this scene of utter desperation has hardly been reported. I observed it with my own eyes, as I took care of their daily life, which consisted of incredibly strenuous training, coupled with cruel and torturous corporal punishment as a daily routine.

Kasuga Takeo never fully recovered from the innumerable beatings he received on the base. His superiors told him that corporal punishment would instill a "soldier's fighting spirit" in him. His letter is invaluable for its description of how desperate the pilots felt the night before their death.

The tokkōtai pilots were supposed to die. From the time they received their assignment, they no longer belonged to this world. They could not return even if they were unable to locate the enemy. A graduate of Waseda University who kept returning without finding an enemy to attack was shot to death the ninth time he came back. Many pilots did not try to ram into an American vessel because that guaranteed an explosion. Some tried to land on water near the shore instead (Fujishiro Hajime, pers. comm., May 25, 2003). It was also reported that, after taking off, some returned and buzzed the officers' quarters as if to dive into them before they disappeared in the sky (Oguma 2002, 33).

Tokkōtai pilots were like the Roman soldiers mentioned in Horace's ode. In the full text (Horace 1997, 161), Horace's famous phrase *pro patria mori* is followed by a warning:

Sweet and proper it is to die for your country,
But Death would just as soon come after him
Who runs away; Death gets him by the backs
Of his fleeting knees and jumps him from behind.

The soldiers had reached a point of no return.

The diaries of these young men offer eloquent testimony that contradicts both the stereotype held outside of Japan and the propaganda circulated by the Japanese military: that tokkōtai pilots died happily for the emperor (Inoguchi, and Nakajima 1953; Ugaki 1991). Some, like Sasaki Hachirō and Hayashi Tadao, rejected and defied the emperor-centered ideology outright. Others tried to accept it but were unable to do so. As Hayashi Ichizō put it: "There must be some peace of mind for dedicating my life to the emperor. . . . To be honest, I cannot say that the wish to die for the emperor is genuine, coming from my heart. However, it is decided for me that I die for the emperor."

Having no choice except to go through with their assigned mission, the tokkōtai pilots reproduced the imperial ideology in action while refusing or failing to embrace it in thought.

COSMOPOLITAN INTELLECTUALS AS PILOTS

A brief description of higher education in prewar Japan is presented here in order to demonstrate that the formidable intellectual level reached by the student soldiers whose writings are presented in this book was not exceptional but represents the norm for this elite group. At that time, those who went to higher schools and universities were the intellectual crème de la crème of Japan. They took Descartes' thesis *Cogito ergo sum* as their motto. They had passed extremely difficult examinations for entrance to the higher schools and then to the nation's top universities. The formal curriculum and the informal education they received in their dormitories from the seniors at these institutions were extremely demanding and thoroughly cosmopolitan.

Higher Schools in Prewar Japan

In 1886 a government decree established the imperial universities, teachers' schools (*shihan gakkō*), and elementary and middle schools. In 1894 the five most advanced middle schools, established in 1886, were redesignated as higher schools. The establishment of a women's high school was decreed in 1899.

By the early 1920s the number of higher schools for men had reached thirty-two. The entrance examinations were fiercely competitive, but the students' success was based strictly on their ability, not on the wealth or pedigree of their families. The higher schools were designed to create the future elites of Japan. The men were housed in dormitories so that they would be nurtured by the total campus culture rather than merely by their classroom instruction. The First Higher School in Tokyo had four dormitories with a total of 109 rooms housing two or three students each (Fujishiro 1981, 49). Graduation from these higher schools often guaranteed entrance to the prestigious imperial universities, although some opted for top private universities, such as Keiō and Waseda. The Imperial University of Tokyo was founded in 1886 and the Imperial University of Kyoto was established in 1897; seven more imperial universities had been set up by the onset of World War II.

At the First Higher School, each entering class numbered 380 members until 1931. This total was reduced to 350 in 1932 and 1933 and to 300 in 1934, when the Ministry of Education reacted to left-wing movements among the students. In 1939 the ministry increased the number to 400 (200 in the humanities and 200 in the sciences) because by that time the authorities figured that students' political activism had subsided (Fujishiro 1981, 49). Perhaps, as Irokawa points out (pers. comm., May 20, 2003), the dissidents were all in jail by then.

During the three years that students spent at the higher schools, they received a cosmopolitan education. Two foreign languages, in addition to classical Latin, were required; English, German, and French were offered. This component of the curriculum was so central that students were grouped into different categories depending on their choice of first and second foreign languages. At the Second Higher School, students who chose German as their foreign language (after the required Latin) were told during the first class to read Goethe's *Die Leiden des jungen Werthers* (*The Sorrows of Young Werther*) in the original German—without being taught the roman alphabet first. Foreign language classes met for more than ten hours per week. Students learned how to read and write very efficiently (Irokawa 2003, 162).

The cosmopolitan character of higher education was not confined to the formal curriculum but was also a product of peer influence. The rite of passage required of incoming students at the Second Higher School was reading Kant's *Critique of Pure Reason*. Freshmen found it impossible to understand this work, no matter how many times they reread it. The task was intended to make them realize how ignorant they were and how hard they must study. In the dormitory, the new students were told by their seniors to read the entirety of *Iwanami Bunko,* a well-known series of world classics in philosophy, literature, history, art, music, and religion (Irokawa 2003, 163). This "pocket book series" was inaugurated in 1927 by Iwanami Shigeo, founder of Iwanami Publishers, after the model of the Reclam series in Germany, which Iwanami had read with passionate engagement. A graduate of the First Higher School and the University of Tokyo, where he majored in philosophy, Iwanami followed the motto of the Japanese philosopher Miki Kiyoshi: "Truth be sought by all and art be loved by all." The first series included about thirty books, including a translation of Kant's *Kritik der praktischen Vernunft* (*Critique of Practical Reason*), Jules Henri Poincaré's *La Science et l'hypothèse* (*Science and Hypothesis*), Adam Smith's *The Wealth of Nations,* Tolstoy's *War and Peace,* and Chekhov's *Uncle Vanya,* as well as Chinese and Japanese literature (Okano 1979 [1995]). The newcomers were told by the seniors in the dormitory to keep a "reading diary" in which they recorded and reflected on what they read. The completion of a book per day was the minimum expectation.

Philosophy and literature were at the core of the curriculum, no matter what a student's major was. Irokawa recalls that when he was a first-year student at the Second Higher School he packed his rucksack with an anthology of Nietzsche but could not crack it. The rucksack became a pillow for his nap, and he returned the book to the library. He tried to read Nietzsche's *Also sprach Zarathustra,* which many of his peers treated like a Bible, in German, but he found the aphorisms extremely difficult (Irokawa, pers. comm., June 3, 2003).

Students discovered how ignorant they were and set a cosmopolitan intellectual horizon as their goal. They aspired to the height of intellectual achievement in the Western and the Asian traditions. These traditions were defined inclusively: Western civilization encompassed the ancient Greek and Roman classics and modern works from western, central, and eastern Europe, including Russia; Asian civilization encompassed India, China, and Japan from the classical period to the present. Students majoring in law or economics read philosophy; the discipline's centrality to the curriculum was assumed. All students were expected to engage in broad and deep intellectual inquiry. The drinking song used at the higher schools was "Dekansho," whose title was an abbreviation of "Descartes, Kant, and Schopenhauer"; this song became so popular that it continued to be sung at universities well into the postwar period.

Music held a significant place in student life. In the dormitory, students heard solo concerts as well as orchestral performances, and they went to see operas in the cities. Some of the student pilots were accomplished musicians. Wada Minoru, the torpedo pilot, was an accomplished violinist. He was the concertmaster in the orchestra at the First Higher School (Wada Tan 1972, 312). Dormitories at the higher schools housed large collections of recordings to which the students could listen at any time. In contrast to their reading, which included many Japanese works, their music was decisively Western. Hardly any students practiced or listened to Japanese music, although the kabuki theater with its accompanying *shamisen* music must have been popular. Sports were equally important. Many students eagerly joined clubs for participating in kendō (fencing), jūdō, karate, swimming, and hiking or mountain climbing. At many higher schools and universities, club members forged close bonds that lasted long after graduation.

When these young men were at the higher schools, Japan's militarism had reached its height. Suzuki Kurazō, an army officer dubbed "little Himmler" after Heinrich Himmler, the Nazi SS leader and chief of the German police during the Third Reich, orchestrated the strict control of speech (Satō 2004). Anyone who protested against the government or showed any sign of dissenting from the prevailing ideology was expelled and jailed. The campuses of the higher schools and universities were supposedly self-governing bodies, and they tried their best to maintain freedom of thought. Irokawa recalls that some students read Marxist literature, which had long been banned; they hid the books above the beams of the ceiling in the dormitory (pers. comm., June 3, 2003).

Although an ivory tower atmosphere prevailed on campus, students were sensitive to political movements outside of Japan, including the rise of German fascism, anti-Semitism, and Jewish Zionism (Irokawa 2003, 162). Nakao and the Matsunaga brothers were troubled by the Dreyfus Affair in France. Sasaki and Hayashi Ichizō expressed serious concern about the civilian casualties that resulted from the Japanese invasion of other Asian countries. The campaign began with the Manchurian Incident of 1931, the establishment of the puppet state of Manchukuo in 1932, and the Shanghai Incident of that same year (Young 1998). Throughout the 1930s, as the elder Matsunaga brother's writings reveal, the war in Asia had claimed many casualties among Japanese soldiers and among Korean and Chinese soldiers and civilians. In April 1939, when it rained as constantly as it did during the rainy season, which in most years comes only in June, students at the First Higher School began to talk about the ghosts of the Chinese punishing the Japanese by causing natural catastrophes (Fujishiro 1981, 5). These young men's awareness of the continuing march of Japan's imperial militarism and of their approaching death is evident even in the writings of the Matsunaga brothers, who attended Kokugakuin University in Tokyo, which was more conservative than the imperial universities.

The appetite with which these students devoured books and the fervor with which they tested their youthful bodies in sports and mountain climbing testify to their determination to live intensely instead of waiting for death (Irokawa 2003, 163). They knew that death was already waiting for them around the corner and that they could not escape their fate. In each and every diary, students who were not yet soldiers expressed their realization of the imminence of death. They all asked themselves why they had to die in their early twenties and sought answers in their reading; when they could find no adequate answers, they searched instead for rationalizations of their fate. This quest led them to intensive and extensive readings (see below).

Reading

The sheer number of books that these student soldiers mentioned and discussed in their diaries is astonishing. The practice of reading extensively, as well as keeping diaries, was instilled in higher school students and continued through their years at the university. In analyzing the complete published writings of four pilots, I tabulated about fourteen hundred books that they listed (Ohnuki-Tierney 2002, 307–40). These constituted only a part of their reading, however, and some of the most commonly read books were not included. In fact, Irokawa Daikichi, Yoshida Teigo, and other Japanese scholars who attended higher schools and imperial universities were surprised by the relatively small number of books listed. According to Fujishiro (pers. comm., May 20, 2003), who edited Sasaki's diary, the 458 books mentioned in the published volume represent only one-tenth of what Sasaki read; large segments of his diary, which discuss many more books in great detail, had to be omitted to limit the length of the publication.

The student soldiers' reading ranged from the works of classical writers such as Aristotle, Plato, Socrates, and Zeno of Citium, the founder of Stoicism, to works by major nineteenth- and twentieth-century literary and philosophical figures in Japan and the West. The French, German, and Russian writers whose works the student soldiers most frequently read— often in the original languages—and discussed include, respectively, Rousseau, Martin du Gard, Gide, and Rolland; Kant, Hegel, Nietzsche, Goethe, Schiller, Marx, and Thomas Mann; and Lenin, Dostoevsky, Tolstoy, and Berdyaev. The Danish writer Kierkegaard was also important. After works in Japanese, those by French and German authors, in that order, were most frequently cited.

The Europeans who had the greatest influence on student soldiers' thinking were (1) post-Kantian Transcendental Idealists, inspired by Kant's first critique, especially Fichte, Schelling, and Hegel; (2) German Romantic Idealists, influenced by Kant's second and third critiques, especially Schiller and Goethe; (3) the German *Romantiker* proper, especially Novalis,

Hölderlin, and Friedrich Schlegel; and (4) Marxists, both German and Russian.

Japan's intense intellectual engagement with the West was heavily mediated by its long history of influence by Chinese intellectual traditions. For example, Confucianism, introduced to Japan during the sixth century C.E., became a powerful basis for ideas of loyalty and sacrifice. Especially in the resurrected form used in the 1880s, this belief system helped prepare Japan to become a modern military nation for which individual sacrifice was essential. Neo-Confucianism, especially the Wang Yang-ming (Ōyōmei) ideology, which was introduced during the seventeenth century, emphasized the individual and self-cultivation, paving the way for the Japanese to embrace Kantian individualism (Bitō 1993 [1996]) and *Bildung* (self-cultivation), which Dumont (1994, 53) sees as the essence of the German philosophical stance. Works by such Chinese scholars as Kuan-tzu, Confucius, Mencius, and Wang Yang-ming had already been naturalized in Japan by that time.

Early on, young men read the works of writers who advocated *vissi d'arte, l'art pour l'art,* or art for art's sake. Sasaki, a rationalist, read the works of Oscar Wilde, who was very influential in Japan at the time; even the prime minister, Konoe Fumimaro, had been a devoted follower of Wilde when he was a student at the Imperial University of Kyoto. Hayashi Tadao and Nakao both read works by French writers who represented this movement, including Baudelaire, Balzac, and Flaubert. The art-for-art's-sake movement was deeply involved with questions of individual freedom from societal restrictions. The student soldiers were most strongly influenced by aesthetics directly linked to concepts and symbols that had profound sociopolitical dimensions. Nakao was inspired by Plato's aesthetics, which transcended mere visual beauty to become an aesthetics of truth. He was also moved by Rilke's discussion of Auguste Rodin; he commented that Rodin's work celebrated the vigor of life and that his aesthetics transcended the self in an age that exposed human "hubris." Takushima refers to Coppé, a Parnassian poet who emphasized commitment to social values and to plebeian life, indicating that he, like Coppé, combined lofty idealism and concern for the poor. Takushima was concerned with discrimination against minorities in Japanese society and the civilian casualties caused by Japanese colonialism. Nakao and Sasaki read the works of Kant with particular intensity, deliberating on his aesthetics in relation to social responsibility. These philosophers and writers offered student soldiers powerful ways in which to comprehend and articulate their dilemmas as cosmopolitan intellectuals in an age of nationalist warfare.

Some students were already aware of the crisis Japan faced in the 1930s, and most were acutely conscious of its perilous position by 1942. As they began feeling the "fate they chose,"[6] they turned their reading toward the more direct questions raised by their facing imminent death. They read the classics extensively. Many espoused the cosmopolitanism advocated by the Cynics and the Stoics. As they examined the meaning of being a member of society, they read Socrates and debated his ethical decisions. Their questions about the individual's responsibility to society also led them to such modern authors as Thomas Mann, Romain Rolland, and Roger Martin du Gard. Burning with idealism, they debated whether patriotism can be understood as the sacrifice of the self for a greater cause.

On the other hand, they began seeking psychological comfort in an aesthetics of nihilism; the aesthetics of death and its symbols, such as dusk, were central themes of Romanticism. When they saw the material and moral corruption that existed on the military base, their reasoning about why they should sacrifice themselves for war-torn Japan was no longer convincing to them. The stance of nihilism offered them powerfully poetic ways to understand or, in fact, to avoid understanding the death in which they lived. As Irokawa observes, "While we could indulge ourselves in nihilism, we were able to delude ourselves into having peace of mind, since it was a very dark period" (2003, 162).

UTOPIAN VISIONS: MARXISM, ROMANTICISM, AND CHRISTIANITY

Marxism

Although disillusionment with communism as a form of revolutionary theory and practice was pervasive in Europe by the 1920s and in Japan by the 1930s, Marxism, especially Leninism, remained a powerful intellectual force in Japan all through World War II and well into the 1980s, especially among university students, academics, and liberal intellectuals. After the war, *Capital* remained almost a sacred text for university students, who memorized its famous fourth chapter, "The General Formula for Capital."[7]

The student pilots' extensive reading of Marxism is quite impressive. Sasaki's diary contains sustained discussions of Marx, Engels, Lenin, Kropotkin, Stalin, and Trotsky. Hayashi Tadao and Sasaki located Marxism in the broader context of political economy, history, and historical materialism. For a more complete understanding of these issues, they also read Simmel and Weber as counterpoints. Both read Marxist literature critically. After reading works by Kawakami Hajime (1879–1946), an influential Marxist professor of economics at the Imperial University of Kyoto who became a member of the Communist Party, Sasaki remarks that writings by Marxists are usually full of propaganda and combative but lack sophistication in their philosophical arguments. Nonetheless, both were committed to Marxism, embracing it as a philosophical conviction and attempting to live up to its principles. Sasaki and Hayashi Tadao's brother came into conflict with their fathers, who, they thought, embraced capitalism and materialism.

Lenin's work made inroads into Japan gradually from the early 1920s onward (Duus 1988). Both Sasaki and Hayashi Tadao discuss the final stage of capitalism, the imperial stage, showing the profound and continuing influence of Lenin's theory on their thinking. At that time, Lenin's warning that capitalism would lead to colonialism and imperialism and his advocacy of the right of nations to self-determination had a powerful appeal in Asia and Africa, where Western colonialism had precipitated a strong surge of nationalism. Similar opinions developed in Japan and in Ho Chi-minh's Vietnam.

Despite the sophistication with which these student soldiers understood and argued about Marxism and historical materialism, Marxism was, in the end, a form of idealism that gave them a tool with which to fight against capitalism. Both Sasaki and Hayashi Tadao wanted to destroy not only the United States and Britain, which embodied capitalism, but also Japan, which they saw as corrupted by capitalism, in order to usher in a new Japan and a new world. Other student soldiers shared this hope.[8] Ironically, although Marx repudiated nationalism and hoped for a peaceful world united by its working class, Marxism served students as an expression of their idealism, and it became an intellectual justification for these young soldiers' patriotism and a rationale for their involuntary participation in an all-consuming military conflict.

Their Marxism was always conjoined with other philosophical and political ideas. Sasaki's utopia was built on the humanitarianism of Albert Schweitzer and the ideas of a return to nature and agrarianism articulated by Miyazawa Kenji. Hayashi Tadao's utopia was filled with his poetic lyricism and references to sublimity.

Nakao was a serious reader of fascism and totalitarianism. But after reading Vilfredo Pareto, Giovanni Gentile, Alfred Rosenberg, Carl Schmitt, and others, he concluded that Nazism and fascism formed the "totalitarian camp which rose against liberalism and materialism" (Nakao 1997, 439–40). He never embraced fascism uncritically, but he found in it a critique similar to the one that other students found in Marxism: antidotes to the competitive individualism, verging on egotism and materialism, that characterized modernity. But Nakao was not a simple right-wing ideologue, as his reaction to Osaragi Jirō's book about the Dreyfus Affair attests (Nakao

1997, 204–5). He was indignant about the way Dreyfus was treated and exclaimed: "The life of an innocent should never be at stake. However, for the military only its honor is at stake." After praising the Clemenceau brothers, Émile Zola, and the judge at the final trial, he declared: "Am I to enter the world of chaos in which one's partisan interests obstruct justice? I should not like to be part of the world which accrues the only justice to the bureaucrats and almighty power to the military. I prefer to remain in the outer field and, like Zola, try to steer the nation toward justice and truth." Nakao also deplored prejudice against the *hisabetsu burakumin,* a minority group within Japan. Although he succumbed to some elements of government propaganda and espoused some of the ideas promoted by right-wing intellectuals, Nakao was never a supporter of the totalitarian and militaristic ideology promulgated by the imperial Japanese state.

Romanticism

Romanticism, like Marxism, was a movement against capitalism, commodity fetishism, and competitive individualism. Marx and Lenin held the anticapitalist elements of Romanticism in high regard, and the Romantics' critique of modern culture resembled Marxist critiques of bourgeois individualism and commodity fetishism. In Japan, as in Europe, Romanticism became part of the struggle to overcome modernity. The student pilots embodied the Japanese historical experience since the Meiji period: profoundly influenced by modernity, which initially wore a Western face, they tried to overcome modernity, including the colonialist designs with which the Western powers approached Japan, at one and the same time. Japanese intellectuals' stance toward modernity was similar, but not entirely parallel, to that of European intellectuals during the late nineteenth and early twentieth centuries. The Romantic movement had a global scope, sweeping through Germany, France, and Russia and reaching as far as China and Japan. That Goethe's *The Sorrows of Young Werther,* the best-known work of the German Romantic movement of the *Sturm und Drang,* was the first book assigned to the German majors of the Second Higher School shows the movement's impact. Nonetheless, it would be erroneous to envision a neat package labeled "German *Romantik*" that traveled from one country to the next. Romanticism took a variety of forms that were parts of the complex challenges of overcoming modernity in each society, on one hand, and were imbricated in the increasing threats of armed conflict between nation-states that escalated into world wars, on the other. In their soliloquies, the student soldiers turned to the philosophers and literary figures whose central concerns involved the questions of the

individual versus society, life and death, aesthetics, and patriotism in relation to cosmopolitanism debated by Socrates, the Cynics, and the Stoics.
These interrelated themes were major concerns of Romanticism but have
also been basic and perennial questions in philosophy and literature since
antiquity.[9]

In Sasaki's declaration of hope that a new Japan would rise like a phoenix from the ashes of the defeat of Meiji Japan and the simultaneous destruction of the Western powers, which were all deeply corrupted by advanced capitalism, we see a complex combination of patriotism, historical
determinism, and a Romanticism whose master trope was irony. A similar
statement is found in the diary of Hayashi Tadao, who hoped for the defeat
of imperial Japan. Yet he called Japan his "ancestral land" (*sokoku*) and
considered it his duty to revitalize and rebuild it. Hayashi did not spell
out his vision of this new Japan, but his writing is replete with references
to sublimity, using various Japanese terms for *sublimity* and *beauty*, and
his utopia seems to have been primarily an aesthetic one. In this respect,
Hayashi was a thoroughgoing Romantic.

Christianity

Some tokkōtai pilots were devout Christians who, like Hayashi Ichizō, carried the Bible on their final flight and sang hymns on their last night,
which were dangerous acts given the strict censorship exercised by the
thought police on military bases.

Christianity promised these young men another form of utopia. Ever
since the early Meiji period, Uchimura Kanzō and other Christian leaders
had become exemplars of principled individuals whose struggle against
the increasing threat of totalitarianism was greatly admired not only by
Christians but by the Japanese generally. Not all Christians followed this
path. For example, Nitobe Inazō worked at the League of Nations with intellectual leaders such as Albert Einstein, Marie Curie, and Henri Bergson.
His cosmopolitan experiences and intellectual engagement notwithstanding, he became patriotic and penned *The Way of the Warrior* in English
in 1899, in which he proclaimed that the way of the warrior was as indig-
enous to Japan as cherry blossoms, thereby unintentionally endorsing the
state ideology.[10] But, by and large, Japanese Christians were political liberals. They strove to create their utopia on earth, to build a society based
on freedom, equality, and fraternity—the goal of the Meiji "restoration,"
at least as they interpreted it. All but one of the founding members of the
Social Democratic Party were Christians. The party was formed in 1901, a
year after the formation of the Socialist Society, which was disbanded by

the government within twelve hours of the publication of its manifesto. Except for Kinoshita Naoe, these socialists were critical neither of the Meiji constitution nor of the role of the emperor (Duus 1988, 659–67). The Social Democratic Party in Japan, like its European counterparts, espoused many socialist ideals and sought a gradual rather than a revolutionary path to change. In the consciousness of many Japanese, social democratic politics and Christianity were entirely compatible.

Hayashi Ichizō relied on his Christian faith as he embarked on his final mission. Yet his Christianity was inextricably mixed with doubt. Kierkegaard's theology was central to the anguished soliloquy in which he questioned the meaning of life and death. He carried Kierkegaard's *Sickness unto Death* as well as the Bible onto his plane, along with a photograph of his mother. As his last day approached, he filled his diary and letters with cries for her. Singing hymns and reading the Bible became his way of feeling close to his beloved and faraway mother, herself a devout Christian.

Other Christian pilots also struggled to sustain their faith as they faced death. On the night before his last flight, Kumai Tsuneo urged his comrades to sing hymns together. They chose hymn number 405, whose words ask God to give them strength "until they meet again." Hagihara Kōtarō, one of those who joined Kumai in the singing, survived and later recalled that singing hymns carried a risk of punishment: "Although we were not explicitly fighting Christianity and thus it was nominally permitted to sing hymns, we could have been in real trouble" (Ebina 1983, 181–82). Amid the severe censorship that prevailed on the bases and the hostile attitudes of some career soldiers toward student soldiers, this final act was a last celebration of the beauty of humanity in the most inhuman of circumstances, a protest against the military aggression, and even a dirge for themselves.

RATIONALIZATIONS

These student soldiers' tortured dialogues with the world's intellectual and spiritual traditions reveal that ultimately they sought rationalizations, rather than meaning in a neutral or positive sense, because they felt utterly powerless in the face of the imminent death that had been forced on them. That they took their death as inevitable even during their mid-to-late teens is almost unimaginable from the vantage point of today, but it indeed was the case. When Japan's police state gave them no power either to express their thoughts individually or to organize collective resistance movements, they rationalized their predicament by means of historical determinism—their own version, not the Marxist or the Hegelian one— and envisioned themselves as caught in the grand flow of world history leading them to their deaths. Alternatively, they reclaimed a sense of individual agency by assigning to themselves the role of destroying the old Japan—Meiji Japan, imperial Japan, feudal Japan, capitalist Japan—in order to protect their beloved ancestral land, to bring about a utopia, or even to create a new world. They sought psychological refuge in the aesthetic of nihilism, as expressed in various literary works of the Romantics. Or they consoled themselves with the aesthetic of the words and melodies of hymns, which they used as dirges, without having a vision of resurrection, redemption, or any form of afterworld.

The student soldiers continued their reading and soliloquizing until the day they perished. All expressed a sense of profound isolation as they came to terms with death. Expressions of loneliness pervade in the diaries. Indeed, one dies absolutely alone—any time and at any place. These young men, however, had received the death sentence at an early age and lived constantly in the shadow of death. This anticipation haunted them with loneliness, and yet they were unable to discuss their feelings openly because they were expected to be happy to die. Notwithstanding their desperate efforts to rationalize their actions, these young men recorded their agony in painful detail. Hayashi Tadao wrote repeatedly in November 1940, "I do not want to die! . . . I want to live!" In September 1942 Nakao composed a poem titled "Stillness" that expresses many pilots' feelings about the passage of time: every moment brought death closer. His and other student soldiers' writings are suffused with mourning for all they have lost, including life itself. In another poem Nakao describes the moon as a "beautiful woman gently crying." Two days after Nakao was inspired by Tanabe Hajime's lecture on the virtues of patriotism and service to the nation, while he was at the Kyoto station en route to Tokyo, he encountered people holding boxes wrapped in white cloth containing only a piece of paper with a dead soldier's name on it. Nakao wrote: "The whiteness of the boxes was painful to my eyes. Were they [the dead soldiers] able to say without hesitation, 'I will see you again at the Yasukuni Shrine'?" Nakao clearly questions the state's claim that the cherry blossoms were the metamorphosed souls of fallen soldiers and also was skeptical of the soldiers' own willingness to sacrifice their lives for the emperor *qua* Japan. Perhaps the most representative expression of the feelings of these pilots occurs in a passage from Miyazawa Kenji's *The Crow and the Great Dipper*, which Sasaki Hachirō quotes as conveying his own thoughts in praying for the arrival of "the day as soon as possible when we welcome a world in which we do not have to kill enemies whom we cannot hate." Miyazawa

Kenji (1896–1932), a poet and author of children's books, was highly influential among young intellectuals at the time. This passage expresses the student soldiers' cosmopolitanism and their utter perplexity when they found themselves engaged in a war they did not believe in—a perplexity shared by many young American soldiers during the Vietnam War (Edelman 1985). It is an irony common to wars that these young men became less patriotic as their final flight approached. Passion of any sort was readily crushed on the base as they witnessed Japan's militarism.

Recently some scholars have sought to explain "terrorism" in various parts of the world by locating its seeds in Western intellectual traditions. This search was preceded by scholars' attempts to find the conceptual basis of totalitarianism in their own intellectual traditions. If Max Horkheimer and Theodor Adorno (2002 [1944]) saw the Enlightenment as serving later totalitarian goals, Isaiah Berlin saw both the Enlightenment and the Counter-Enlightenment as having had a pernicious impact on later politics. On the one hand, Berlin saw some of the most important figures of French Enlightenment, such as Jean-Jacques Rousseau and Claude-Adrien Helvétius, as having provided the conceptual tools that facilitated totalitarian goals (Berlin 2003), and, on the other, he viewed Fascism and Communism as "Romanticism in its inflamed state" (Berlin 1959, 202) and Johann Gottlieb Fichte, a German Romanticist, as one of the six enemies of human liberty (Berlin 2003). Essays in *Nietzsche, Godfather of Fascism?* (Golomb and Wistrich 2002) deliberate on the role of Nietzsche's philosophy in German fascism.

More recently, we have witnessed a flurry of publications pointing out that non-Western revolutionaries of the twentieth century and contemporary terrorists are not the poor and the uneducated but are sometimes highly educated intellectuals, and that the ideological sources of their actions are found in Western intellectual traditions, especially Counter-Enlightenment philosophies and literature, including Romanticism. The political philosopher John Gray, the author of *Enlightenment's Wake* (1995), writes in *Al Qaeda and What It Means to Be Modern* (2003, 22–23, 25): "No one did more in laying the intellectual foundations of radical Islam than the Egyptian thinker Sayyid Qutb. . . . The central theme of Qutb's writings is the spiritual emptiness of modern western societies. . . . The intellectual roots of radical Islam are in the European Counter-Enlightenment." Ian Buruma and Avishai Margalit (2004, 143) see the ideas of the French Revolution in the Islamic revolutionary movement and in the failed experiments in state socialism in Egypt, Syria, and Algeria. According to them, later models for Arab progress were Mussolini's Italy, Nazi Germany, and the Soviet Union, while Marxism and German Romanticism provided the intellectual inspiration for many non-Western political leaders such as Pol Pot. They argue: "This is why it was such a misfortune, in many ways, for the Middle East to have encountered the modern West for the first time through echoes of the French Revolution. . . . Most revolts against Western imperialism, and its local offshoots, borrowed heavily from Western ideas" (143).

In these discussions, as in those concerning earlier totalitarianism, Nietzsche's nihilism looms large. Some link it directly to contemporary terrorists. According to Navid Kermani (2002), *not* the Quran but Nietzsche's nihilism—that is, the "will to nothingness"—was the key spiritual source for some suicide bombers. Kermani sees 9/11 as an extreme expression of modernism. Farhad Khosrokhavar, who penned books about the Iranian revolution (Khosrokhavar with Vieille 1990), tells us that Heidegger, mediated by Henri Corbin, had a crucial influence on neoconservative Iranian intellectuals (Khosrokhavar 2001).

The quotations from the diaries of the Japanese student soldiers pilots may be traced, intertexually, to the Counter-Enlightenment philosophers, the Romantics, and especially Nietzsche. Sasaki's and Hayashi Tadao's images of the destruction of the old Japan and the birth of a new Japan may be read as having direct reference to the theme of death, destruction, and rebirth in many of Nietzsche's writings, including *The Birth of Tragedy* and *Also sprach Zarathustra*. These two works were musts for young men at the time. Nietzsche's phrase "the hour-hand of the clock of your existence" (Nietzsche 1927,1084) may have been an intertextual reference for what Irokawa (2003) reported as a common practice among the student soldiers drafted to become tokkōtai pilots: grabbing the clock and stopping it in their desperate effort to stop the time ticking away inexorably toward their death. The poem in which Nakao remarked "How lonely is the sound of the clock" may be another echo of Nietzsche's clock. Sasaki's desire to find an "idol" could have come from Nietzsche, although his direct reference is to Watsuji Tetsurō, a professor of philosophy at the Imperial University of Kyoto. Hayashi, Sasaki, Nakao, and Irokawa all read Nietzsche.

But their enchantment with Nietzsche had nothing to do with the Japanese military aggression orchestrated by political and military leaders. We must clearly distinguish the leaders and executors of atrocities, such as Pol Pot, and active collaborators, such as Goebbels and Speer, from those who were unwittingly caught in the political and military machinery of the regime. Fascists and other authoritarian dictators, such as Hitler and Goebbels, strategically deployed the rhetoric of Germany's rebirth from economic ruin and wounded pride after World War I. But the veneer of their adherence to Nietzsche or Counter-Enlightenment philosophy stops right there. They were true believers in the righteousness of the course Germany took and hoped until the end that Germany would win, without its destruction, except in their delusion during the final moments of the war. In Japan, some leaders were intellectuals under the influence of Counter-Enlightenment philosophies and literature. For example, the wartime prime minister Konoe Fumimaro, while a student at the University of Kyoto, published a translation of Oscar Wilde that was banned by the government (see Ohnuki-Tierney 2002). But many, such as Tōjō and Ōnishi, the inventor of the tokkōtai operation, went straight to the idea of the supremacy of Japan and Japan's victory. For that goal, they sacrificed young men by sending them off as tokkōtai pilots who, they hoped, would bring about a miraculous victory even as American bombers were dropping firebombs day and night on Tokyo and other cities.

These leaders utilized the young men's idealism and patriotism, which were embedded in cosmopolitanism and pluralistic nationalism along the Herder-Berlin line of thought, to the advantage of their state nationalism, just as Stalin appealed to the idealism of Soviet intellectuals such as Sakharov and transformed it into patriotism.[11]

More immediate factors that led them to patriotism are shared by many other peoples. First, outside of European political centers, the threat posed by Western colonialism was indeed real, but it was also utilized by various national governments to fan popular sentiment for their own purposes, as the Japanese state had done since the end of the nineteenth century. We see this in the young men's diaries. Second, toward the end of the war, the certain prospect of a homeland invasion—which became an immediate reality with the bombing of Tokyo and other cities, well before the final devastation wrought by atomic bombs—served as a powerful force behind the last-minute rationalization of these young men's inevitable deaths, as vividly described in the diary by Hayashi Ichizō. When wars are fought not by armies encountering one another on the battlefield but by the massive destruction of cities and the deaths of civilians, people's patriotism is strengthened, and those who had not previously hated the enemy often come to share that popular sentiment. Even people who are skeptical about the current government's policy and the virtues of its military, as Hayashi Tadao certainly was about the "brutal" Japanese army, may feel compelled to unite with their people under such circumstances. Nothing stirs the patriotism of the people and hatred of the enemy more powerfully than the homeland attack, be it the German bombing of Coventry or the Allied bombing of Dresden (Buruma 2004; Dyson 2005). Most recently, it was conspicuously demonstrated after 9/11 in the United States and also in Iraq after the American and British invasion and occupation.

A LONG ROAD TO THE POINT OF NO RETURN

The Role of Aesthetic in Authoritarian Regimes

Why and how did these highly intelligent young men either succumb to some aspects of the military ideology or fail to recognize the government's strategy until they reached the point of no return? The mobilization of aesthetic by totalitarian regimes is a well-known phenomenon. Nazi Germany, Mussolini's Italy, Franco's Spain, and Lenin and Stalin's USSR were infamous for their conspicuous use of art, music, public performances, political rallies, parades, and monuments. In Japan, nothing comparable to Wagnerian opera, Nuremberg rallies, or the fascist March on Rome was staged. No posters of the emperor or, for that matter, of Tōjō were used, in contrast to the glorification of Hitler, Stalin, and Mussolini. Nevertheless, the Japanese government mobilized the aesthetic of cherry blossoms, even more intensively than Hitler used roses and bouquets of flowers, as a means of securing public acceptance of its military actions. The aestheticization of nationalism, aggressive or imperial expansion, and warfare is a pervasive feature of modern nation-states, be they totalitarian or democratic. As for democratic states, we are familiar with the emphasis on "beauty" attributed to patriotism, which is symbolized in the Stars and Stripes by American governments past and present, with a very conspicuous example occurring after September 11, 2001.

The Militarization of Cherry Blossoms in Japanese Culture

The successive Japanese military governments used the cherry blossom as their master trope. Japanese people from the country and the city and from all walks of life have loved cherry blossoms for centuries. Each spring, gorgeous full blooms cover the entire Japanese archipelago, starting early in the south and moving progressively northward, in a pattern that was seen as analogous to the vitality of the Japanese people. The exact time of blooming is unpredictable, and the blossoms last only a short time; many Japanese today, as in the past, eagerly anticipate their displays and go to view them, fervently appreciating their beauty from bud to full bloom. Under the cherry blossoms they dance, sing, masquerade, and eat and drink, becoming intoxicated literally and figuratively. The flower also offers a medium for soliloquy. Individuals reflect on life and death, love and loss, and other important matters in their lives while composing poems in which the cherry blossom serves as the medium for their deliberations. Poetry composition is an integral part of the ritual of cherry-blossom viewing and was especially important in prewar Japan.

The field of meaning of the flower is rich and complex (Ohnuki-Tierney 2002, 27–58). At the level of the individual, the flower represents processes of life, death, and rebirth and relationships between men and women, as well as production and reproduction. The most salient characteristic of the cherry blossom is their gorgeous but very brief life—a powerful basis for the ontological and emotive appeal of the flower. In literature and art it has been closely linked to the sublimity of pathos and ephemerality: *mono-no-aware*. On a more abstract level, it represents a subversion of the norm, its inversion and subversion, or the antiself. For example, the ritual of viewing is often accompanied by changes of social identity through the wearing of masks and costumes. Some Japanese believe that people lose their minds under a cherry tree in full bloom. That same image seen against a blue sky represents young women and their reproductivity as well as warriors, who were at the apex of Japanese society and were dubbed "humans among humans" in a well-known proverb. White blossoms at night against the dark sky, in contrast, symbolize geisha, who represent nonreproductive sexuality—the antithesis of the normative society, for which reproduction is the key to continuity.

At the collective level, each social group in the mosaic of Japanese society has developed its own tradition of cherry-blossom viewing. Over time, the flower became a dominant symbol of the Japanese people as a whole. It rose to the consciousness of Japanese intellectuals, artists, and other creators of high culture during the ninth century through their discourse with the Chinese, against whom they sought to establish a distinctive identity. They chose cherry blossoms in opposition to Chinese plum blossoms, which had been espoused by the Japanese elite. Ever since, the Japanese have made strenuous efforts to construct the flower as unique to Japan. Toward the end of the Edo period, masters of woodblock printing portrayed Japan as the land of cherry blossoms. The tradition of using cherry trees as Japan's state gift was inaugurated in 1912, when the First Lady, Mrs. William Howard Taft, requested the cherry trees that were subsequently planted along the Potomac River in Washington, D.C., where their blossoms still attract throngs of viewers every spring. Cherry blossoms have long been intensely involved in conceptions and representations of the Japanese self, at both the individual and the collective levels.

Since the beginning of the Meiji period, successive governments aestheticized their military operations and the deaths of soldiers on the battlefield visually and conceptually. The symbolism of cherry blossoms became the master trope of Japan's imperial nationalism. The aesthetic of the cherry blossom was deployed in numerous ways, especially as a symbol of soldiers' sacrifice for the emperor *qua* Japan. The visual aesthetic of the flower was transferred to the "Japanese soul" (*yamato damashi'i*), an exclusive spiritual property of the Japanese that endowed young men with a noble character, enabling them to face death without fear. The metaphor was intensively and extensively deployed by the military in its effort to promulgate the dictum "Thou shall die like beautiful falling cherry petals for the emperor."

Although the state effort to mobilize the masses by militarizing cherry blossoms began during the Meiji period, it developed throughout Japan's modern history. The militarization of Japanese culture intensified from the 1920s and 1930s, when the military seized state power, until the end of World War II. The government's aestheticization of militarism and its imperial ambitions with this flower was propagated by its relentless control of popular culture, including school songs and textbooks and popular songs, films, and plays. At the same time, the state carried out an intensive program of censorship. These strategies of propaganda and thought control were quite successful. The state's deployment of nationalist symbols penetrated even into the minds of people who consciously opposed government policies. For example, Inoue Takeshi, a progressive, antimilitary, and pro-Western thinker, authored a highly acclaimed elementary school reader in 1932 that was dubbed "The Cherry Blossom Reader." It opens with images of cherry blossoms, the rising sun flag, toy soldiers, a battleship, and a plane—that is, a series of nationalist and military symbols. During the process of imperial expansion, cherry trees representing the Japanese soul were planted all over Japan's colonies in order to transform the colonized spaces into Japanese spaces.

The Yasukuni National Shrine, where the souls of fallen soldiers had been commemorated since the beginning of the Meiji period, featured the cherry tree as its emblem. The shrine was constructed to centralize rituals honoring the soldiers who died fighting on the side of the emperor against the shogunate, which resulted in the establishment of the Meiji government. Originally the cherry trees were planted so that the beautiful blossoms would console the souls of fallen soldiers. As the process of militarization accelerated in the early twentieth century, this symbolism underwent a basic transformation so that falling cherry petals represented soldiers who sacrificed their lives for the emperor. The cherry blossoms at the Yasukuni National Shrine became their metamorphosed souls. Not only was their apotheosis guaranteed, but they would be honored by the emperor's regular visits to the shrine. This shift in the meaning of the flower from consolation of fallen soldiers to the celebration and encouragement of sacrifice for the emperor was reflected in the name of the shrine. In 1933 it was changed from the "shrine to invite the souls" of fallen soldiers to the "shrine for the loyal souls." The cover of *The History of the Loyal Souls at the Yasukuni Shrine* (Kamo, Kaigun, and Rikugun 1933–35), the official history of the shrine, shows ten pale pink petals falling against a deep blue background. Militarism was ascending rapidly in Japan during the early 1930s, at the same time that Hitler and the Nazis were rising to power in Germany.

The mobilization of the aesthetic of cherry blossoms to encourage sacrifice reached its height with the tokkōtai operation. A single cherry blossom was painted in pink on a white background on both sides of the tokkōtai airplane, while various Japanese terms for cherry blossoms were used as the names of the special attack corps. Cherry trees were in full bloom in southern Kyūshū in April 1945, and some pilots flew off with branches of blossoms on their helmets and uniforms (see photo 10). Others referred to cherry blossoms in their last poems and letters. A well-known photograph shows female high school students, who assisted with the daily work on the base, waving flowering cherry branches as they bid farewell to pilots taking off on their death missions (see photo 11).

The diaries in this book tell us that most of them neither embraced the emperor-centered ideology nor subscribed to the militarized meaning of cherry blossoms as it was articulated in the state ideology. On the other hand, they did not directly confront the militarized meaning of cherry blossoms, either. In fact, they did not even notice the fundamental transformation that the imperial state had wrought in the significance of this important cultural symbol.

The Absence of Symbolic Communication

The cherry blossom provides an excellent example of how we do not always communicate in our communication, whether with words or objectified symbols. This is the case especially when there are a great number of meanings for a given symbol: within the same social context individuals can draw different meanings without ever confronting the fact that they do not share the meaning, or, more technically, the signification. In many Western cultures the rose is perhaps as rich in meaning as the cherry blossom is in Japan. One can read passion, sacrifice, martyrdom, death, resurrection, political power (a Roman emperor's rose wreath worn as a crown), and a host of other meanings, unless the context specifies one. The Nazis also extensively used the aesthetic of roses. "Misrecognition" (*méconnaissance*) is a ubiquitous phenomenon in our communication because people do not know whether they are indeed drawing the same meaning from a word or an object.

In ordinary circumstances, misrecognition remains inconsequential. But it takes on an enormous significance when it is involved in the dissemination of the authoritarian ideology. Aesthetic, in the deployment of cherry blossoms in the Japanese case and roses in the Nazi case, played a crucial role in this phenomenon, both enabling the state to inculcate its ideology and concealing the way in which it did so. Wars and killing are presented as sublime, as succinctly expressed in the dictum "Thou shall fall like beautiful cherry petals after a brief life."

From Cultural Nationalism to Political Nationalism

Cherry blossoms originally grew in the mountains, the most sacred natural space in Japan. The sublime is most often ascribed to "nature" as a symbol of the purity and beauty of a nation and its people. Aestheticized nature as homeland occupies the central place in Romantic literature and philosophy. In these representations, idealized nature is both a spatial and a temporal representation of the self and the nation. It is "our space" as well as "our primordial past," that is, "our history," imagined as free from the contamination of modernity and, in Japan, also free from Western influences (Ohnuki-Tierney 1993a, 1993b). Schiller's "disenchantment of the world," a phrase made well known by Weber, expresses this negative attitude toward modernity and the longing for a pristine past. Sasaki's reading follows this line of aesthetics and modernity from Kant to Rousseau and Schiller. Hayashi Tadao and Nakao read Balzac, who located this point of origin in an idealized Rome, in which he saw pristine Frenchness.

The cultural nationalism symbolized by nature can shift easily to political nationalism, because the choice of a primordial past was just as often an expression of the nationalist aims of a state; for example, the Meiji government sought to elevate the emperor and retroactively establish a firm foundation of absolute monarchy in antiquity. As a plethora of examples from various countries attests, the Romantic search for an alternative to modernity might unwittingly mislead intellectuals and artists to a particular kind of nationalism in which cosmopolitanism is not incompatible with patriotism and nationalism (compare Appiah 2004). Many European Romantics espoused cultural nationalism while criticizing political nationalism. On the other hand, Fichte, an enthusiastic student of Kant and an influential member of the German Romantik school whose work all the student soldiers read, developed political nationalism by transferring the concept of the ego (*Ich*) to the German nation, thereby elevating Germans to the status of "a primordial and unadulterated *Urvolk*" (Wolf 1999, 211). Fichte's nationalism was radically different from that of Herder, who saw many different *Volk*s as equal in principle (Berlin 1959 [2002]).

In political nationalisms, an unadulterated Volk or Urvolk is often symbolized by unadulterated nature. This combination of nature and nationalism, a seemingly innocent pair, can quickly turn lethal by becoming a part of the machinery of political nationalism. In late nineteenth-century Germany, the soil, which represented agricultural communities, became the spiritual and economic source for the *völkisch* movement, and the *Heimat* (homeland), as the utopian symbol, became an instrument of their race theory (Mosse 1964 [1981], 108–25, 155, 169; Koshar 1998, 26–28, 47–48, 54). It was Rudolf Darré, the Reichsminister of Agriculture, who coined the Nazi motto *Blut und Boden* (Blood and Soil); he also pushed the *Naturschutz* (promotion of nature) as a state policy (Schama 1995 [1996], 81–100).

Aesthetic value is assigned to the symbols that stand for the most cherished values of the people: their land (space), their history (time), their idealism, and their moral codes of purity and sacrifice. People respond powerfully and deeply to aesthetic values, interpreting them in terms of their own idealism and experience of sublimity, while the state can use the same aesthetic and symbolism to coopt people. This line of analysis has been most extensively developed with regard to European fascism. Writing about Nazi Germany, Mosse argues that "the 'aesthetics of politics' was the force which linked myths, symbols, and the feeling of the masses" (1975, 2). Similarly, but in reference to fascism in general, Walter Benjamin discusses the uses and abuses of *l'art pour l'art* by totalitarian regimes: "[Mankind's] self-alienation has reached such a degree that it can experience its own destruction as an aesthetic pleasure of the first order. This is the situation of politics which Fascism is rendering aesthetic. Communism responds by politicizing art" ([1958] 1968, 242). Benjamin's view sheds a disturbing light on both the Japanese state's use of aesthetic values to propagate its imperialist militarism and the sublimity sought by the tokkōtai pilots whose vision of the destruction of Japan and its adversaries was, in their tortured rationale, to be followed by rebirth of a new Japan or a new world but culminated in their own death.

It is deeply alarming that aesthetic in realpolitik can be so dangerously beguiling as aesthetic moves a symbol from an innocent cultural space to a dangerous political space and puts it into the service of a state ideology. "Nature," when used as a political symbol of "our homeland," can be dangerous: its idealized beauty disarms people because they interpret nature in terms of their own familiar associations, while the state construes the meaning of nature in terms of its ideology. In Japan, as in many other societies, nature and nationalism, which were both embodied in cherry blossoms, formed a dangerous liaison. And here, as in countless other cases, misrecognition prevented the tokkōtai pilots and other student soldiers from coming to terms with the discrepancy between what they perceived and what the state intended.

In the final analysis, the tokkōtai pilots' patriotism and the state ideology were imbricated *in action,* even though there was a gulf *in thought* between the two. It was the student soldiers' quest for aesthetic, their Romanticism and idealism, that carried them beyond the point of no return. They developed their worldview and their aesthetics in large part from their reading. These young men would have been able to hold their own intellectually against the political nationalism orchestrated by the state if it had been presented to them directly and openly. But when it was mediated by the lofty intellectual traditions of the West, they failed to recognize the transformations wrought by promilitary political and intellectual leaders. They were well armed to resist the naked propaganda of the motto *Ein Volk, ein Reich, ein Führer.* However, when the "general will," transformed by the Nazi and the Japanese states, was presented as the general will that Rousseau and Kant defined, they were disarmed. Few student soldiers noticed or suspected the wicked hand of manipulation. Others eagerly embraced beautiful nature in the works of Rousseau, Beethoven, Goethe, or Thomas Mann, never suspecting that the Nazis also mobilized the aesthetic of nature in their motto "Blood and Soil." Like many young European men who fought in World War I, the student pilots memorized Nietzsche's *Also sprach Zarathustra,* recited Baudelaire's *Les Fleurs du mal,* and expressed their agony by referring in German to the two souls in *Faust.* Inspired by Emerson's inspirational motto, "Hitch your wagon to a star," they identified the star as their intellectual and spiritual idealism, not as earthly ambition. Their political innocence and intellectual idealism in fact made them defenseless against the clever manipulation of ideas and symbols by the military government and, because they were situated in this particular time and place, they only sent them even more swiftly to certain death.

In this book I use the terms *beautiful, sublime,* and *aesthetic* interchangeably. For Burke (1757) "an eternal distinction" between the Sublime and the Beautiful is that the former is founded on pain, thus capable of producing the strongest emotion that the mind is able to feel, whereas the latter is founded on pleasure (Burke 1757, 86–87, 157; see also 101–2, 128–29). For Immanuel Kant, there are two types of judgments: logical and aesthetic; each in turn is reflective or determinate (Brent 1977, 119). Both the Beautiful and the Sublime are judgments of reflection, rather than of sense or logic, and thus depend neither on a definite concept nor on a sensation (Kant 1790 [2000], 101). The "[r]emarkable difference between the two" is that "[t]he Beautiful in nature is connected with the form of the object, which consists in having [definite] boundaries. The Sublime . . . is to be found in a formless object, so far as in it or by occasion of it *bound-lessness* is represented, and yet its totality is also present to thought" (1790 [2000], 101–2; emphasis in original). "Sublimity, therefore, does not reside in anything of nature, but *only in our mind*" (129, emphasis added) and thus can lead to "no need of society." (For a detailed discussion of the Beautiful and the Sublime, see Brent 1977, esp. 118–23, 132–52). Kant explicitly states that it is incorrect to call any object of nature sublime but correct to call many objects of nature beautiful (1790 [2000], 103). Unlike other scholars of aesthetics whose concern is exclusively with the aesthetics of art, Kant's "judgment of the beautiful is meant to apply to *objects*, of nature as well as art" (Brent 1977, 132; emphasis in original). Although Kant's distinction between the Beautiful and the Sublime is most helpful, I do not strictly apply the Kantian distinction between the two primarily because the distinction in each instance is not critical for the purpose of presenting the thoughts in the diaries.

What is crucial for analytical purposes is the implication of the aesthetic judgment in relation to polysemic symbols. Because aesthetic judgments do not depend on a definite concept but on an indeterminate reference to concepts, they are able to refer to any number of concepts, as in the case of the aesthetic of polysemic cherry blossoms. As Brent (1977, 125) points out, the transcendental imagination is a productive imagination, rather than a reproductive imagination, and thus it leaves room for individual play as well as collectivity: "Kant's identification of the lack of absolute creativity of the productive imagination does not prevent it from providing collective *forms* for empirical intuitions. Indeed, in regard to aesthetic ideas, which are not, certainly, merely individual representations, we are tempted to say that they provide the form of possible empirical images" (emphasis in original). Thus, Kant's notion of reflective judgment without dependence on a definite concept and his notion of transcendental imagination identify the very space where individuals in a given culture read their own meaning in the symbolism of cherry blossoms, for example, within a culturally defined field of its meanings, as the young men discussed in this book did, while also acting on the field, possibly by expanding it, as the Japanese military did. Indeed, it is this space where misrecognition takes place.

CONCLUSION

Ironically, the portrayal promoted by the Japanese military government corresponds closely with the stereotype of kamikaze outside of Japan, presenting these young men as the modern incarnation of the warriors happily sacrificing themselves for the lord, now the emperor. The diaries presented in this book offer a salutary correction, allowing us to listen to the student soldiers' voices and helping us to understand the dilemmas they faced. The tokkōtai pilots were forced to volunteer. None of them whole-heartedly espoused the emperor-centered military ideology and willingly sacrificed his life out of loyalty to the emperor *qua* Japan. The pilots carried out the mission that the military had designed and assigned to them, diving or ramming into American vessels, but they did so without subscribing to the military ideology. It is indeed remarkable, as well as deeply tragic, that in their struggles to face their fate they drew on all the resources of Asian and Western literature, philosophy, and history that were available to them to try to find some meaning and rationalization for their approaching death, which they knew they could not avoid.

The kamikaze continue to be the Ur-model for contemporary suicide bombers *qua* terrorists as they are represented in the Western media. It is difficult to make valid comparisons between the tokkōtai pilots and contemporary suicide bombers. *Suicide bomber* and *terrorist* are blanket terms referring to a wide variety of individuals and the social-political groups to which they belong. Their "religious background" is too varied and complex to specify it as Islamic. Pape (2005) considers that the suicide terrorisms around the globe are responses to occupation or foreign control of their homeland, with religion playing only an aggravating factor. Khosrokhavar's (2002) finding is that the suicide bombers in Britain are the second generation highly educated Pakistanis who feel victimized in British society, establish their identity with their parents' country of origin, and seek a prophetic role in the new Islamic world. In a recent review of seven books on "suicide bombers," Caryl (2005) points to complexities in their motivations and circumstances, and differences among the so-called suicide terrorists. But we have no personal information about them as individuals, in contrast to the massive information we have on the tokkōtai.

As mentioned in the Preamble, the planes at Pearl Harbor in 1941 were fully equipped to return but the pilots were shot down. The pilots in 1944–45 attacks were placed by military order on planes without the fuel to return. "Suicide" and "volunteering to die" involve complex issues. Did the high-ranking warriors of medieval Japan who were ordered to commit suicide by the shogun indeed commit suicide, or were they murdered by the shogun? Did the French or German soldiers in World War I who were ordered to charge into enemy territory through a shower of artillery shells commit suicide, since they knew their death was guaranteed and yet obeyed orders? Or were they murdered by their commanding officers? And did some of the very young children among contemporary suicide bombers really volunteer to die? Or were they murdered by those who brainwashed them?

Some of these complexities aside, basic differences between the two groups nonetheless exist and must be reiterated, while taking care not to portray the tokkōtai pilots as good and contemporary suicide bombers as evil. Although in 1944 and 1945 they were assigned one-way missions, neither the pilots nor other Japanese thought that these young men committed suicide. As some of the pilots and their surviving relatives bluntly put it, they were "murdered" by their government. They acted as members of a regular uniformed military in wartime and acted on orders issued from above, rather than making a personal decision to strap on a bomb and turn themselves into explosive projectiles. The tokkōtai pilots were involuntary servants of a nation-state. They attacked military targets, rather than skyscrapers, transportation systems, cafés, and schools filled with innocent civilians. This distinction is straightforward enough but somehow was missed by a historian when Niall Ferguson (2001, 77–78) proposed that the Japanese pilots of 1944 and 1945 were the models for "the use of violence by nonstate organizations in the pursuit of extreme political goals" and for "the tactic of flying planes directly at populous targets." Cumings (2001) cautions us against "the staying power of this flawed and disturbing analogy," citing, for example, its use by Bill Moyers, a leading liberal commentator. The remainder of this book is dedicated to elucidating the distinction by detailing the lives and thoughts of the young men who died in the 1944–45 operation.

None of the major religions practiced in wartime Japan offered any vision of an afterlife; the Japanese had long ceased to believe in Buddhist reincarnation, and Shintoism was a religion for this world, not for the afterlife. The supreme reward that the Japanese military government offered to soldiers for loyal sacrifice was metamorphosis into cherry blossoms at the Yasukuni National Shrine, which none of them believed in. Today, the manifestos circulated by some leaders of so-called terrorist groups and factions that claim credit for so-called suicide bombings and the Western media that call them by these names (which they firmly reject for themselves) assert that those who die in the commission of these acts are promised a reward in heaven. Yet these manifestos and mass media reports must be taken with caution. After all, during World War II the propaganda spread by Japanese military leaders, who sent these young men to death without risking their own lives, and the American military's construction of kamikaze as the utmost Other presented a consistent portrait of the tokkōtai pilots that does not accord with their own understanding of their position and the meaning—or meaninglessness—of their acts.

The tokkōtai pilots were indeed similar to those who fought in the modern wars during which soldiers were sent right into a shower of artillery shells, machine gun fire and grenades, knowing very well that their chance of survival was close to nil. There is an uncanny parallel between these young Japanese men and the British soldiers who fought during World War I. Fussell (1975 [2000], 155–90) eloquently relates that when they had a bad day the Oxbridge graduates as well as uneducated privates turned to Ovid, Keats, Shakespeare, and others, and he points to "the unparalleled literariness of all ranks who fought the Great War." Their Japanese counterparts consoled themselves by reading Remarque's *All Quiet on the Western Front* (1928) and Witkop's collection of letters by German student soldiers. It is striking that the letters sent home by American soldiers during the Vietnam war (Edelman 1985) contain poems and exquisitely poetic passages as they express their deep thoughts through their observation of the beauty of nature in Vietnam. None of them committed suicide; they were killed in action. As they anticipated their imminent death, many turned to the poetics of humanity.

Past events often lie buried in the dustbin of history, only to be resurrected by what Benjamin calls the "angel of history" (after Paul Klee's Angelus Novus), usually because of some contemporary interest in the issues they involve or the occurrence of what seem like comparable phenomena in the present. In the immediate aftermath of 9/11, the U.S. government resurrected a remembered ca ricature rather than historical knowledge, portraying the attack on the World Trade Center as an assault on the homeland similar to the purported kamikaze attack on the U.S. Pacific Fleet at Pearl Harbor and the beginning of a global war. The tokkōtai case is not a matter of being exiled from history or the usual form of "forgetting." The deliberately distorted view of these young men as fanatical suicide fighters not only has remained but has been reinforced intentionally, time and again, as the the prototypical peril posed by the Other. If knowledge production is mediated by geopolitics, so is the purposeful reproduction of caricatures as historical facts. The roots of this phenomenon are embedded in the geopolitics of World War II and its aftermath, when the United States asserted a monopoly over world power (Kelly 1998, 2003).

We cannot exonerate those who commit grave crimes against humanity, be they Hitler and the officers of the SS and the German Army or Ōnishi Takijirō and the other military leaders who mercilessly cut short the lives of the tokkōtai pilots. But we must also recognize our frailty, which leads us to participate unknowingly in such totalitarian and entirely destructive operations. We must be aware of how easily we, including these youths and others who become involved in armed conflicts, can be led *not* to recognize the clever manipulations carried out by military regimes. I hope that this work contributes to an understanding of how vulnerable each one of us is to historical forces that lead us to participate in—or to misrecognize or ignore, and thus unknowingly condone—human tragedies on a colossal scale.

This book introduces the anguished voices of young men whose ardent quest for purity of spirit and idealistic vision of humanity were brought to a premature end by their death in meaningless wars. Their letters, diaries, and memoirs remain as testimony to their humanity; their voices are too powerful to be buried for good. Not because they were Japanese but because they were human beings, I find it inexcusable to dismiss them from our knowledge and replace them with an inhuman caricature.

I offer no apologia for the deaths inflicted by the tokkōtai pilots. This book does not exonerate Japan for the atrocities that the imperial nation's military inflicted on its enemies and on colonized peoples during its wars and other armed aggressions. Nor should this book be read to condone acts of murder committed by suicide bombers or terrorists anywhere. Rather, this book is a plea to reflect on each and every individual who becomes a victim in meaningless wars. As I finished work on this book in mid-December 2005, more than 2,100 American soldiers had lost their lives in Iraq, almost 16,000 had been grievously injured or maimed in action, and about 30,000 Iraqi civilians, many of them women and children, had been killed. The total number of dead and injured should not be the only concern. We must reflect on each individual whose hopes for the future came to a sudden and permanent stop. The ubiquitous presence of the American flag on everything from men's boxer shorts and car radio antennas to the halls where the political conventions were held has created a heightened sense of the beauty of patriotism. Yellow ribbons express support for the soldiers in Iraq and the sacredness of the sacrifice of those serving in the military during this war. Cherry blossoms and the rising sun flag did much the same work for Japanese people during the darkest period of their recent history. As an American Vietnam veteran remarked: "Patriotism is easy, but the war is hard."

> Mountain cherry blossom, its splendor in its reflection in the purity of snow in a deep mountain.

Born in 1922, Sasaki Hachirō was drafted as a student soldier from the Imperial University of Tokyo in December 1943 and volunteered to be a tokkōtai pilot on February 20, 1945. He died as a navy ensign on a tokkōtai mission on April 14, 1945, at the age of twenty-two years and nine months.[1]

A Testament of the Youth: Diary and Love, in the Absence of Life by Sasaki Hachirō (1981) is a 466-page book devoted to his diary and to letters, essays, and poems he wrote between 1939 and 1945. The title indicates that it was written by Sasaki as a testament (the literary meaning of *isho* is "will") left by a young man, consisting of his diary and expressions of his love toward his family members, friends, and Japan even though he is no longer alive. The diary starts on March 16, 1939, when Sasaki was sixteen years old, shortly before his entrance examination for the First Higher School (Ichikō) in March 1939. It ends on December 8, 1943. The diary he kept during the period of his life spent on the military base, from December 9, 1943, until April 14, 1945, is not included, but some letters and diary excerpts from this period are appended to the book. His writings also appear in edited volumes.[2]

Sasaki was born to an upper-middle-class family; he had two brothers (one deceased) and a younger sister. After the death of his older brother, Sasaki was brought up as the eldest son. He was very close to his younger brother, Sasaki Taizō, whose published article about his brother was most helpful (Sasaki Taizō 1995). He read the whole of this chapter and offered me invaluable comments. Their father had a successful lumber business, for which he traveled extensively to north China and Manchuria. Right after the great Kantō earthquake in the Tokyo area in 1923, the father moved his business from Kobe to Tokyo, where lumber was greatly needed for the reconstruction. Hygienic conditions were still very poor, and the oldest child, Gorō, contracted amoebic dysentery and died within a few days. The parents were devastated by his death (Sasaki Taizō, pers. comm., May 5, 2005). The father tried his best to dissuade Sasaki Hachirō from volunteering to be a pilot. Failing to do so, he never spoke to his son again; it was too painful for him. Even when Hachirō returned home before his final flight, his father left the house and did not return that evening (Sasaki Taizō 1995). After the war ended, the family received notice of Hachirō's death, together with a medal and a small mount of money. Without a word, the father took the money to a local liquor store, brought back a large bottle of sake, and drank it all. Having lost his beloved first son at the height of his business success, and then, years later, being unable to dissuade his second son from volunteering to be a pilot, he became disillusioned with life and never worked a single day after the end of the war. In order to support the family, the mother took in lodgers and sold ties and *obijime* (accessories for the kimono sash), which she wove with a special technique called *kokonoeori*. Until the father's death at the age of seventy-four, no family member ever mentioned Hachirō; it was too painful for them. For the same reason, the family held neither a funeral nor a memorial service for him; nor did they bury his "ashes" (his remains, needless to say, were never recovered) in their family tomb or elsewhere (Sasaki Taizō 1995:77–78; pers. comm., June 26, 2005).

In 2003 I visited the site of his house in Den'enchōfu, a wealthy suburb of Tokyo. It stood on a hill overlooking a nature preserve. On fine days Mt. Fuji was visible from this hilltop. In the yard, there used to be an old cherry tree with abundant blossoms. It was cut down when the house was sold to accommodate two large houses.

After graduating from the First Higher School in March 1942, Sasaki entered the University of Tokyo, where he majored in economics. His academic career was the most successful any Japanese male could dream of at the time. Not only did he excel in intellectual pursuits, but he also was an avid member of the mountain climbing club at the First Higher School, which was the most elite student club.

Those of his good friends who survived the war became intellectual and business leaders in postwar Japan. His younger brother, Sasaki Taizō, became a professor of physics at the University of Tokyo and a prominent figure in the field. Ōuchi Tsutomu, one year ahead of Sasaki and his close friend, became a well-known economics professor at the University of Tokyo. Ōuchi Tsutomu's father, Ōuchi Hyō'e, a famous professor of economics at the same school, was wrongly accused twice, in 1920 and 1938, of collaborating in left-wing activities and was imprisoned and stripped of his post at the university, although he returned to the post after the end of the war. Hirasawa Hideo, Sasaki's other close friend, became CEO of Japan Airlines and then president of HSST (the high-speed railroad company). Sasaki repeatedly expressed his appreciation of his friendship with Ōuchi Tsutomu, Hirasawa Hideo, and his younger brother. He tried to be cerebral in his relationship with his parents. Sasaki was obviously pleased by his mother's love and respect for him, expressed in her emotional outbursts at the time of his successful entrance to the First Higher School and to the University of Tokyo, when she became very excited about attending the ceremony held for new students. He was both bemused by her excitement and embarrassed by her boasting (309–10).

Until he entered the navy, Sasaki was antagonistic toward his father because in his eyes his father was a true believer in and practitioner of capitalism—the worst offense, according to the opinions of idealistic university students at the time. His father became enraged on hearing of his decision to join the navy. Sasaki accused his father of being happy to see others volunteer to fight and yet selfishly wanting his own son to take care of him in his old age (387–88, 393–94). His brother Taizō, on the other hand, believes that their father, having seen during his business trip to north China the meaningless atrocities inflicted by the Japanese army on the Chinese, was naturally unwilling to have his son give his life to a war he did not believe in (pers. comm., June 26, 2005). But Hachirō did not understand the reason for his father's anger.

Sasaki was one of five hundred students from the University of Tokyo drafted during a three-day period in December 1943. At that time, a total of about six thousand students were drafted. On January 28, 1944, Sasaki was sent to the Yatabe Naval Air Base, where professional soldiers known as the "demonic prison guards" (*oni no shigoki*) were waiting. Sasaki was placed in Group No. 6 under an officer nicknamed "Ishioka the Demon." With only the slightest of excuses, officers inflicted corporal punishment on student soldiers or ordered them to run around the air base many times. Some were hit so hard that they lost consciousness, and their faces were swollen from the beatings (Fujishiro 1981, 448–51). On February 20, 1945, all the student soldiers were summoned into a hall and were asked to write down their names if they wished to "volunteer" to be tokkōtai pilots. It was hardly a free choice (Fujishiro 1981, 455).

Sasaki had a voracious appetite for learning. According to Fujishiro, the works discussed in the published volume represent only one-tenth of what he recorded in his diary. As the list of readings given at the end of this chapter shows, Sasaki's reading ranged from Plato and Socrates to Rousseau and those who lived for "art for art's sake," such as Oscar Wilde and Tanizaki Junichirō. He read German proficiently. The German intellectual tradition had a profound impact on Sasaki. He listened mostly to music by German composers, although he was familiar with Bartók (Hungarian), Smetana (Czech), and Sibelius (Finnish). His favorite was Beethoven, whose music gave encouragement and solace when needed.

This essay explores Sasaki's diary and other writings, organizing them thematically within a chronological sequence in order to follow his thoughts as they changed over time.

ENTRANCE TO THE FIRST HIGHER SCHOOL

Sasaki's diary begins with the examination for entrance to the First Higher School on March 16, 1939. He was quite cheerful after the examination and delighted in spending his time going to plays and movies and reading. He saw films ranging from *Popeye* to *Bolero* and read a variety of books: Alexandre Dumas's *The Lady of the Camellias* (*La Dame aux Camélias*), Ivan Turgenev's *Virgin Soil*, Fyodor Dostoevsky's *Crime and Punishment*, Anton Chekhov's *The Duel* and *The Wife*, Pearl Buck's *The Good Earth*, and Tanizaki Junichirō's *The Tale of Genji* (March 16–26, pp. 11–13).

On March 27, 1939 (13–15), the result of the entrance examination was posted. He went to see the announcement, accompanied by his mother and his younger brother, Sasaki Taizō. After finding his number, he bid farewell to them and went to Kabukiza to hear *Carmen*. Sitting next to the orchestra, he was enormously impressed by the "genius" of Georges Bizet and Prosper Mérimée. He found the performance so exciting that he had a hard time falling asleep that night.

On March 30, 1939 (15), he underwent the physical examination and an oral examination at the First Higher School. He listed Beethoven and General Nogi as people he admired. General Nogi was a commander who did not spare his sons' lives during the war against Russia and committed suicide together with his wife when Emperor Meiji's body was taken across the bridge and out of the imperial castle (Bitō 1994). Sasaki writes that when asked by a senior in his dormitory about his thoughts regarding the "current political situation,"

I was aghast and annoyed. I resorted to some meaningless abstract statements. He kept shouting at me, preaching how we should recognize the responsibility of being able to study under the current political situation and expounding on the importance of spending three years in earnest.

"Of course," Sasaki sarcastically remarks, obviously disdaining someone who takes himself so seriously as a privileged member of the elite.

On April 4, 1939 (16–17), he was awoken by footsteps on the stairway to the second floor of the family's house, where his bedroom was located. It was his mother:

> She ran up to my room, fell onto my bed, and, while holding my hands firmly, she said, "Thank you. Thank you. It is all because of your effort." . . . Then, she began to cry. It turned out that Mr. Mineo (professor at the First Higher School) had sent her a telegram notifying her of my successful entrance to the First Higher School. I tried my best not to cry, since a man with a great future should not show emotion for this sort of thing. So, I just listened to her. But, it was hard to control my emotion when she told me that she made pilgrimages [to a shrine to pray for his success] for twenty-one days, even on the days of rain and high wind.[3]

FIRST HIGHER SCHOOL DAYS

Sasaki's experience at the First Higher School was crucial to his later decision to become a tokkōtai pilot, for during this period he realized that the students at the school were the future leaders of Japan. The school cultivated his pride and sense of responsibility to society. The diary entry for April 17, 1939 (20–21), begins:

> Since everyone was getting up early, I woke up at 6:30. . . . After talking for a while with my roommates, I continued my reading of Gide's *The Immoralist* [*L'Immoraliste*]. The ceremony for the entrance to the dormitory started at 9:00 A.M. After some speeches, the head of all the dormitories gave a speech: "We who were able to enter the First Higher School are better than those who did not make it only because we know how to take exams better. The rate of the graduates from the First Higher School [going on] to the Imperial University of Tokyo is going down. The reason why the First Higher School is the best lies elsewhere [than the intellect]—that is, in the friendship among students and the bond between the teachers and their disciples."

> After listening to the fifty-year history of the First Higher School . . . when all of us, including the President, sang "Gyokuhai" [the school song], I shed tears, unexpectedly. The members of the entire school put our efforts together in order to build our country. This is how the graduates of the First Higher School carry out the role of leading the nation.

This sense of pride and responsibility as a future leader of the country played a part in Sasaki's decision to sacrifice himself for the country.

Sasaki was quite happy with the school. The schedule left him a great deal of freedom to pursue his own studies (22), and he resolved to train his body and discipline himself for learning during the three years to come (23). He was active in sports, including tennis and skiing. Sports clubs were important socially as well as athletically. His diary mentions invitations to join the baseball club and the mountain-climbing club. Student life was punctuated by frequent "storms," in which a group of intoxicated students went around singing loudly, and *konpa* (a Japanese version of "company"), when students gathered over food and drinks brought or paid for by the participants. Although Sasaki was quite happy to be part of life at the First Higher School, he always kept his head rather than blindly falling in love, participating overenthusiastically in events, or zealously espousing new ideas.

Sasaki expressed sympathy toward other Asian peoples during his higher school days and took two extended trips to the Asian continent, quite an unusual activity for young people when such travels took a long time and were costly. From August 10 to September 3, 1939, he visited Manchuria, and between October 12 and 29, 1939, he traveled to Shanghai, Qingdao, Tianjin, and Beijing, China. As shown by his direct acquaintance with other parts of Asia at a time when access to othr countries was quite limited, he was remarkably outward looking and adventurous.

Sasaki was most passionately involved in mountain climbing and devoted a great deal of effort to reviving the mountain-climbing club. The attitude that this activity was a spiritual and physical challenge pervades his description of a very serious accident in the mountains (109–10), which, however, did not deter him from continuing to climb after his recovery. On July 20, 1940, in early evening, at the upper reaches of the Kurobe gorge in Toyama Prefecture, he fell, along with a large rock on which he was standing. Since he suffered severe memory loss, the details of the incident were supplied by his brother (Sasaki Taizō 1995, 70–71). He was with two other students; one stayed at the site, while the other went down to get help. Okamoto Matsujirō and other construction workers in the mountains rushed to his rescue although it was midnight, and they reached the site of the accident only in the morning. The load Sasaki was carrying on his back had fortunately got caught on a tree, and Sasaki, unconscious, was dangling from a branch. As he fell, he was injured all over his body and face, including his eyes. His memory of the past six months, including the incident, was blacked out. His mother hastened to the scene with a doctor from Tokyo. Sasaki was treated at the Red Cross Hospital in Toyama and then spent a month in a hospital in Azabu, Tokyo. Feeling immense gratitude to Okamoto Matsujirō for saving his life, he became a lifelong friend and visited the Okamoto family whenever he was in the vicinity. At the time when he was drafted, he asked his brother Taizō to visit the family whenever possible. On hearing of Sasaki's death, Mrs. Okamoto carved out a wooden Kan'on Buddha and prayed for his soul for thirty years until her own death. The Okamotos and the Sasakis became good friends and remained in touch after the war.

During the early period of his life, just before and after he entered the First Higher School, Sasaki thoroughly enjoyed life. He listened to the classical music of Western Europe, in particular works by Beethoven and Mozart, buying recordings and frequenting the symphony and the opera. On January 20, 1939 (58), for example, he went to hear the Shinkyō Orchestra perform Beethoven's Symphony no. 3, op. 55, in E-flat major ("Eroica"). His diary comments in detail on the performance, evaluating different sections as well as the successive movements. On January 30 (59–60), after going to the movies with his friends Ōuchi and Hirasawa, he rushed to catch a recital by Leonid Kreutzer (1884–1953), a Russian-born pianist who, after being deprived of his German citizenship by the Nazis, came to Japan in 1935, held the post of professor at the Tokyo School of Music, and nurtured many Japanese disciples. Sasaki listened to his performance of Beethoven's Piano Sonata no. 8, op. 13, in C minor ("Pathétique"), Chopin's Preludes, op. 28, and Liszt's "Mephisto Waltz," "The Dance of the Dwarfs," and Hungarian Rhapsodies, op. 8. "As [Kreutzer] continued to play," he writes, "his performance shone more and more and I could not help but utter a sigh [in awe]." Sasaki's taste in music inclined decisively toward the classical of Western Europe. He declared the first Japanese performance of a work by Bartók by the Shinkyō Orchestra boring and without melody and concluded that he could not appreciate modern music (May 10, 1939, 27–28).

HIGHER EDUCATION AS AN ARENA OF STRUGGLE BETWEEN LIBERALISM AND CONSERVATISM

One of the most fascinating features of Sasaki's diary is that he recorded his responses to many lectures that he attended and books that he read.

During the time he attended the First Higher School, Japan had been at the mercy of thought control and the "red hunt," the persecution of suspected subversives, all of whom had been jailed by then. Ultranationalism and militarism were increasingly gaining control over people's thinking and driving out radicalism and liberalism. For example, on November 10, 1939 (44–45), at the urging of his friend, Sasaki went to hear Matsuda Fukumatsu preach about how the Westerners were always thinking of the "yellow peril" and that their view of the Japanese was discriminatory. He comments that although it is necessary to attack those who unconditionally worship the West, which attempts to exclude Japan, it is nonsense to condemn the Western view outright.

During the 1940s Sasaki engaged in extensive reading and deliberation about the Kyoto school of philosophy, which attempted to transcend Western philosophy and establish Japan's own philosophical school while carrying on an extensive dialogue with Western philosophers.[4] He began to read Nishida Kitarō's *An Inquiry into the Good* (*Zen no Kenkyū*), commenting that "it was in general dogmatic, although there is much to learn from it" (January 20, 1970, 58; see also October 20, 1940, 121; October 11, 1942, 337).

Sasaki's comments on Watsuji Tetsurō illuminate his thoughts concerning the question of the individual and society. Watsuji was a leading scholar of the Kyoto school who wrote about Nietzsche, Kierkegaard, and Heidegger. His philosophy of ethics increasingly emphasized ethnonationalism and the aestheticization of what he thought of as the Japanese proclivity toward collectivism. After reading Watsuji's *The Revival of the Idol* (*Gūzō Sūhai*), Sasaki writes:

> Watsuji explains the difference between individualism and egotism and then emphasizes that ethnonationalism must be based on individualism. . . . There is some more room to think about his proposition. (March 31, 1940, 79–80; see also March 25 and 26, 1940, 76, 78; October 11, 1942, 337)

Sasaki read the work of Tanabe Hajime, another member of the Kyoto school of philosophy, who attempted to transcend both Hegel and Marx (112, 115, 132, 134, 137, 156, 297). Tanabe had a powerful influence on young students at higher schools and universities, and in the end his advocacy of political activism as a means for individuals to change society indirectly encouraged them to go to war. Sasaki finished reading Tanabe's *Historical Reality* (*Rekishiteki Genjitsu*) on September 25, 1940 (111–12), and on October 12 (115–17) he referred to his *Between Philosophy and Science* (*Tetsugaku to Kagaku no Aida*) and *Outline of Philosophy* (*Tetsugaku*

Tsūron). On November 1, 1940 (130–34), in a long discussion of historical practice, Sasaki writes:

> For those who live in the twentieth century, it is necessary to come to a synthesis between the most passive and the most aggressive poles of rationalism and activism. Here the dialectic proposed by Tanabe in his *Historical Reality* plays a role. That is, rationalism is too objective and activism is too subjective. As Heidegger claims, we are *in* history. It is not that there is history first and we enter it. At the moment we are born, we are in history. We are the subject that lives in the object. Development (according to rationalism) is construction (of activism), growth *qua* practice—that is history.

Sasaki's most revealing comments about Tanabe's work come at the time of the entrance examination for the University of Tokyo in the field of economics on March 1, 1942:

> Today the entrance examination begins. I wore my usual old uniform, but my underclothes were nice and clean. I thought I wrote unique opinions on the questions on national history and Western history. I think I was quite bold in my answer to the question on contemporary literary criticism. So, I don't know how they will evaluate it. Of course in retrospect I could have done better, but if they don't pass me, it means they cannot fathom my ability. A question on contemporary literary criticism was from Tanabe Hajime's *Historical Reality*. Isn't it depressing to think I was once so impressed by such a book! The book is full of loose ends. Dogmatic at that. It is nothing but empty reasoning.

Like many intellectuals at the time, including Nakao and Hayashi Tadao, Sasaki read the works of the influential Kyoto philosophers, but Sasaki's final appraisal of Tanabe was quite negative, and he made his criticism explicit in an examination. Given that Tanabe was the most revered philosopher at the time, one can appreciate that Sasaki was quite an independent thinker.

AESTHETICS: NATURE AND IDEALISM

Sasaki's passion for mountain climbing and the fulfillment he felt while gazing at the beauty of nature from high peaks were coupled with his reading of works by Japanese and European Romantics. In his happy early days at the First Higher School, his favorite leisure activity was to go to a coffee shop and listen to music while reading Hermann Hesse's *Beautiful Is Youth* (*Schön ist die Jugend*), *Peter Carmenzind, A Journey on Foot in Autumn* (*Eine Fussreise in Herbst*), *Knulp: Three Tales from the Life of Knulp* (*Knulp: Drei Geschichten aus dem Leben Knulps*), *Beneath the Wheel* (*Unterm Rad*) (April 19, 23, 25 and May 1, 1940, 87, 88–89, 90, 92), and *Demian* (November 16, 1940, 142). Sasaki writes that he understands how Hesse could not understand his fellow humans and wandered in nature (89). But, he concludes, Hesse is ultimately a sentimental author.

Of the works of Johann Christoph Friedrich von Schiller, Sasaki read *The Robbers* (*Die Raüber*), *Intrigues and Love* (*Kabale und Liebe*), *Theory of Beauty and Art, The Gods of Greece* (*Die Götter Griechenlands*), and *The Artists* (*Die Künstler*) (February 12, 16, April 27, and May 17, 1940, 184, 186, 188, 228). A year after remarking that Schiller's aesthetics in *Theory of Beauty and Art* is "a complete replication of Kant's aesthetics" (April 27, 1940, 90), in May 1941 (228), he writes:

> I read Schiller's poems. I find common threads between his longing for the Greeks and our quest to return to the *Manyōshū* [the oldest collection of Japanese poems], although I find a contrast between the sunny power of the Greek mind and the solid power of the *Manyōshū*—a contrast between the West and the East? In Hegel I sense beauty, truth, freedom, and an intuitive rationality of the Greeks. As Kierkegaard suggests, Hegel offers something more than German philosophy—Greek-like Romanticism? I read Schiller's *Die Götter Griechenlands* and *Die Künstler*. Beautiful and powerful. I feel a surge of strength in my whole body. The eighteenth and nineteenth centuries were not completely dominated by rationalism.

Romanticism seemed to Sasaki to revivify a world disenchanted by rationalism.

Sasaki's interest in the writers belonging to the "art for art's sake" movement continued throughout his life. On January 1, 1942 (275–76), he read Oscar Wilde's "The Portrait of Mr. W. H.," "The Model Millionaire," and "The Canterville Ghost." He found them "beautiful" and read them without interruption. He was thoroughly impressed by Wilde's concept of aesthetics.

Sasaki's extensive reading in European Romanticism did not lessen his interest in Japanese Romantics' aesthetics, which held great appeal for him. For example, he praised Tanizaki Junichirō, the author of *In Praise of Shadows* (*In-ei reisan*), because of his "quiet idealist aesthetic in the shadow, Japanese aesthetics, sensual beauty unlike that of ancient European aesthetics" (January 9, 1941, 172). He read Satō Haruo, who wrote some pro-war jingoistic poems as well as many novels and poems that were thought to have high literary quality. Sasaki pronounced *The Star* (*Hoshi*) "beautiful" and found its "art for art's sake" premise convincing (202).

Sasaki read Kunikida Doppo's *Musashino* (named after a district outside Tokyo), which aestheticized Musashino as the ideal of nature untouched by civilization. This famous novel made Musashino synonymous with nature and implicitly contrasted to nearby urban Tokyo. Sasaki's quest for beauty, in nature and in the ideal world, explains how he became engrossed in the novels of Kawabata Yasunari, a Nobel prize–winning novelist whose work is imbued with the exquisite beauty of nature and an aesthetic of sensuality.

Sasaki greatly admired Miyazawa Kenji, in whose writing he finds his own voice. After four years of teaching at an agricultural school, Miyazawa Kenji spent the rest of his life on a farm, subsisting on its products while writing and teaching farmers how to improve their methods. He wrote poems as well as children's books. Miyazawa's idealism, the purity of his spirit, and the self-sacrifice for humanity expressed in his work won him posthumous fame, and many young intellectuals became enthusiastic readers of his works and ardent followers of his principles (Miura 1996, 495). Miyazawa stood for the uncontaminated nature of Japan. In the cultural imaginations of many peoples, whether in France, Germany, Russia, China, or Japan, agriculture, the rural, and the peasantry stand for the primordial self of the people before their contamination by urbanization, industrialization, and foreign influences (Ohnuki-Tierney 1993a, 1993b).

Sasaki's quest for beauty featured cherry blossoms, whether experienced directly or depicted in various literary oeuvres. During a 1940 bus trip along Lake Yamanaka, Sasaki became intoxicated by the spring scenery, especially Mt. Fuji and cherry blossoms (82). The following spring, he expressed his amazement at cherry blossoms that had appeared overnight and worried that a strong wind might scatter them (206). A few days later he went on a trip without a fixed itinerary. On the island of Ōshima he composed two poems that treat the fallen cherry petals as a metaphor for the passing spring (209–10). At Shimoda in Shizuoka Prefecture, he observed that the cherry trees were still blooming, while the petals of the mountain cherries on Ōshima had already fallen. Referring to two famous poems by the well-known poet Wakayama Bokusui in praise of mountain cherry blossoms, Sasaki composed a poem in which he describes the "loneliness of the flower after the peak" (April 10, 1941, 210–11). In March 1942 he admired mountain cherries in full bloom and associated them with "youth," which in Japanese is written in two characters that mean "blue spring." He noted that when he walked down the street, women in spring attire looked attractive (308–9). The cherry blossom became a metaphor for youth, women, beauty, and himself. At the same time, cherry blossoms reminded him of the fleeting quality of spring and its transient beauty, which he associated with pathos.

Sasaki exclaims that the cherry blossoms whose petals have partially fallen, enveloped in the morning mist at Shinobazu-no-ike in Ueno, in Tokyo, are refreshing. After accusing the government of utilizing the popularity of actresses who were selling government bonds at the Imperial Theater, he praises mountain cherry blossoms that he sees from his house. He is touched by their "modest beauty" and composed two poems praising cherry trees, which bloom by themselves without seeking fame (311–12). A few days later, he composed a poem in which double-petaled cherry blossoms on a single tree against a background of green captures the entirety of spring (312). In these passages, cherry blossoms become the counterparts of a Japan engulfed in war fever and are used to critique government policy.

Shortly before his final sortie, Sasaki was given special permission to visit his home. He confided to his friend, Hirasawa, that he had "volunteered" to be a tokkōtai pilot, although he had not told his parents. Hirasawa begged Sasaki not to throw his life away but to try to fly back to the base even at the risk of facing shame. The two went to take photos, and then Sasaki gave him a lock of his hair. This was their last meeting (Fujishiro 1981, 457). Sasaki later sent Hirasawa a poem in which he directly links himself to mountain cherry blossoms: "Mountain cherry blossoms, its splendor in its reflection in the purity of snow in a deep mountain" (Fujishiro 1981, 458). Blaming himself for seeking honor and recognition, he affirms that his ideal is purity of spirit, which blooms even when no one notices its presence.

At the time of Sasaki's final mission, cherry trees at the bases in southern Kyūshū were in full bloom. Fujishiro (1981, 462) notes that the pilots adorned themselves with cherry branches on their last mission but does not mention whether Sasaki did so. In a letter to his friend Hirasawa, after describing double-petaled cherry blossoms in full bloom, Sasaki reports that one after another the tokkōtai planes had taken off for an all-out attack. During his last days at the Kanoya air base, Sasaki writes a number of poems in which cherry blossoms figure. One refers to those that fall just as spring passes away after enveloping the "Place under the Sun"—that is, Japan—with their fragrance (Ebina 1983, 185). He sent seven of his poems to Hirasawa. In one, he describes the tokkōtai pilots taking off with cherry blossoms as ancient warriors. In another, after thanking Hirasawa for his friendship, he vows to "fall like cherry blossoms" after sinking an aircraft carrier (Fujishiro 1981, 462–63). After his death, his sister also composed a poem in which she referred to him as a mountain cherry blossom (Fujishiro 1981, 465).

The writings of a student pilot such as Sasaki, an avowed Marxist, are important for our understanding of the symbolism of cherry blossoms. We would expect to find this symbolism within the context of the ideology of sacrifice for the emperor *qua* Japan in the writings of conservative soldiers. But this symbol also featured in the writings of political liberals. I examine the range of meanings Sasaki assigned to the flower and ask whether its more nationalistic meanings penetrated his thoughts.

Before the war reared its ugly, menacing head, Sasaki's cherry blossoms stood for spring and youth. His later poems reveal his more complex responses to the atmosphere in which the Japanese were thrown into a wild craze regarding the war and every individual was compelled to be patriotic. For Sasaki, cherry blossoms represented the counterpoint to what was happening in society and the ideal he tried to emulate: to maintain one's own integrity and remain pure and beautiful without succumbing to the temptations of society and the quest for fame. The flowers formed a transcendental mirror showing what he aspired to be, knowing very well his own weakness for others' praise. Toward the end of his life, the falling cherry blossoms served as a metaphor for the pilots, including himself, who "fall" for the country, but without any references to the emperor or to cherry blossoms as the souls of fallen soldiers at the Yasukuni National Shrine.

IDEALISM: THE SEARCH FOR A GREATER CAUSE

Sasaki's quest for purity and beauty in nature, ideas, and people is part and parcel of his idealism and search for the meaning of life in dedicating oneself to a greater cause, transcending the egotistical fulfillment brought by worldly fame and fortune. Reading *The Revival of the Idol,* in which Watsuji explains how "the Greek idols were destroyed by Apostle Paul," prompts Sasaki to reflect on his own yearning for "the ultimate"—God or an equivalent (March 10, 1940, 73–74). Having read *Uncle Tom's Cabin,* he writes:

> The words of Mrs. Stowe—"because I am loved by God," "I am with God"—
> How much do I wish to have an absolute authority! But, I cannot believe in
> Christianity. Any other absolute authority? (April 2, 1940, 80–81)

Sasaki's quest for the "ultimate" culminated on the mountain peak of Kamikōchi. He writes:

> We entered Kamikōchi and greeted the Hodaka mountain peaks in the morning. Leaves of larch and birch are reflecting the morning sun and it is like looking at a scroll painting. I found my absolute authority here. If man did not possess a political nature, I would not mind sacrificing my life for this absolute authority [beauty and nature]. (April 4, 1940, 81)

This statement should be compared with one written on October 12, 1940 (115–17): "Idealism is neither a fixed ideology nor an absolute authority."

While Sasaki found his "ultimate" in the beauty of nature at the psychological level, he deliberated on idealism at the conceptual level as well. A statement written on November 1, 1940, although somewhat contrived, reveals his quest for his idealism at the time Japan was marching toward authoritarianism:

> I prefer to think that "inevitability" is more important than "necessity." One must always strive for *stirb und werde!* ["die and become!" or growth through death]. I am truly grateful for being alive. . . . We cannot detach ourselves from the present condition. It is *in Welt sein* [the presence in the universe] of Heidegger. . . . The most important thing is the freedom of will, freedom of spirit, amidst the chaos at present. . . . Blind obedience without free will is not an answer to our chaos. Chaos is not so simple as to be resolved by a Führer. (130–31)

He likes Goethe's phrase *Stirb und Werde* and proclaims that a human being must always be youthful (January 28, 1941, 180).

An important principle for Sasaki was the individual's responsibility toward a greater cause. His greater cause became the good of the social group to which he belonged: the Japanese. Sasaki's conception of Japan combined a blurred image of his ideal Japan and the actual Japan, which he saw as corrupted but nonetheless facing the greatest threat in its history. The question of responsibility toward society was not an abstract concern for Sasaki and his peers, because the choice to live for themselves meant life, whereas the choice to serve society meant death. He and other student pilots chose the latter. But the choice was made only after anguished philosophical debates about happiness and death from Socrates, the Cyrenaics, and the Epicureans to the Cynics, on one hand, and the notion of social responsibility from Aristotle, Kant, Mann, and Rolland, on the other.

In the final analysis, it was their idealism—sacrifice of the self for a greater cause—and the sense of social responsibility cultivated at the First Higher School that led Sasaki and his peers to take the course leading them ultimately to death, through which they hoped to bring about their utopia: a new Japan without egotism and free from capitalistic corruption. Sasaki's vision of the new Japan derived from the philosophical idealism that runs through the works of Rousseau, Kant, Fichte, Schilling, and Goethe in *Wilhelm Meister*—which he read eagerly. His idealism constituted a complex set of deliberations on the nature of human beings. Inspired by a lecture given by Asanaga Sanjūrō, he traces the development of the consciousness of the self:

> Beginning with Socrates, it was rediscovered during the Renaissance, transformed in Kant's transcendental idealism, became the absolute self in Romanticism only to be abandoned during the latter half of the nineteenth century, and was revived by the neo-Romanticists of southwestern Germany. (207–9)

He is torn between giving priority to rationality or to emotion: "Rationality, a ghost. Desiccation of emotion" (118). Yet after reading Nietzsche and Rousseau he states: "Only after emotions subside, deliberations come through" (137).

In his quest to understand what was happening to Japan, Sasaki read a large number of books about philosophy, political economy, history, and related subjects. He often read them as counterpoints to the Marxism of Marx, Engels, Kropotkin, Lenin, and Trotsky which, of all the philosophical schools, had the greatest influence on him. Marxism identified the ills of Japan at the time. Yet it did not provide him with a utopia, and he was never a blind believer in Marx. As a congratulatory gift on his entrance to the University of Tokyo, his friend Ōuchi sent him *Friedrich Engels: Sein Leben und Werk* by Evgeniia Akimovna Stepanova in Japanese translation. Sasaki opted for reading the original in German and was deeply moved (304). He also read *Das Kapital* and noted, "After getting into Volume 2 of *Capital*, my progress is very slow. It is not well organized and the writing is obtuse" (351).

He criticizes Japanese Marxists:

> All books written by [Japanese] Marxists are demagogical, combative, or like a composition written by a higher school student who encountered philosophy for the first time. It goes without saying that it is just about impossible to understand their texts. I no longer have the naïveté to lose myself by their

demagogy. I feel sorry for Marx for being propagated by these fellows. (June 5, 1942, 320–22)

Repeatedly calling Marx a "craftsman (*kōsakunin*)" (200), he disapproved of him for scientifically measuring human happiness (331). He was impressed by the activist stance of Lenin and Stalin and wished that "we had someone like them in Japan" (351).

While Marxism provided Sasaki with a way to identify evil, Miyazawa Kenji and Albert Schweitzer shaped his vision of utopia. For the last class reunion of the First Higher School on November 10, 1943, Sasaki wrote a long essay about Miyazawa (1896–1932), the poet who dedicated his life to helping farmers. Sasaki's essay, "Love, War, and Death—On Miyazawa Kenji's *The Crow and the Great Dipper*," centers on passages by Miyazawa that expressed Sasaki's own feelings. The first is the crow's prayer to the Great Dipper, its guardian deity, on the eve of its war against the mountain crows:

I don't know if I am supposed to win this war but I will fight as much as I can, leaving my fate in your hands. . . . I pray that we will see the day as soon as possible when we welcome a world in which we do not have to kill enemies whom we cannot hate. For this end, I would not mind my body being ripped innumerable times. (Fujishito 1981: 418–19)

Choosing to emphasize this passage in November 1943, just a month before he and his university classmates were to be conscripted into the military and sent to war, was a significant political and intellectual act.

Schweitzer's humanitarianism served Sasaki as a sustaining source of inspiration and strength. While still in the First Higher School, he began reading Schweitzer's *Out of My Life and Thought: An Autobiography* (*Aus meinem Leben und Denken*) in German. At the age of twenty-one he admired Schweitzer's motto: "To devote oneself to scholarship and art until age thirty, and afterward to devote oneself to those who are unfortunate." Inspired by Schweitzer's "non-romantic humanitarianism," Sasaki felt a surge of strength inside (362–63). He quoted Schweitzer to express his determination to "recognize the value of any task and devote oneself to it with full sense of responsibility" and to renounce heroism in one's action (376–77).

OPPOSITION TO WAR AND MILITARISM

Sasaki admired Uchimura Kanzō, a Christian who refused to bow toward the emperor's signature on the *Imperial Rescript on Education* when, on January 9, 1891, the First Higher School celebrated its centennial. Uchimura regarded this act as idol worship. He was dismissed from his teaching position there (90, 113, 260). A major strategy of the state from the beginning of the Meiji period was to transfer the notion of love, loyalty, and indebtedness from parents to the emperor, who was constructed and represented to the people as their father, with the entire population of Japan constituting one family. The government policy of posthumously promoting tokkōtai pilots by two ranks greatly increased the amount of financial compensation provided to survivors, so dying enabled the pilot to support his parents as if he had lived to take care of them in their old age. When a soldier was faced with imminent death, such a reward for his parents offered him a rationale to plunge to his death, especially if his parents were not well off, even when neither the pilot nor his parents espoused the idea. Sasaki was able to see through the state strategy and made sarcastic remarks about this promotion.

He was shocked to see his good friend Hanzawa, who was utterly devoted to Nietzsche, salute toward the Meiji Shrine from a train and remarked: "If he were thoroughly converted to Nietzsche, he would not have done so" (December 19, 1940, 156–57). On December 9, 1941, Sasaki writes:

> Somehow I just can't be euphoric over Japan's victories in war. I feel anxiety. I am also concerned about what will happen to capitalism after the war. (262)

A few days later, he remarks:

> Being able to live well in this emperor's state under his benevolence, I would not refuse to be drafted if it is his order. I am not so weak as to be crushed by the war. However, I resolutely declare my anti-war stance. I will attempt to eliminate wars. (December 15, 1941, 263–64)

Sasaki is concerned about the right wing's utilization of patriotism to enlist the populace at a time of national crisis:

> At the time when Marxism was in vogue, people, especially upper-class people, poured sympathy over the proletariat. It was fine. But they were unable to see beyond it. They were unaware of the devil's hand of the right wing. . . . A new national system, unification under the emperor—these are slogans. . . . Now we see a sudden surge of patriotism and concern over our country. It is quite natural for anyone who is conscious of being a Japanese

to have such feelings. However, we cannot allow an ugly hand to capture the pure soul. . . . To be utilized by them will prevent us from achieving our goal for our nation. (March 7, 1941, 192–93)

On September 14, 1941, he observes:

It is reported that all Japanese must work for the industries important for the war effort. That means that there are people who are sucking sweet nectar while ignoring struggle, human dignity, the humanity of the Japanese. What is patriotism? What do you mean by "ancestral country" [*sokoku*]? How can we tolerate the killing of millions of people and depriving billions of people of basic human freedom under the banner of such abstract notions [as patriotism and homeland]? (249)

Sasaki continued to wrestle with these questions after he was drafted.

Sasaki questioned why the military ignored unethical conduct in its own ranks, such as torturing men who refused to go to war and working soldiers on the base to death in the name of "training" (January 22, 1942, 281). He is upset by the Japanese occupation of Singapore, which the Japanese greeted with a frenzied celebration:

Finally we invade Singapore. There must have been a large number of civilian casualties inflicted by the operation. Cruelty of war. Blind to such matters, history marches on day by day. (February 10, 1940, 292)

Sasaki then records a poem, although it is not clear whether it is his own composition or one by the Czech religious reformer Jan Hus (1369?–1415; known as John Huss): "How heavy is my heart, thinking of all these people who fight not knowing what the war is about" (February 10, 1942, 292–93). This sentiment echoes that of Miyazawa Kenji's work portraying the crows not knowing why they had to fight.

After he entered the University of Tokyo in April 1942, the tone of his diary becomes darker. As the incident of the purging of economics professors, including Ōuchi Hyō'e, his friend's father, indicates, the government intensified its attempt at thought control. By 1942 the power of the state was so pervasive that economics students who held a research meeting were arrested. The department was regarded as a hotbed of Marxism, and only a small number of students chose the subject as their major, although both Sasaki and Ōuchi Tsutomu did so. Students could not utter such words as *capitalism* and *inflation,* and meetings of reading and research groups were prohibited (Fujishiro 1981, 431–32).

On April 5, 1942 (310), Sasaki speaks of spring as an annoying season, a complete turnabout from his celebration of spring on March 26, before he entered the university. His shifting mood was connected with the changing political situation. On April 6, 1942, he deplores hypocrisy in the celebration of "the Japanese spirit" and "the imperial country" (*sumera mikuni*). He uses an exclamation mark when he writes: "The military—A Big Fool! [*Gunbu no ōbakayarō*]" (310-11). The following day he harshly criticizes the newspapers for the fanfare they gave to the nine soldiers who rammed into American vessels at Pearl Harbor (*gunshin*). The government did not disclose that the tenth soldier had been captured by the Americans but elevated the nine soldiers to deities. He is especially annoyed by the media's praise of mothers for having raised their sons to be "splendid soldiers" (311). He sees through the state "strategy," which misleads people into participating in the war effort by "forcing" loyalty (*chū*) to the emperor by its praise of mothers. Referring to someone who proclaimed that he was ready to die because Prince Takamatsu talked to him in person, he declares that one does not die simply to be granted a meeting with a prince or a posthumous promotion by two ranks (403-4).

Sasaki's attitude toward Germany becomes increasingly negative as he learns about Nazism. In 1941 he can find no "beauty" in *Heimat*, a famous German film (182). His reaction to the Nazi propaganda film *Triumph of the Will* (*Triumph des Willen*) by Leni Riefenstahl is extremely negative. He finds the repetition boring. He understands how people might be moved to join the patriotic effort because of the way the Nazis presented the collective life of "one people." But their techniques—sanctifying labor for the collectivity, turning people into idiots, and having them perform for the dictator—appall him. He regards these techniques as being "against humanity and against history" (March 7, 1942, 301-2). In passages written during July and August 1942, Sasaki describes his loss of faith in Germany and finds both Germany as a country and the Germans as a people distasteful. He declares that it will be a matter of days before Germany and Italy surrender (380-82).

NATIONALISM: PARTIAL PENETRATION OF STATE IDEOLOGY?

Despite Sasaki's critical stance toward militarism, he remains deeply patriotic. He believes in an idealized Japan, which becomes a cause larger than himself. Thus, it would not be accurate to portray him as completely uninfluenced by the ideological propaganda promulgated by the state. Early in his school years, Sasaki's patriotism almost verges on the ideology epitomized in the slogan "die for the emperor." When the war begins, Sasaki writes that because he was living a good life in this imperial nation (*teikoku*) because of the emperor's grace (*kō'on*), he would not refuse the draft (December 25, 1941, 263–64). His favorite poem is the one by Yoshida Shōin: "Knowing its consequences, I do what I do, compelled by the Japanese soul [*yamato damashii*]" (Fujishiro 1981, 446).

The commemorative celebration of the legendary first emperor's enthronement twenty-six hundred years earlier, *kigen nisen roppyakunen,* was the Meiji government's transformation of myth into history in its effort to build one nation under one imperial father. On November 11, 1941, the date assigned for the celebration, Sasaki returns to the Den'enchōfu train station to go home. He finds men whose faces are red from drinking sake wearing the uniform *yukata* (a cotton kimono, usually worn in summer) and a yellow headband carrying a portable shrine along the street. He remarks:

> I felt happy looking at how energetic they were. There are people who derive utmost joy from such a thing and wildly parade in the streets. In their own way they are feeling the joy of the celebration of the two thousand six hundred years. We [he and his fellow students] certainly cannot do something like that. But there is not one right way to celebrate it. Even if we have different approaches, the important thing is that our feeling is the same. As long as they feel "how happy to have been born in Japan," it is all right. It would be wrong to exercise control over behavior. We must celebrate happily and freely. (139)

In other words, although Sasaki and his fellow students would not celebrate in such a frenzied manner, he approves of others' joining in the spirit of celebration. Most important, he is uncritical of the propaganda of state nationalism: be proud and grateful to be born a Japanese.

Sasaki's statements about nationalism contain contradictions, indicating that he does not see through the strategies of the government in a systematic way. This tendency increased as the war escalated, threatening the Japanese homeland. Although he criticized Japanese people's euphoria at the victories in the Sino-Japanese and Russo-Japanese wars, Sasaki was quite moved when he read about the mass suicide of the Japanese soldiers on the Attu Islands. He believed the propaganda news report that the wounded who no longer could fight bowed in the direction of the imperial palace and committed suicide, after which the rest attacked the enemy in the dark with a firm belief that their behavior would set a model for other Japanese to follow, leading to Japan's eventual victory. Sasaki was moved to tears when reading the testament (*isho*) left by Captain Yamasaki, who led the last assault. He hopes that the war would last long enough so that after finishing his university studies he would be able to join the military. He proclaims: "We must fight to the end so that the Japanese can create a new era by ourselves. We cannot succumb to the 'Red Hair and Blue Eyes' [kōmō hekigan] (the Europeans)" (June 1, 1942, 363–64).

At the time of his entrance to the University of Tokyo, Sasaki's uncle had given him a great deal of money (¥1,000) as a gift. After stating that he would most likely not fulfill his uncle's expectations that he would become a successful man, Sasaki writes: "Although I do not want to disappoint my parents, if I must do so in my pursuit of a larger cause, I have no choice. However, I hope it will not happen." In other words, he knows that his father, his uncle, and other relatives expect him to be successful, but he is willing to serve his country even if it means forfeiting his obligation to his parents (March 31, 1942, 310). After the date for joining the navy is set, he expressed his belief that enlisting in the navy to protect his country amounts to caring for his parents (October 2, 10, 1942, 391–94). Sasaki purposely chooses to be a tokkōtai pilot although he could have used his status as an elder son to secure a desk job as an accountant on the base.

On the other hand, Sasaki does not equate his country with the emperor, and he makes explicit statements against the emperor-centered military ideology. For example, he calls the concept of chūkō icchi, which equates loyalty to one's feudal lord or emperor with loyalty to one's parents, a vestige of medieval times (306). When he did not attend the ceremony commemorating the emperor's birthday (tenchōsetsu), his father criticized him for not having the national spirit (kokka seishin). He concedes that no one can be free from societal rules and that thus he will follow the example of Socrates, but maintains that he will not have anything to do with the national spirit (313).

On June 11, 1943, Sasaki recorded his difference of opinion concerning the war with his friend Ōuchi (364–65; Fujishiro 1981, 434–36). In a letter to Sasaki, Ōuchi opposes the war unequivocally and hopes for Japan's defeat. For Ōuchi, the war is for Japanese capitalism, imperialism, and Japan's rulers, not for the people. He cannot understand how Sasaki, who is so bright and knowledgeable, does not understand it as he does (Fujishiro 1981, 436). He tells Sasaki not to die in the war, because a wish to die in such a war derives only from a sense of heroism or from momentary sentimentality; it is an act of stupidity (364–65).

Sasaki, too, believes that Japan has become corrupted by capitalism. But Japan remains his homeland (sokoku). His solution is to destroy it in order to bring about a new Japan. Disagreeing with Ōuchi, he says that the war is justified because the United States and England represent the evil forces of capitalism (364–65). He believes that the Japanese still retain some feudal elements, such as the way of warrior (*bushidō*), which protects them from becoming simply the prey of capitalists, although he keenly feels the danger of "illogical spiritualism" (279).

The news of the American landing on the Attu Islands prompts Sasaki to engage in a long soliloquy about capitalism and Marxism in which he expresse the conviction or, perhaps, the hope that capitalism is in its final stage:

> There is some sign of a new ethos for a new era. However, even though the material foundation for the new era is already being built, we cannot help but notice the legacy of old capitalism. If the power of old capitalism is something we cannot get rid of easily but if it can be crushed by defeat in war, we are turning the disaster into a fortunate event. We are now searching for something like a phoenix which rises out of ashes. Even if Japan gets defeated once or twice, as long as the Japanese survive, Japan will not be destroyed. It looks as though we are "carp on the cutting board" (*sojō no koi*). I am not being pessimistic, but we cannot deny reality. We have to move on, overcoming the times of difficulty. (359–62)

This passage reiterates his patriotism; he welcomes Japan's defeat because it means the death of "old capitalism" and the birth of a new Japan free of its shackles. He identifies his purpose in life: "At the critical juncture in history we cannot let old capitalists and irrational military men cling to the old regime. We [young men] ourselves must shoulder the responsibility of bringing in the new world" (377).

A phoenix rising out of the ashes of destruction was a favorite metaphor among young intellectuals at the time. For Sasaki, the phoenix was a new Japan, brimming with love for humanity and free of the capitalistic corruption that had transformed individualism into egotism (365). Sasaki sees death in the war as honorable for a young man, and he wishes to die after fulfilling his duty and responsibility to help create a new Japan (365). His declaration that he will join the navy has an idealistic yet fatalistic tone (391–94):

> Finally I will join the Navy on December 1. In anticipation, I have trained my body by swimming, gymnastics, and target practice. I am confident about my strength. We must now be the shield to protect the eternal life of our nation by going to the front to prevent the enemy's advance as much as possible. Scholarship is important. But our discipline [economics], which is pragmatic and socially relevant, will become even better when we are trained in the military. Even if I fall, society does not rely on one individual. I am not concerned and shall eagerly go to the front.

The term *shield* comes from the ancient term that the border guards used to refer to themselves in the eighth-century collection of poems *Manyōshū*: they were the shields for the emperor. Since the beginning of the Meiji period, the state attempted to propagate this term and the concept behind it (see also chapter 4). Sasaki, however, speaks of himself and his fellow soldiers as shields for Japan and as dying for their country, rather than for the emperor *qua* the nation.

In addition to this cerebral rationale for sacrificing himself, Sasaki shows us a state of mind that many young men experienced at the height of militarism, when the state created a frenzied atmosphere in which patriotism was praised as the utmost virtue. Tokkōtai pilots were elevated as "heroes among heroes," and their friends and people in the community lavished them with respect and praise for their bravery and virtue. This praise had a powerful psychological impact on many pilots. In this atmosphere, those who considered the war effort—including the tokkōtai operation—to be futile could not voice their opinions in public, so dissenting or skeptical views never reached these young men.

There is no question that Sasaki enjoys praise from others, including the acclaim he has received because of his extraordinary brilliance and academic success. He uses the German word *Ehrgeiz* to refer to the Japanese concept *kōmyōshin*, the desire for fame. He repeatedly refers to being torn between his wish for Ehrgeiz and self-doubt (278). He vows to pass the entrance examination to the University of Tokyo with the top score so that he can dismiss those who seek acclaim (286). In other words, precisely because he seeks to overcome his own weakness for praise, he is especially critical of those who perform well for the sake of earning praise. The diary entry for the day before he entered the navy makes it clear that Sasaki derived much satisfaction and self-assurance from the praise of his friends and relatives, who held an elaborate farewell party, writing their "true feelings" on the national flag as a farewell gift to him. He was quite touched when former members of the mountain-climbing club of the First Higher School came to bid him farewell. His best friend Hirasawa even gave him a haircut, which moved him deeply (404–7).

One of the recurrent themes in the writings by student soldiers is their sense of their identity *as men*. They saw their sacrifice for the country as a masculine duty, which included the protection of their beloved women— mostly mothers, but also wives, lovers, and young women in the abstract, since many of these young men had not had a relationship with a particular woman. Sasaki praises *kyōkaku*, a type of man during the Edo period who helped the weak and fought against the strong and was romanticized in later periods. Sasaki wishes to live as a man and die as a man, just as a kyōkaku did. He repeatedly uses *otoko* (man), a term that emphasizes the masculinity of men (February 2, 1941, 289–91). The Japanese state since the start of the Meiji period, like Nazi Germany, had deliberately used the strategy of appealing to young men's sense of masculinity to encourage them to take up arms and emphasizing the role of women who produce and nurture such young men.

Sasaki continues to defy the military government and seeks a utopian Japan. But, as astute and bright as he is, he cannot see how he has misinterpreted the propaganda of the government and translated it into his own idealized Japan. Sasaki is deeply patriotic. For the sake of his ideal country, he is willing to forgo his obligation to his parents.

LIFE IN THE SHADOW OF DEATH: AGONY AND AMBIVALENCE

A striking fact that emerges in Sasaki's diary is that he was always aware that his death in the war was inevitable. This consciousness is already visible in 1940. In response to hearing of the suicide of the son of Shimamura Hōgetsu (a well-known literary figure and a professor at Waseda University), Sasaki writes:

> If one thinks of a young life who dies in a state of purity and beauty, one even regrets that a human being is essentially a political animal. I know it comes from sentimentalism, but if one must die, one wishes to die beautifully. (April 13, 1940, 84)

As Sasaki's patriotic commitment to sacrificing his life for a new Japan deepens, he becomes more keenly aware of the imminence of his own death. The 1941 section of the diary opens with his motto for the year: "Live each moment as the ultimate. If one did so, one would live a life without regret, even with pains, pleasure, life and death" (167). Such an existential statement from a person only eighteen years old shows the dark shadow of war that hangs over him and other young men.

He mocks government propaganda newsreels in which photos of the so-called heroic souls (*eirei*) of brave soldiers (*yūshi*)—that is, pilots—are shown, pointing out that as long as they are someone's fathers and elder brothers they can be sacrificed. He states:

> I find contradictions. How many really die 'tragic deaths' in this war? I am sure there are more comical deaths under the disguise of tragic deaths. The two are the same on the surface. But comical deaths cloaked as tragic

deaths involve no joy of life, but are filled with agony without any meaning or value. That is, it is doubly negative, and that is why it is comical." (April 16, 1941, 219)

Sasaki's sense of the macabre may insulate him against government propaganda, but it does not diminish his agonized awareness of the meaningless waste of human life.

His awareness that he was destined to die became intensified in 1941 when international politics deteriorated and diplomatic negotiations between Japan and the United States no longer promised a solution, Sasaki met with his brother Taizō in June of 1941 and told him to major in science. He reasoned that Japan would certainly go to war and that university students would be drafted unless they were science majors. Explaining how important it was for their parents not to lose both their sons, he convinced his brother to follow his advice, even though the idea of a science major came as a complete surprise to Taizō (Sasaki Taizō 1995:72).

Sasaki's continual struggle to come up with a rationale for his own death appears explicitly in the diary. On January 10, 1942, he writes a poem marked by deep sadness and a sense of desperation: "Realizing how I have no more meaning for my life, I shall find the rationale in dedicating my life for others" (278). The notion of self-sacrifice is one of several rationales with which he tried to convince himself to accept his fate. Two days later, his diary entry ends: "I don't care what happens anymore. I just want to die" (279–80). He had arrived at this point of total resignation by 1942, four years before his death. On January 26, 1942 (285), he begins his diary entry by stating: "Since I may die any time, I make my living quarters neat, live a well-organized life, and take my photos [for posterity]."

His diary entry for March 4, 1942, includes a painfully sad reading of an incident during a walk as an allegory of the situation in which he and the rest of the Japanese are placed. On this day he went to the Tama River with his dog in order to read a book of poems by Wakayama Bokusui (1885–1928). He cites a romantic poem by Bokusui about longing for a person at the time when dandelions bloom on the sandy bank of the Tama River, proclaiming that in this year this sort of longing is no longer his— and implying that he has felt such longing before. Sasaki's thought is now focused only on how his days of study are numbered just when he feels that his study should be devoted to finding ways to lead his society, which has been wrecked by the war. He then notices a spider on the book:

It is a small spider. Feeling mischievous, I put a cigarette I was smoking near the spider. It frantically ran away. I put my cigarette just in front of it. It ran again. I put my cigarette near the spider again. I repeated this several times. The spider stopped running. I let it be for a while. But, feeling mischievous again, I put my cigarette above it. It ran. I put my cigarette in front of it. I continued this for about two minutes, or a bit longer, perhaps. Then it became weak and motionless. Even though it never touched the heat of the cigarette, it curled up its legs and stopped moving. Perhaps for this spider, the size of the book is like the size of Japan and five minutes may be five to ten years. During this time within this space, wherever the spider went there was fire and it could not escape no matter where it went. When it stopped, fire came from above. It could not stand still even for a second. If this happens to a human being, he or she will go insane. Above all, the spider could not understand where the heat was coming from. Human beings too would lose sanity if they could not understand the cause of the trouble they are suffering. I wish to be a man who can, even while struggling, objectively identify the cause of the trouble and transmit that knowledge to the next generation. I wish only then to die.

The allegory, as I interpret it, is a painful portrayal of the people in wartime Japan who do not understand what is going on and run amok seeking to find a way out of the impossible situation caused by the war. Sasaki wants to help take the lead in finding a way out of the war for the Japanese—and he wishes not to die until he has done so.

Sasaki also expresses his ambivalence and agony in references to novels by Natsume Sōseki (1867–1916), a major intellectual figure whose literary output was very influential. Highly educated in English and American literary traditions, Sōseki was concerned with how to reconcile one's integrity with one's responsibility as a member of society. Affirming his belief that literature and art should not be influenced by political authority, he refused to accept a doctorate in literature offered by the Ministry of Education. In 1942 Sasaki expressed his own doubts and anxieties when writing at length about two novels by Natsume Sōseki: *Kōjin* (*The Traveler*) and *Kokoro* (*The Soul*). The solitude of human existence and the struggle for life and death are the major themes of these novels. Sasaki identifies himself with their protagonists, repeating statements such as "To die or to go insane" (from *Kōjin*) and echoing their dilemmas concerning whether to live according to their own convictions or to meet the demands of society. By means of these references to Sōseki, Sasaki portrays his utter despair at being unable to decide which course of action he should choose. He is indecisive about sacrificing himself for the war; just as he thinks he is able to face death, he begins to enjoy life. He is torn and tormented by doubts. Sasaki also read Mori Ōgai (1862–1922), another well-known novelist who wrestled with the questions of modernity and of life and death in relation to one's responsibility to society. Referring to the time when he took the entrance examination for the First Higher School, he states: "At one time I even embraced General Nogi; perhaps it is better to go to war; things will be more clear-cut" (June 27 and July 1, 1942, 324–26). This is a statement of desperation: preferring death to the agony of indecision.

In his search for meaning in life, Sasaki tears a photo of Engels from the book Ōuchi has given him and puts it on his desk. He writes that he has come to appreciate Engels, who played second fiddle to Marx all his life. In stating his envy of Engels for being able to devote himself to another person, Sasaki expresses his torment about his struggle between living for himself and dying for Japan (340). The same issue emerges in Sasaki's reaction to a stage production of *The Forty-Seven Retainers*. He is moved to tears by the men's singular devotion to the cause of avenging their master (351). By World War II, this play, which originated as an eighteenth-century antiestablishment play, had been completely transformed into a morality play to support the ideology of dying for the emperor *qua* Japan (Ohnuki-Tierney 2002, 142–51). Even though Sasaki shrewdly saw through the state's manipulation of the nine deified soldiers of Pearl Harbor, he was moved by this morality play. He was desperately searching for a greater cause worthy of his sacrifice.

Sasaki's reaction to the news of the death of Admiral Yamamoto Isoroku (1884–1943) reveals his anguish. Yamamoto initially opposed Japan's entry into the war, declaring that Japan would prevail for only six months to a year. However, he was assigned to be in command of the Pearl Harbor attack and the battle of Midway. He became a hero after his plane was shot down by the Americans. On hearing of his death, Sasaki feels an impulse to volunteer to be a pilot and die. He writes, "It may give a more stable feeling," expressing the sense that he would rather die than go through the agony of his indecision (362–63).[5]

Sasaki expresses his ambivalence most poignantly in a meditation on a well-known statement from Goethe's *Faust* ("Before the Gate"):

Zwei Seelen wohnen ach in mein[em] Herz!! (Ah, two souls [*tamashi'i*] reside in my heart [*kokoro*]!!) After all I am just a human being. Sometimes my chest pounds with excitement when I think of the day I will fly into the sky. I trained my mind and body as hard as I could and am anxious for the day I can use them to their full capacity in fighting. I think my life and death belong to the mission. Yet, at other times, I envy those science majors who remain at home [exempt from the draft]. Or, I think of those fellows who did not pass the draft examination as "having managed cleverly." I envy those who became bookkeepers or those who work at the headquarters. I am drawn by my second soul to the earth. Perhaps this is inevitable. These two souls of mine are hidden in me but each raises its head as external stimulations work on my mind. When I talk to my comrades who are also going on the mission, when I have full confidence in my body and my mind, when I visit my relatives who encourage me and thank me, then I become filled with desire to protect them by becoming a shield for them. When they publicly announce at the base "Sasaki Hachirō, Kō Pass" [passing with the top score], and the Army tries to persuade me to quit the Navy and join them, then I find meaning in my life. I become excited and wish to work as hard as possible. On the other hand, when I hear that those in bookkeeping or at the headquarters are talked about as if they are the ones with good academic records, or see those without talent becoming engineers and doctors, working at safe places and being pampered, then I realize that we are the ones who are placed at the most dangerous spot. I am reminded of workers [in the capitalist system] who become discouraged when they realize how the management takes advantage of them. I feel like a fool to be proud of my fitness as a pilot. Those who skillfully escaped by not qualifying in the examination and took shelter in bookkeeping, engineering, and medical tasks must be the real clever ones. One of my souls looks to heaven, while the other is attracted to the earth. I wish to enter the Navy as soon as possible so that I can devote myself to the task. I hope that the days when I am tormented by stupid thoughts will pass quickly. (397–98)

CONCLUSION

Sasaki's writings offer us extraordinary insights into the complex thought processes of a young tokkōtai pilot and how they changed during the escalation of Japanese militarism. His writing also reveals some important thought processes that were common among such young men, as we will see in other diaries.

Perhaps most astonishing is that Sasaki and the others knew they had little hope for life and accepted this fact stoically. Of all the student soldiers introduced in this book, Sasaki was the most vocal in opposing the war, and his comments on the military and the Japanese government at the time were blasphemous. In advising his brother to choose a science major, his message was "Don't you die" (Sasaki Taizō 1995, 72). Yet he himself was resolute, and he never tried to avoid his fate. He felt the inevitability of death in early 1940 when he was only seventeen, exactly five years before he died. Just before he was drafted, he copied all the essays he had written during his Higher School and university days, including the one on Miyazawa Kenji, and wrote a testimony—all of which he handed over to his brother (Sasaki Taizō 1995, 74), a clear sign that he knew he would not survive the war. His existential wrestling with his fate is unimaginable from the viewpoint of today. It is chilling to realize that, since the end of the nineteenth century, the Japanese state had managed to penetrate the minds of the people so successfully that they accepted and resigned themselves to their fate. In this respect Japan contrasts with Nazi Germany, whose state ideology did not promote soldiers' acceptance of their own death; the German soldiers were told to kill.

It is in this context of a young man's resignation to his inevitable—that is, imminent—death that we must understand the quest for idealism and beauty that characterizes Sasaki's life and writings, as well as those of others. Sasaki's idealism took the form of a quest for beauty in nature and in human beings and their ideas. He saw beauty in purity of spirit. His idealism led him to seek meaning in life that is greater than simply satisfying himself. Tragically, this quest only reinforced his patriotism.

Sasaki's patriotism was a result of a tortured struggle to justify his own death for his beloved country. Informed by the global intellectual currents of the time, especially Marxism and Romanticism, he located beauty and human dignity in his ideal of a new Japan, which he envisioned rising like a phoenix from the ashes of the old Japan, corrupted by materialism and egotism. This belief led him to affirm that there was some virtue in destroying the United States and England, and even Japan, in order to usher in a new era of humanism and idealism for Japan and for the world. Or, perhaps, this hope itself became one of many rationales with which he tried to convince himself that his death, from which he could not escape, had some meaning.

The idealism that led Sasaki to his death was part of a complex philosophical debate in which he engaged with his friends. Two of his closest friends, Ōuchi and Hirasawa, opposed Sasaki's volunteering to die as a pilot. In the pages of his diary, he struggles to understand the individual's duty to himself and his responsibility to society. This sense of special responsibility was cultivated at the First Higher School, where young men were told to be the leaders of the future Japan.

Most remarkably, as he came close to dying for the sake of "his" Japan, Sasaki became less patriotic and was full of sarcastic remarks about the military and Japan. He died for a Japan he disdained, rationalizing that he would help bring a new Japan into being. His decision to become a tokkōtai pilot was as complex as his patriotism. Far from any sustaining act of volition, it was riddled with conflict and agony. Above all, Sasaki had reached the point of no return, and his death was guaranteed even if he changed his mind.

Sasaki died like the spider he found on his book by the Tama River. Rather than fulfilling his wish to help the Japanese find a way out of their situation, he died without finding a way out even for himself. It was an extraordinarily sad ending for this brilliant young man. We will see that his was not a unique case but one that represents a common pattern.

Sasaki's thoughts often seem contradictory, at least from the vantage point of today. His basic stance was in opposition to the emperor-centered ideology and especially the military ideology of the state. Yet he had embraced some aspects of the nationalist ideology in his earlier years, as is evident in his youthful admiration of General Nogi, his reference to the warrior's way (*bushidō*) as a counterpoint to capitalism, and his occasional identification of loyalty toward one's parents with loyalty to the country. These contradictions suggest that the state had been at least partly successful in its effort to inculcate the ideology that soldiers should die for the emperor even in the mind of such a brilliant young man and critical thinker. Yet in the end he did not die for the emperor. He admired Nogi and the forty-seven retainers more because they acted decisively from unswerving devotion to a higher cause than because they had an unflinching loyalty to the emperor.

Sasaki's idealism and love of beauty led him to a quest for the primordial soul of the Japanese as expressed in nature before it was contaminated by capitalism. The cherry blossom was an important "flower for thought" for Sasaki, who assigned various meanings to it. The way these meanings changed at different periods of his life is most illuminating. First, the flower embodied the spring of life, full of beauty, when Sasaki was celebrating his youth. Yet it also held pathos for the brevity of spring and youth, as if he were anticipating his own early death. When he was looking for an answer in his struggle between the virtue of individual integrity and the demands of society, the cherry blossom became the mirror reflecting the purity of an individual who keeps his principles in spite of the worldly desire for acclaim. The flower was the symbol of his ideal vision. Toward the end of his short life, the falling cherry blossom became the metaphor for himself and his death. Of these three sets of meanings, the second one—the strength of the individual against the tide of society—came from Sasaki's imagination, yet other Japanese could readily understand this meaning. His identification with falling cherry petals derived more from the symbolism in Japanese culture in general than from cherry blossoms as a part of the emperor-centered ideology. For Sasaki, the cherry blossom was a powerfully evocative symbol, but it did not stand for sacrifice for the emperor or the metamorphosed souls of fallen soldiers. The flower was above all a symbol of his idealism, whose most important dimension was aesthetic.

PARTIAL LIST OF SASAKI HACHIRŌ'S READING

History, economic history, economics—German: Erich Maria Remarque, Wilhelm Windelband; *English:* William James Ashley, Alfred Marshall; *Italian:* Benedetto Croce.

Philosophy, including economic and political philosophy, and ethics—German: Wilhelm Dilthey, Friedrich Engels; Ludwig Feuerbach, Johann Gottlieb Fichte, Georg Wilhelm Friedrich Hegel, Carl Hilty [Swiss], Emmanuel Kant, Karl Johann Kautsky, Theodor Lipps, Karl Marx, Friedrich Nietzsche, Leopold von Ranke, Arthur Schopenhauer; *Classical:* Plato, Socrates; *English:* Jeremy Bentham, John Stuart Mill, Adam Smith; *French:* Jean-Jacques Rousseau; *Russian:* Vladimir Ilyich Lénin, Lev Davidovich Trótsky; *Italian:* Gabriele D'Annunzio; *Japanese:* Nishida Kitarō, Tanabe Hajima, Uchimura Kanzō, Watsuji Tetsurō

Science—German: Albert Einstein, Max Planck; *English:* Isaac Newton.

Sociology—German: Max Weber; Georg Simmel.

Literature—German: Johann Wolfgang von Goethe, Hermann Hesse, Thomas Mann, Johann Christoph Friedrich von Schiller; *English:* George Noel Gordon Byron, Thomas Carlyle, Charles Dickens, Lafcadio Hearn, William Shakespeare, H. G. Wells, Oscar Wilde; *Russian:* Anton Chekhov, Fyodor Dostoevsky, Nikolai Gogol, Leo Tolstoy, Ivan Turgenev; *French:* Romain Rolland; *Japanese:* Abe Yoshishige, Arishima Takeo, Higuchi Ichiyō, Kawabata Yasunari, Kunikida Doppo, Miyazawa Kenji, Mori Ōgai, Natsume Sōseki, Tanizaki Junichirō, Tayama Katai, Yamamoto Yūzō

Now it is before the dawn. It is 3 o'clock at night. 3:00 A.M.
I do not want to die! I will try to live a full life. . . . I want to
live. No, I don't want to die. . . . I feel lonely. I don't know why
I feel so lonely—Being isolated? Feeling the poverty of the self?
Homesick?

November 26, 1940

Exquisitely erotic
Her smile for me
The image of the maiden
How distant it is now.

1945

Dusk, that most beautiful moment . . .
With no pattern
Appear and disappear
Millions of images
Beloved people.
How unbearable to die in the sky.

July 27, 1945, the night before Hayashi's final flight

Hayashi Tadao died on July 28, 1945, at the age of twenty-
four. Born in Tokyo in 1922, he attended the prestigious Third
Higher School in Kyoto and then the Imperial University of
Kyoto in western Japan. He was drafted as a student soldier
on December 9, 1943. Hayashi sought training as a scout
pilot, and in May 1944 he became a Navy Air Force pilot with

the rank of ensign. While on a scouting mission off Shikoku Island, his plane was shot down by an American fighter plane that took off from an aircraft carrier he had sighted. In a tragic twist of fate, he was killed two days *after* the Allied Forces had delivered the Potsdam Declaration to Japan.

My Life Burning in the Moonlight: Hand-Written Diary and Other Writings by Hayashi Tadao was compiled and edited by his elder brother, Hayashi Katsuya, who chose the title to portray how he died—as his plane exploded in the moonlight among scattered clouds (Hayashi Katsuya 1967, 220). The book includes diary entries from April 6, 1940, to July 14, 1944, covering his years at the Third Higher School (Sankō), at the Imperial University of Kyoto, and in the Navy Air Force. Parts of his diary are quoted in four other publications.[1] The volume also includes poems and letters written in 1945 and two essays, one on Thomas Mann's *Buddenbrooks*, which he wrote during his first year at the Third Higher School, when he was eighteen, and the other on the economic history of modern Europe, written at the Ōi Naval Air Base.

The collection closes with two recollections of Hayashi, one by his elder brother, Hayashi Katsuya, and the other by Ōchihara Yutaka, a Sanskrit scholar at the University of Kyoto who had attended the Third Higher School and the Imperial University of Kyoto with Hayashi Tadao. Both were written in 1967, when the book was published. In his essay, self-consciously titled "Hayashi Tadao in My Recollection," Hayashi Katsuya explains his reasons for waiting twenty years after his brother's death before publishing these writings. First, right after the end of the war, the American occupation forces imposed strict censorship. The atomic bombings of Hiroshima and Nagasaki could not be discussed in public. At that time it was not possible to publish any portion of diaries like Hayashi's. If one attempted to do so, the original could be confiscated. In fact, a rumor about an attempt to publish unauthorized material could lead to severe sanctions. Second, Hayashi Katsuya wanted to wait long enough for the Japanese to come to understand how their nation entered World War II and why it resorted to sending university students to war before he published the diary. He hoped that when the Japanese came to terms with these issues they would be able to understand the thoughts and feelings of young men such as his brother who perished. During the war the two brothers had engaged in extensive discussions about a variety of political issues, and Hayashi Katsuya wanted to see how their answers to these issues might appear in retrospect. For example, they debated the rise of Nazism as a result of Germany's defeat in World War I, the significance of Japan's militarism and imperial expansion, how Asia might change after

World War II, and what role Japan might play in changing Asia. Envisioning a starting time twenty years after the end of the war, Hayashi Katsuya did not pursue the last two volumes of his brother's four-volume diary, covering his time in the Navy Air Force, which remained in the possession of a friend. Only in 1966, on the anniversary of his younger brother's birth, was the last half of the diary returned to Hayashi Katsuya.

Hayashi Tadao began keeping a diary as soon as he could write. Hayashi Katsuya, wanting to share his brother's diary in order to show how he earnestly pursued his quest for truth, omitted the early writings that had no bearing on the quest. The entries in the published volume start at the time of Hayashi Tadao's entry into the Third Higher School at the age of eighteen. Hayashi Katsuya's essay provides information about the family's history.

The Hayashi family lived in a large mansion on a hill in Kanagawa overlooking the Bay of Tokyo. According to Hayashi Katsuya, their father was a "feudalistic" patriarch. As was the custom, the eldest son was given special privileges but was disciplined very strictly, with the expectation that he would succeed his father as head of the Hayashi family. Their mother followed the tradition of a samurai family, as in the saying "a samurai family which has at least one attendant following the master with a spear" (*yari hitosuji no iyegara*). She even taught her firstborn son the proper manner of committing *seppuku* (harakiri, or ritual suicide), which was a samurai tradition. As was not unusual for a younger child, Hayashi Tadao was indulged by his mother. He could go to her, looking for comfort, at any time and for any reason. He had very little to do with his father, who died in 1935 when he was only thirteen (Hayashi Katsuya 1967, 223–24).

Their father's death was the result of a stroke that he suffered during a verbal confrontation with Hayashi Katsuya, who could not stand what he called his father's "Meiji-style" combination of "hypocritical progressiveness with feudalistic arrogance." During the confrontation, the elder son addressed his father as "you" (*anata*) and asked to sever his tie to the family. His father could not tolerate being addressed with the form used for equals rather than with the respectful term for "father" (*chichi*), much less his son's defiance and refusal of family responsibilities. Swearing that he would kill Katsuya, he grabbed the family's sword (at that time most families with some stature kept a sword as an heirloom). At that moment he suffered a massive stroke. Hayashi Katsuya felt extremely guilty, and for an entire year he gave up everything to care for his father, feeding him, giving him shots, and even performing some minor surgery under the direction of three medical doctors who attended him. When he drew his last breath, his father thanked him: "Katsuya (the elder brother) is my doctor" (Hayashi Katsuya 1967, 225–26).

The Hayashi family's fortunes declined precipitously after his death. The father had left an enormous amount of debt. The electricity, water, and gas were cut off because payments were in arrears. The elder brother worked in a factory during the day and sold *oden* (a plebeian dish with vegetables, tōfu, and various other ingredients in a broth) from a cart on the street at night. Doctor Suzuki Umetarō, a well-known member of the Japanese and German academies of science, recognized Hayashi Katsuya's talent and hired him to work at his chemistry lab. The pay was low, and he was allowed only one meal per day, which he supplemented by helping himself to the guinea pig feed. After Katsuya left home to work at the lab, his younger brother sent him a postcard requesting his return lest Tadao and their mother die of starvation (Hayashi Katsuya 1967, 226–27).

The family's situation improved markedly when the elder Hayashi brother secured a full-time position at the navy's Basic Research Institute. He was strongly opposed to Japan's militarism. Although the government did not draft university students in the fields of science and education, and thus Hayashi Katsuya could remain a civilian as long as he worked in the lab, he considered leaving the lab and even staged an act of sabotage. The navy decided to close its eyes as long as he relinquished any privileges accorded to government scientists and disclosed no information about the research taking place in the lab, all of which had potential military applications. Baron Ōkura Kihichirō became Hayashi Katsuya's patron, and he began to receive a handsome salary. He became able to support the family and to provide for younger brother's higher education. In 1939, Hayashi Tadao passed the examination for entrance to the Third Higher School with literature as his major (Hayashi Katsuya 1967, 226–27).

Hayashi Tadao and his elder brother, Hayashi Katsuya, did not get along during the period of abject poverty that followed their father's death. The two later became very close, however. They shared a deep commitment to Marxism and a love of Western classical music, listening to recorded symphonies at the elder brother's house. They discussed life and death, philosophy, the war and Japan's situation, and many other subjects (Hayashi Katsuya 1967, 228).

Hayashi Tadao was always close to his mother. In his last letter to her he recalls that they had talked about living together after his graduation from the university. They had planned to settle in Kyoto, which seemed to him a "peaceful and plebeian" place (196), in contrast to Tokyo. Now, he tells her their dreams have been swept away by historical events. He expresses regret that she will have to live without him in the face of the destruction of everything she had believed in.

Shortly after the war, the family received a wooden box on which were written the words "The Heroic Soul of the Late Ensign Hayashi Tadao." In the box, instead of his remains, there was a small paper with the word *remains* (*ikotsu*) written in calligraphy. At the news of his death, his mother lost her will to live and began to "wither" visibly. She died the following year, on February 16, 1946. Disillusioned about his country, Hayashi's elder brother, a chemist of great promise, chose to live in a remote mountain village and tutor children instead of trying to establish a career as a chemist in the city. His pupils built a wooden casket for his mother in which he placed the box with his brother's "paper remains" (Kaigun Hikō Yobi Gakusei Dai-14-kikai 1966a, 194; Hayashi Katsuya 1967, 230).

I have selected passages from Hayashi Tadao's diary and other writings to illuminate the major themes of his thought, organizing them chronologically within the major phases of his life at the higher school, at the university, and in the Navy Air Force.

ENTRANCE TO THE THIRD HIGHER SCHOOL, 1940

April 6, 1940

After leaving his home in Kanagawa, near Tokyo, to settle in Kyoto at the age of eighteen, Hayashi Tadao felt homesick. In the very first diary entry, he recalls the warm atmosphere of the family home and expresses his admiration for his elder brother. He vows to study English fourteen to twenty hours per week and the German language and German intellectual history fifteen hours per week, in addition to the formal school curriculum. His study of European languages and philosophy prepared him to read both widely and deeply.

> At night, I read Herman Hesse's *Beneath the Wheel* [*Unterm Rad*, or *The Prodigy*]. The young soul [of Hans Giebenrath], a young bud, tries to grow against the oppression of the education at the monastery. He leaves the monastery and tries to cultivate his own path. But unfortunately Hans falls ill. Beauty and ephemerality of his spirit and soul, leading to the sad ending of his life. The undercurrent of impermanence. Breath of growth, beautiful but fragile soul of the youth, and death.

Hayashi is touched by the spirit of life and growth in Hans bursting against the ever-present forces that try to thwart it. He emphasizes the ephemeral sublimity of Hans's beautiful and fragile soul and body. Hayashi feels that Hans was drawn toward death.

This entry announces the themes that were central to Hayashi throughout his brief life: the quest for beauty—in nature, people, and ideas—and the haunting thought of death, which he aestheticizes; and the struggle to understand individual freedom in relation or in opposition to the individual's obligation to the group.

Hayashi reflects on the nature of human bonds, both sexual and intellectual, referring to individuals only by an initial in the Latin alphabet:

> Human beings have sexual desire. . . . Love, pleasure of the body—they are so far away from me. I am afraid of love. I cannot be confident that the physical union can be achieved with purity. Perhaps love is possible only with someone like M. Physical union with purity and pure pleasure are in the realm of gold hunt. It is so far removed from me.

"Gold hunt," written in English, seems to refer to a difficult quest that is seldom successful.

In addition to his restrained but intense desire for a woman, Hayashi is tormented by his need for intellectual companionship with male friends:

> Among my friends, I respect and love S most. But, I am sure he does not have respect and love for me. He is mysterious. My foremost effort today is to try to be worthy of his friendship [if it happens].

Throughout his diary, he pours out his intense desire to find a real friend with whom he can engage in intellectual discussion.[2] (6)

April 15, 1940

To master the English language and to identify a principle which will intellectually uphold me—which is none other than liberalism—are two important tasks in my search.

Waste of thought processes—in my case there is a great deal of it. For example, in vain I ask, "How long will I live?" (6–7)

May 23, 1940

My daily assignment to myself is to read 5 pages in English and 100 pages in Japanese. . . . During my higher school days, my assignment to myself is: (1) to read 300 books in Japanese, and 15 books in English; (2) to master English to the level of my Japanese; (3) to improve my physical stamina—daily exercise for 30 minutes, but not to read when I rest.

In order to carry out this self-imposed schedule, he plans to buy a watch. (12)

July 1940: Essay on Mann's *Buddenbrooks*

Thomas Mann's work had a powerful influence on Hayashi. Before he took the entrance examination for the Third Higher School he had become engrossed in Mann's *The Magic Mountain* (*Der Zauberberg*) and *Buddenbrooks*, about which he wrote a lengthy essay for his own satisfaction. He later read Heinrich Mann's *Enttäuschung* (*Disillusionment*) (January 1, 1944, 106) and Thomas Mann's *Tonio Kröger* (June 20 and 25, 1944, 149, 155); he also reread *The Magic Mountain* (August 31, 1940, 20; January 3, 1944, 107). The essay about *Buddenbrooks* succinctly expresses the struggle between the fulfillment of the self, which for young men in Japan at that time meant life, and their service to society, which meant death:

> Mann is said to be the novelist of life and death. Sometimes he is said to be the novelist of decadence. It is also said that he was saved from death because of his commitment to "citizenship," which has a hundred-year history [in Germany]. . . . Mann uses the terms *life, death,* and *citizenship* in his own way, which is very different from the "meaning of death" of Paul Bourget. . . . What is death for Mann? And, life? . . . His "citizenship" is the healthy vitality for life and it sustains life, whereas his death is the state in which citizenship is lost and has lost its vitality. Mann's "decadence" is eroticism over death or the state of death. It is citizenship which saves decadence.

Hayashi is critical of Mann's inconsistency in not always foregrounding the duality of life and death in *Buddenbrooks*. He tries to find an answer to his agonizing question—whether to die for his country or to avoid death—by reading Mann, who, he understands, maintains that service to one's society and to humanity enables one to transcend the problem of life and death. (201–4)

November 12, 1940

He finishes reading Plato's *The Apology* and Nietzsche's *Thus Spake Zarathustra* [*Also sprach Zarathustra*], but notes that he cannot say that he really understood them. (26)

November 26, 1940

While Hayashi attempts to convince himself to accept death, he cries out for the affirmation of life, as shown in the epigraph to this chapter.

The haunting thought of death makes him extremely lonely, as it does most people. But rather than identifying the source of loneliness in the approaching death itself, he tries to locate it elsewhere. He wonders whether it relates to his sense of isolation from friends with whom he could share his deepest thoughts, his spiritual self, which had not developed as he thought it should, or to homesickness. (26–28)

AT THE THIRD HIGHER SCHOOL, 1941–1942

January 28, 1941

Hayashi discusses his feeling of being threatened by death, claiming that death hangs over his life. Yet he tries to convince himself that life on the cutting edge of a sword—that is, with a constant awareness of death—is the only life that moves forward and bears fruit. (32–33)

April 19, 1941

There is some truth in the indulgence in emotions and eroticism for human beings. Humans have a lonely existence. Even if it is nothing but a union of two bodies, human beings are instinctively destined to feel that they cannot live without the companionship of another human being. Of course, eroticism does not arise simply from loneliness. Is there something else in the desire to seek a companion? But, this interpretation is simply to aestheticize eroticism. . . . I cannot deny the presence of eroticism. (38–39)

April 30, 1941

"A human being is a member of a social group. At the same time, in one's consciousness one is independent. The two are not incompatible." In context, this statement seems more a brave attempt to convince himself of this truth than an experiential conviction. (41–42)

June 22, 1941

Hayashi notes that Germany has declared war against the Soviet Union and asks, "What will happen to Japan?" (54)

June 28, 1944

"Death is immoral and to live is absolutely moral." (56)

August 31, 1941

"Japan, why don't I love and respect you?" (59)

October 12, 1941

The nation is an entity possessing an enormous power to control. . . . I cannot praise Japan any longer. The war is not to protect the country but the inevitable result of the way Japan has developed into a nation.

Within the same paragraph, Hayashi resigns himself to his lot:

I feel that I have to accept the fate of my generation to fight in the war and die. I call it 'fate,' since we have to go to the battlefield to die without being able to express our opinions, criticize and argue pros and cons of issues, and behave with principles, that is, after being deprived of my own agency. . . . To die in the war, to die at the demand of the nation—I have no intention whatsoever to praise it; it is a great tragedy. (63–64)

October 16, 18, 1941

With the announcement of the dissolution of Prime Minister Konoe Fumimaro's cabinet on October 16, Hayashi expresses disgust with Japanese politics. Konoe tried to solve international tensions by peaceful means, including a proposal to meet President Roosevelt, that did not bear fruit. His resignation was due in large part to opposition from the ministries of the army and the navy, which were ready to declare war. On October 18, Hayashi interprets the emperor's appointment of the army general Tōjō Hideki as prime minister as heralding the rapid acceleration of the machinery of war: "We came where we were destined to arrive. What can we expect any more? Our fate is now determined." (64, 65)

November 8, 1941

In a detailed discussion of history and historiography, Hayashi notes:

History is the basis of our Weltanschauung. . . . Mannheim said: "In order to come to true understanding, we must grasp reality with Historismus und Dynamismus [sic]. . . . History provides us with the foundation for practice and a worldview. (72–73)

January 20, 1942

The following statement in *Jean-Christophe* really struck a chord in my heart: "Life consists of continuous and relentless struggle. If one wishes to become a human who is not ashamed of himself, one must fight against invisible enemies, natural disasters, overwhelming desires, dark thoughts; they all deceive people, demean them, and try to destroy them." (76)

May 3, 1942

Following an anniversary celebration at the Third Higher School, Hayashi went with his friends to a restaurant in Kyoto for a drink. The students all wrote their thoughts in the same notebook. This practice, called *yosegaki,* was a customary way to express comradeship. Hayashi wrote two characters standing for Life-Dream (*Sei-Mu*). These conjoined characters should perhaps be understood to mean "a dream of life" or "to live for a dream." Hayashi's diary entry of July 14, 1944, makes it clear that he uses the term "dream" to mean "ideals." (81)

June 18, 1942

Hayashi went to hear Tanabe Hajime (see chapter 1) speak. He writes:

I heard a lecture by Professor T. His voice was so small that it was hard to hear. He said, in sum, "Philosophy is a training for death. Reality demands death, that is, the sacrifice of one's life. One does not die according to his own volition." (87)

He makes no other comment on this day but discusses Tanabe in detail in the diary for May 21, 1943.

AT THE IMPERIAL UNIVERSITY OF KYOTO, 1942–43

September 10, 1942

Hayashi finished his second reading of Martin du Gard's *Les Thibault* in the original French. The first time, he had read it straight through. But he had realized that his French was not up to a level that satisfied him, so he reread the work very carefully and took down all the major themes. Hayashi also read Stendhal's *Le Rouge et le noir* (*The Red and the Black*) and Shimaki Kensaku's *Regional Life* (*Chihō Seikatsu*). (91)

September 23, 1942

Bildung—that's right—human life must be *Bildung*. We must make effort to reach our goal in life.

Bildung refers to self-cultivation, that is, a constant effort to improve oneself (see "Conclusion," below). (91)

September 30, 1942

At this time, Hayashi frequently agonizes about his sexual desire.

I must be honest. Sexual desire—it is painful. I stare at myself longing for the physical unity. Then I fight it as dirty and ugly. It is my anger at not satisfying the desire. On the other hand, I dream of: breathing [of a lover], smell of her sweat that excites you, the smell of the body of the opposite sex, the touch of a warm body, the joy of the embrace of two in love, playing around without the feeling of shame, frenzied dance of love, and falling asleep in her arms, and a pleasant feeling of waking up [beside her]—all these thoughts and images descend on me. Perhaps it is a bad dream after reading novels. . . . I daily struggle with this pain. Conquer yourself; take control of yourself! (91–92)

May 21, 1943

On the 19th I listened to the Monday lecture by Professor T [Tanabe Hajime] on "Death-Life (*Shisei*)." He explained that the Stoic School views death as a natural phenomenon, not to be controlled by our will, whereas Heidegger's existentialism sees death as a realistic possibility—the possibility of rebirth that comes from our ability to face death. He explained that neither will save us from the torment of the life and death problem. The only salvation for us, according to Professor T, is to realize that one must die. In other words, we should not think of death with a possibility for life. We should live our lives prepared to plunge into death at any moment. Thus, death is not *Sein* (being) but *Sollen* (ought to be). Professor T's theory is clearly adapting to the reality of our nation today. . . .

Professor T continued to say that humans and God do not come into direct contact. Instead, a nation mediates between the two. The totality consists of mutual relationships among these three entities. But since they can be separated easily, we must strive to hold them together at all times. All three are constantly changing and moving. The meaning of scholarship lies in its ability to hold all three together.

The announcement of the death of Yamamoto Isoroku, commander in chief of the Combined Fleet, compels Hayashi to reassess Japan's military situation. (96)

June 16, 1943

While reading *Memoirs of a Revolutionist* [by Pyotr Alekseyevich Kropotkin], I was struck by the spiritual strength of the Russians, which was demonstrated by those women of pre-revolutionary Russia. Despite persecution by the government, they sought to learn, sometimes by going overseas, and finally founded a medical academy for women. We find in them the true character of the Russians. When we think of the Russians, we tend to envision the miserable world depicted in *The House of the Dead* by Dostoevsky. But, this strong intellectual passion for truth also existed. We see a unique characteristic of the Russians, who are often seen to have an enigmatic ethnic culture, in which these two trends coexist.

DRAFTED AS A STUDENT SOLDIER, 1943–44

On December 1, 1943, between two and three hundred thousand student soldiers were drafted (the exact number is unknown). On December 9, 1943, Hayashi was one of sixty-three hundred students who were sent to the Takeyama Naval Air Base in Yokosuka. He became a private second class. From this point onward, he increasingly voices doubts about and condemnations of the military and the war in his diary.

December 19, 1943

The days go by fast. Yet, each day feels very long. . . . One cannot fight alone in contemporary wars. Each must become a cog for the wheel. . . . Just because I acutely feel that the war is *Totalkrieg* (total war), I have to approve every activity as necessary. (103)

December 25, 1943

Resolutely I must keep my diary. But *Geist* (spirit) must be *frei* (free). Since we strive to have *Freiheit des Geistes* (freedom of spirit), we feel we are *beschränkt* (controlled).

In order to be the *Träger* (someone who shoulders responsibility) for the protection of the country, one must have a firm conviction for [the idea] *pro patria mori* [to die for one's country], build one's physical strength, and master the technical skills. (103)

December 28, 1943

Hayashi realized the grave prospect that Japan was facing: "As the year 1944 is approaching, a great *Katastrophe* is ever closer." He explains that the cause of the coming catastrophe lies in the military. "We can directly relate to our country with our feelings. But, we cannot relate to our country mediated by the military." He cries out in German: *"Leben, Leben, nur Leben*: To live, to live, only to live!" (104)

January 1, 1944

Deliberating about the fate of Japan, the military, and what it is like to be a soldier, in his first diary entry for 1944 Hayashi reveals several of the major characteristics of his thought: anticipation of his own death, aestheticization of death, and historical determinism as an explanation for his death.

> What is waiting for us in the future is perhaps a great *Enttäuschung* (disillusionment) and, for our society, a pervasive *Anarchie* (anarchy). Not looking at ten or a hundred years from now and closing our eyes from the distant future, we must anticipate their arrival and thus burn all our energy for our goals at the moment. . . . Not for the apotheosis of history, but for the realization of world history, we must sacrifice ourselves for its momentary intention. Is it that history needs the invisible "carriers of sacrifice"?

Hayashi contemplates his place in this historical trajectory by referring to Japanese and European writers' reflections on death and beauty, following the association of his thoughts through a series of allusive images. Hayashi first quotes a famous haiku by Matsuo Bashō from his *Okunohosomichi*: "'The summer grass. The remains of the warriors' dreams.' Isn't this a true expression of historical *Tragödie* (tragedy)?" He then quotes the opening sentence of Heinrich Mann's *Enttäuschung* (*Disillusionment*), with its praise for a strange sort of *Schönheit* (beauty): "The sun in a truly clear sky is dazzlingly bright in its lead color." In his own words he goes on, "What I dream is to stretch out on the waves of the sea under the sun on a spring day to become intoxicated with random thoughts as my body bobs over the waves." Recalling Paul Valéry's *The Graveyard by the Sea* [*Le Cimetière marin*], he writes:

Cimetière de la Mer. . . . Ah, have I started to lose my French already? . . . I yearn for blue sea, green fields, black soil, white pebbles, vast ocean, gentle breezes and warm sun. . . . Somehow I suddenly remember *Souvenirs de la Maison des Morts* [Dostoevsky's *The House of the Dead*]. That scene— at dusk in the summer against white sky, the prisoners are shoved into the cell.

The entry concludes: "I live in solitude." (105–7)

January 3, 1944

"In this peculiar organization of the military, one must completely abandon the self in order to act spontaneously." Hayashi feels that the military needlessly stifles the sense of individual selfhood:

I do not avoid sacrifice. I do not refuse the sacrifice of my self. However, I cannot tolerate the reduction of the self to nothingness in the process. I cannot approve it. Martyrdom or sacrifice must be done at the height of self-realization. Sacrifice at the end of self-annihilation, the dissolving of the self to nothingness, has no meaning whatsoever.

He describes himself: "I am a weak person—sentimental, vain, weak against the carnal desires. *L'homme n'est qu'un roseau faible,* . . . *mais c'est un roseau pensant*—Man is but a fragile reed, . . . but a thinking reed." He is alluding to the well-known quotation from Blaise Pascal (*Pensées,* section 6, no. 347): "Man is but a reed, the weakest in nature, but he is a thinking reed." (107–10)

January 16, 1944

Hayashi believes that Japan and capitalism are both at a critical phase of historical development: "Japan is now developing into *Hochkapitalismus* (advanced capitalism) and is ready to move on to the next stage of the mechanization of the world." (111–12)

January 17, 1944

He expresses admiration for a group of jailed Japanese Marxists and Communists for their courage and mental strength. He then wonders whether he can maintain the same mental fortitude on the base, because he is confronted with daily pressure to nullify or dissolve his self. (112–13)

January 22, 1944

"The military kills passion and transforms a human into a cog in a machine." Both "passion" and "machine" are written in English. (113)

January 23, 1944

"*Antoine, laissez moi seul* (Antoine, let me be alone)"—this plea by Jacques Thibault. His voice, imprisoned by *le pénitencier* (penitentiary), is identical to my voice now. All of us are pessimistic about the possibility of returning home. If I cannot go home and if I cannot get out of this navy life, I will go insane. . . . At the moment, I really want to read books. In this condition, there is no way I can fight in the war. Death is, for me, *coup de théâtre* (an unexpected event). . . . I have no passion. Loss of self in *indifférence*. I don't care what happens any more. The most painful and unbearable feeling comes from this life of forced indifference, a life in which we bump into a brick wall even as we walk one step. . . . The hard part is not death, but to live. At the height of life, life is terminated, the curtain goes down. Maybe it is splendid. After the climax the messenger of death arrives without notice. This is a splendid scenario. But, it is unbearably miserable if one dies after a life in which one cannot devote oneself to one's task and one cannot express oneself. (113–15)

January 26, 1944

Anticipating the following day's announcement of those selected to be pilots, he expresses his hope of being chosen for training as a scout pilot. (116)

SERVING AS A SCOUT PILOT, 1944–45

Hayashi passed the physical examination and was selected as a reserve pilot. He was sent for training at the Tsuchiura Naval Air Base, which was notorious for the brutal treatment of soldiers, on January 28, 1944.

February 6, 1944

How I was stirred by patriotism during my days at the university. We felt the tension when we were coming to the point of no return. Now, it is quite the opposite. I have no more passion. The military kills passion and transforms people, making them indifferent, turning them into cogs that turn a wheel mechanically. (117–18)

April 2, 1944

I pray that this life in the military will end as soon as possible. But, when we listen to the Imperial Rescript to Soldiers and the emperor's proclamation on the Greater Asian War, I feel some lofty inspiration.

An astute observer, Hayashi notes that even he, a political liberal, falls prey to some government propaganda, on this occasion feeling moved by imperial proclamations concerning the glory of Japan's colonial expansion, disguised as the liberation of other Asians from Western colonialism. (120–21)

April 18, 1944

When he was going out on leave carrying *Customs and Lives in Sakhalin* (*Karafuto Fūbutsushō*), a book by Taniuchi Rakubun, he was stopped, and his privilege of leaving the base was revoked. He writes: "The military law is an ethos that forces an individual to be a part of a machine." Later, on May 23, 1944, he gave up reading this book, having found it intensely romantic but of low intellectual quality. (122–23)

May 1, 1944

"Beautiful May arrived. May is the symbol of the gorgeous tapestry of *Natur* (nature). I thoroughly indulged in *schöne Natur* (beautiful nature)." His deep appreciation of the arrival of May was undoubtedly due in part to his pending departure from the Tsuchiura Naval Air Base, which he describes as a road to *Freiheit* (freedom). He writes:

> For us, the statement by Yoshida Shōin [a political activist writing at the end of the Shogunate period] that to die for the country is to live through death is far from our feeling. The military kills one's passion. We move according to the military rule, only. . . . Although I conform to the military on the surface, in my mind my will to move forward has disappeared. What motivates my action is neither *Patriotismus* (patriotism) nor the inner will, but a wish not to make waves. (130–31)

May 4, 1944

Hayashi was chosen be a scout pilot and sent to the Ōi Naval Air Base. He was pleased, and he thought his mother and brother would be pleased as well. The base was located near his home, and his elder brother was living across from the base on the other side of the Ōi River. (131–32)

May 8, 1944

Individualismus (individualism) is not just an 'ism' but is an innate principle of humans. I really hate the military. The only meaning I recognize for it is its role as the protector of our *Volk*. (132)

May 19, 1944

I am drawn to the issues of loneliness, prayer, indebtedness and social responsibility, but not *Liebe* (love), which to me is too remote at this time. I know there is a saying which probably refers to *Leben* (life) symbolized by young cherry blossoms [which fall beautifully after a short life]. But I don't like that sort of "purity" of falling without hesitation. A human should not die easily. (134–35)

May 22, 1944

In my opinion, to die right now is to do so without intervention. In other words, to die at this moment is an obligation imposed by history. (136)

May 23, 1944

There is very little possibility that I will return home alive. No, no possibility whatsoever. Even more so, there is no possibility to use foreign languages. However, even now I have not given up my quest for an answer to "What does Europe stand for?" and am still determined to pursue it. My *Lebensprobleme* (lifetime task) is to understand the nature of European societies and European social sciences, which arose from those societies. (136–38)

May 31, 1944

What if I get a day off and can go home? What a feeling it would be to read aloud the books in German! The books I need to read are: Goethe's *The Sorrows of Young Werther* [*Die Leiden des jungen Werthers*], *Über Helden und Heldenverehrung in der Weltgeschichte* [probably Thomas Carlyle's *On Heroes, Hero-Worship, and the Heroic in History*], John Stuart Mill's *Autobiography*, Aldous Huxley's *Chrome Yellow*, and Maruyama Kaoru's *God Who Wept* (*Namidashita Kami*). What I want most is to study foreign languages—English, German and French. (139–41)

June 2, 1944

Listened to No. 9 [Beethoven's Symphony no. 9, op. 125, in D minor]. I was moved. It is indeed a great piece of music. It intensified my desire to read books. (141)

June 8, 1944

I predict that Paris will fall within one and a half months. Now the whole-sale attack by the enemy with enormous material superiority begins. The last *katastrophisch* (catastrophic) stage described in *All Quiet on the Western Front* [*Nichts Neues im Westen*] is soon to approach. . . . In the south, the enemy, occupying Biak Island, is trying to recapture the Philippines. (143–44)

June 9, 1944

I started to read Chapter 1, Mignon, of Goethe's *Wilhelm Meister* [*Wilhelm Meisters Lehrjahre*]. I can read one page a day, but at this rate it will take *all of* September. I will try to finish it in July so that I can move onto *Werther* in September. (144–45)

June 12, 1944

"The enemy is now approaching Saipan. They are said to be approaching the eastern Sea of Japan." He refers again to "Mignon." Although his reading of it is going slowly, he has found a new source of invigoration and pleasure in his life. He again vows to finish "Mignon" in July and reiterates his plans for reading books in the original language, concluding: "If one is determined, even a devil would go away." (147)

June 16, 1944

Air raid on Saipan, Tenian Island, and the Bonin Islands. The situation is tense indeed. But, for me it is all right for Japan to be destroyed. It is too tedious just to wait. . . . Historical necessity led to the crisis of our people. We rise to defend our people and the land we love.

Again Hayashi resorts to historical determinism as an explanation not only for his own sacrifice but also for the imminent defeat of Japan. (147–48)

June 20, 1944

Calling *Tonio Kröger* one of Mann's "most beautiful and sweet fruits," he records his response to it: "My soul trembles at its tapestry, with a hint of loneliness, exquisite sensitivity, and almost threatening sublimity." Hayashi is apparently drawn toward the nihilistic aesthetics in Mann's work. (148–50)

June 25, 1944

On the base, reading books became prohibited. He comments: "What are they trying to do by issuing such a stupid prohibition? It only exposes their stupidity."

Hayashi struggles with his feelings of doubt and ambivalence, which derive from the military's effort to stifle the sense of the individual self. He describes the contradictions within himself as a struggle between Yoshida Shōin and Tonio Kröger. Yoshida Shōin (1830–59) was a scholar and politician deeply involved in the political struggles taking place at the end of the Edo period who is revered for his integrity and purity of spirit. Yoshida "recklessly" ventured into various activities against the Shogunate, leading to his imprisonment and execution. Tonio Kröger is the protagonist in Thomas Mann's novel of the same name. Hayashi writes that when the Tonio Kröger inside him wins, he sinks into a deep sense of despair. But then the Yoshida Shōin inside him cries out to him, urging him not to give up. (153–56)

July 8, 1944

It does not seem likely that I can acquire W. I. Lenin's *State and Revolution* [*Staat und Revolution—die Staatstheorie des Marxismus und die Aufgaben des Proletariats in der Revolution*]. . . . So, my plan now is to memorize Wilhelm August Schmidtbonn's *The Last Woman* [*Die Letzte*] and Rilke's *The Apostle* [*Der Apostel*]. (161)

July 14, 1944

I am finished with my diary. It is the first *Frucht* (fruit) of my impoverished spiritual life. Confusion and chaos only. *Moi, cette confusion et anarchie, c'est moi*—Me, confusion and chaos, that is me. What attract me are questions about the nature of modern society, its European characteristics, Japan's modernization, and Russia's modernization. . . . To live or to die—we don't know." Hayashi tries to resolve his dilemma by means of deliberations about spiritualism and materialism. "In this diary, I exposed my weaknesses. This *misérable* human, in its entirety, is portrayed in the diary. The writing of the diary was a way of finding meaning for me, as I am trying not to be swept away by the vertigoes of the time and trying to live *aktiv* (actively).

I think that a most suitable life for me is to walk along the streets of Moscow with a hunting cap over my head, study *Weltpolitik* (international politics) and *Weltwirtschaft* (international economics) at the *Bibliothek,* or engage in theoretical analysis of the directions which Japan should take. If I live, I shall accomplish this. If I die, well, it will turn out to be just a dream. I should like to think of this diary as Chapter 1 of the record of a human being with only a big dream who, without finding a solution, tried his best to achieve his dream. The End. July 14, 1944, 9:40 A.M.

Hayashi Tadao gives no reason for terminating his lifelong practice of keeping a diary. Neither does his brother, Hayashi Katsuya, or his friend, Ōchihara Yutaka. Two passages from Hayashi Katsuya's memoir imply that Hayashi Tadao simply gave up hope for himself and for Japan. According to his elder brother (Hayashi Tadao 1967, 200), when Tadao arrived at the Miho Air Base in April 1945, he saw "the death struggle of what made Japan rotten from the core." At one of the last meetings of the two brothers in June 1945, Tadao told his elder brother: "All finished. No more hope." (164–65)

ESSAYS, LETTERS, AND POEMS, 1945

February 26–March 11, 1945

Hayashi wrote an essay titled "The Economic History of Modern Europe," which he labeled "unfinished," while he was stationed at the Ōi Naval Air Base. Impressively broad in scope, the essay traces the rise of the mercantile economy in Europe and the spread of European empires to the Americas. Given Japan's imperial expansion and its apparent failure, Hayashi seeks to understand the historical development of European imperial expansion. (205–15)

Late May 1945

Before he left for the Miho Naval Air Base, Hayashi begged his older brother to lend him Lenin's *State and Revolution.* Since the book was officially banned, his brother was quite reluctant but bowed to his insistent requests. Hayashi told his brother that after closely reading each page while in the toilet, he tore it into pieces and threw it into the toilet or sometimes ate it, for fear of being caught (Hayashi Katsuya 1967, 229).

"Random Thoughts in 1945" (not individually dated)

A collection titled "Random Thoughts in 1945" consists of a large number of poems addressed (as if sent in letters) to people who were important to him, including his mother, his brother, his sweetheart, his aunt, and his close male friends, especially Ōchihara. All the poems are written without a set form, and most consist of three or four lines. I have attempted to reproduce their form as well as their meaning as faithfully as possible. Some poems are grouped together under titles. The collection ends with a poem written the night before his death and his last letters to his mother and brother.

How I am drawn
To the blossoms
That fall, losing their color and fragrance
With a wind.

Exquisitely erotic
Her smile for me
The image of the maiden
How distant it is now.

This ephemeral world.
As mindless wind blows
Petals falling down
Sadness of its fragrance.

On a sandy beach
White moon in a star-studded sky.
Flowers falling down
As wind blows.
. . . .

Love, after all
Reminds you of difference [between you and me]
To overcome it
We struggle

That is love as well
And love
A painful experience.

The night fell. Autumn, already.
Streams of light, faint and dim
Far off, two, three shooting stars.

The unconditional surrender of Germany
A lonely moment in world history
Its tragic efforts
For five years and eight months, with its result
Only an unconditional surrender.

My conviction of our defeat
Since 1942
It is now becoming reality
Who would understand this loneliness?

Adieu
Adieu
All will disappear.
All will be destroyed
It is all right
Isn't it all right,
A very natural process?
. . . .

The control over the sky over southern Kyūshū
Already in the hands of our enemy.
Our ancestral land
Ready to crumble.

Those of us who received our lives in this country
Why should we hesitate to give our lives to it?
Stupid Japan
Indecisive Japan
You, although quite foolish
[We] who belong to this nation
Must rise to your defense

Oh, Remarque, from a boy to an old man
Bypassing youth
Destroyed by war
The fate of our *Geschlecht* [generation]
The irony of historical fate
Plays the melody of a finale on the Western front
Prophet Nietzsche
Forever follows after Germany
Forever returning
This *Purgatorio*.[3]

. . . .

Mother, my elder brother
As running water that never returns
Please give up on your wandering child.

In the human world
But outside the comfort of emotional support, she must walk all alone
My aged mother, how painful to think about her.

How I wish to embrace her in my arms
To console her
But, it is now impossible to do so.

Counting only on me
To care for her
Only on me
All this time
I anguish in sorrow thinking of her.

Like your own son
You raised me, my brother
Even you I must leave behind and go alone.
(166–98)

Some addresses are written in prose but have poems interspersed within them. The longest is addressed to Ōchihara Yukata, his best friend, identified by the letter O (174–75):

You who made my university days so rich in learning. And you, who taught me the beauty of friendship. You will be in the center of my altar celebrating my past. While you were reading *Hitopadeśa,* I was trying to master [Alphonse] Dopsch. So, we spent every winter and summer day—the whole year—together, only the two of us, in the library. You, who follow the right path, were learning Latin grammar, whereas I was trying to memorize writings by Caius [Julius Caesar] in order to understand the inductive method. Do you still remember, O, the phrase from Caius? *Gallia est omnis divisa in partes tres; quorum unam . . . Aquitania, . . .* (Gaul is divided into three parts, one of which . . . Aquitania). . . . Émile Faguet's *The Art of Reading* [*L'art de lire*]. Nietzsche—our headache but full of [intellectual] flights and dynamism. You wanted me to explain his *Vom Nutzen und Nachteil der Historie für das Leben* [*On the Advantage and Disadvantage of History for Life*] since you could not understand it. But, we both resonated with Goethe's saying: "It is bothersome to teach without breathing life into it." . . . Ah, the two of us—young *Philologe* [philologists].

A letter to his sweetheart, whom he identified by the initial *I,* follows his addresses to his aunt, teacher F, friend K, and Ōchihara. She is not explained in either his diary or the essays by others. His particular beloved realized the ideal of his youthful imagination, but the fulfillment of love still seemed beyond reach (180):

You are a beautiful human being. You are too clever to be my friend. Your mind and every move of your body are so "refined" [English word in Japanese transliteration]. Why should a man like me deserve the interest of someone so *Mannigfaltigkeit* [*sic*] (talented in many ways)? Your affectionate manner of late—ah, it feels like a dream, too fortunate for me to be true. I love you. . . . Love tortures the person in love. But, my love, the pain of love is happiness itself. As Rilke says, illness is itself happiness. . . . Friendship is to devote one's soul and body, without expectations of return, knowing that love is painful.

The following is but one example of the many times his thoughts turned to women whom he would never have the luxury of having. His imagination is both romantic and sensual. After a long poem titled "Past and Present," he writes in prose (181):

How I wish to read Baudelaire's *Paris Spleen* [*Le Spleen de Paris*]. . . . Read again "The Stranger" [*L'Etranger*], *Vocations* [*Les Vocations*], and *Beautiful Dorothea* [*La Belle Dorothée*].[4] The dark-skinned woman Dorothée—walking at high noon on the white sandy beach.

A long poem titled "The End of Imperial Japan" expresses his feeling of desperation. Here are the beginning and the final stanzas (188–89):

The End of Imperial Japan

Ruining and crumbling, Decadence
Nothing will be left
The end of all
This fall
Lonely and chilly wind will blow
There will be nothing left.

. . .

All will crumble
Japan will meet its finale
That taboo
Catastrophe.

"Finale" considers the same subject in prose (190–91).

All that existed in the past is falling down and being swept away. As all the authorities and the orders are sinking into chaos, the images of those who met me in the past vanish without a trace.

Ah, the Past. It is fading away like a shooting star. . . .

Collapse!! Japan is following the road to its destruction. We are heading toward the *Todesmeer* (the sea of death).

Those who struggle—it is hopeless. . . . Japan of the past will be destroyed.

Destruction, what a sweet project. Decadence! Withering of a comfortable life. Bobbing and sinking. You—you are alive only by the eroticism of death.

In a long poem titled "Premonitions," he takes his fate for granted and comes to terms with death (193-95).

Premonitions

Catastrophe
Decadence
Rest is an invitation to death
Well, now
All who appear in my vision
Farewell
All is lost now.

My plane
Earlier today, it tried to take off
Turned sharply to the left
It twisted, twisted sharply
At that time, I thought to myself
It is all right with me to die now
If one must go, it is better to go quickly
It has been such a long day of struggle and pain.

Preparing himself for death, he mourns the ephemeral beauty that foretold the end in the following poem and then writes his last letter to his mother (195–96).

The Night before Death

. . .
Dusk, that most beautiful moment . . .
With no pattern
Millions of images
Appear and disappear
Millions of images
Beloved people.
How unbearable to die in the sky

Hayashi Tadao's last letter to his mother, dated May 30, 1945, reads:

Mother, you often talked [about] how we would live together in Kyoto after my graduation from the University. . . . Kyoto is really a very peaceful and plebeian city. You and I—it is the best place to live together, while continuing to learn. Mother, there is no hope [of living] together now that we are swept up in the torrents of the world. How are you going to live? What from the past can you use as moral support for your life? What moral strength can you depend on to continue to live? My aging mother to whom I cannot offer my love. I cannot bear the thought of you—my poor mother. (196)

CONCLUSION

Hayashi Tadao and Sasaki Hachirō followed similar paths, and their thinking developed along similar lines. Having attended elite higher schools and imperial universities, they had broad intellectual horizons. Both read very widely in economics, history, literature, and philosophy. Hayashi's heart lay with literature, especially that in French and German. The breadth of his intellect is illustrated by his reading of *Hitopadeśa*, a collection of children's stories in Hindi, and André Du Bouchet, a French poet who experimented with fragmented forms.

Why did Sasaki and Hayashi become patriotic even as they openly criticized the military government? Why did they acquiesce in the draft rather than find a way to resist? This alternative was not altogether impossible at that time. Some young men were clever enough to fail the physical examination. Sasaki's best friend, Ōuchi, did not join in the war effort, condemning it as a capitalistic endeavor. Hayashi's elder brother refused to be a "designated chemist" for the government. Both suffered as a result of their refusal to fight in the war, but they managed to avoid being turned into cogs in the military machine. The life histories of Sasaki and Hayashi illustrate the more common pattern among young men. When these idealistic youths were at the higher school and the university, they were swayed by government propaganda about the beauty of patriotism. They unknowingly conflated loyalty to their beloved Japan with loyalty to the imperial Japan for which the government wanted them to sacrifice their lives.

Even when they were beguiled by the government's version of the virtue of patriotism, they felt the shadow of approaching death. Hayashi Tadao's diaries show this knowledge quite clearly. In 1940, Hayashi was already acutely aware of the danger encroaching on Japan and the real threat to his life, asking, "How long will I live?" He desperately fought against accepting even the thought of death, declaring, "Death is immoral and to live is absolutely moral." In late 1940, before he had heard that a draft notice for his elder brother had arrived, he wrote in agony: "I do not want to die. . . . I want to live!" He predicted Japan's defeat as early as 1942. After being drafted, there was no point of return for anyone. Hayashi Tadao thought that the military stifled the individual self and stripped him of all feelings, let alone passion. He contended that any meaningful act of sacrifice must come at the height of self-realization, not when the self is reduced to nothing. As Hayashi approached his death, he became more and more disillusioned by the military, and his sense of patriotism was greatly diminished.

Hayashi's abiding philosophical question was the problem of life and death in relation to the fulfillment of the self, on one hand, and the obligation of service to one's society and to humanity in general, on the other. Sasaki formulated the issue in a similar way. In exploring this question, Hayashi was heavily influenced by such writers as Romain Rolland, whose book *Jean-Christophe* was widely read in Japan for decades after its publication. Hayashi cites a section from the first volume in which Jean-Christophe advocates constant struggle for idealism against the temptations from within himself and from many enemies in society, embracing Rolland's thesis "one against all"

Hayashi's thinking about the problem of life and death, self and society was also deeply influenced by Thomas Mann and Roger Martin du Gard. Mann's consideration of life and death in relation to citizenship offered Hayashi a way to deliberate about the problem in relation to the general question of one's responsibility to society. He became even more engrossed in the works of Roger Martin du Gard. Although he read *Confidence africaine,* Hayashi was most intensely drawn to *Les Thibault,* the eight-volume work for which the author received the Nobel Prize for Literature in 1937. Jacques Thibault sacrificed his life to fight against war and revolution. Hayashi read *Les Thibault* twice in the original French and frequently mentioned it in his diary. The most sustained discussions of the book occur after he experienced the life at various navy air bases where he was daily exposed to the myriad of petty rules and regulations aimed at controlling soldiers' behavior and their thoughts. When Hayashi was driven to desperation, he found solace in Jacques Thibault's cry to be left alone when confined in a penitentiary.

A subtle but significant transformation occurred in Hayashi's thinking, as it did in Sasaki's. When these young men realized that they had no choice about whether they lived or died, they began to turn their idealistic philosophical deliberations toward finding a rationale for their fate. Marxism was extremely influential in Japan as a liberating force when the feudal system collapsed at the end of the nineteenth century. For many, Marxism became a form of idealism, serving as a counterpoint to capitalism, which Hayashi called "advanced capitalism" in German, and to self-centered individualism. It offered a vision of society without class oppression, which had permeated Japanese society from the very beginning. Hayashi's Marxism was not confined to Marx and Engels. The book he read on the base, at very high risk to his own safety, was Lenin's *State and Revolution.*

For both Hayashi and Sasaki, however, the vision of utopia that Marxism promised after the defeat of imperialism turned into a rationale for war as Japan was nearing its final collapse. Using the metaphor of a phoenix, perhaps derived from Rousseau, both student soldiers articulated the idea that the old Japan, which had been corrupted by capitalism, had to be entirely destroyed so that a new Japan would rise like a phoenix from the ashes. Both sought a glimmer of hope amid catastrophe. This utopian ideal was entirely selfless, since both knew they would perish in the cataclysm. Hayashi and Sasaki used historical determinism to explain their predicament to themselves; they were helplessly caught up in the grand historical flow. As Hayashi put it, "to die at this moment is an obligation imposed by history."

Hayashi was, above all, a poet. He believed that although humans are not beautiful by nature a person should aspire to become beautiful through self-reflection and that a person's worldview must be beautiful in order for life to take the right path. He read countless novels and poems, including those of Hesse, whose work is imbued with lyricism. Hayashi's writing is far more lyrical than that of Sasaki; he composed a large number of poems, some very long. The Japanese word for *beautiful* (*utsukushii*) and the German word *schön* or *Schönheit* recur like a refrain throughout his poems, letters, and diary. He sought beauty in nature, love, life, death, and human beings. For him, *Tonio Kröger* is one of Mann's "most beautiful and sweet fruits"; his heart trembled at "its tapestry, with a hint of loneliness, exquisite sensitivity, and almost threatening sublimity." This statement is worth repeating, since it succinctly expresses Hayashi's aesthetic sensibilities.

Hayashi's frequent references to the ephemeral beauty of dusk show his close reading of Novalis and other literary Romantics. But his poetics was far more sophisticated and complex than that of other young men. Hayashi experimented with the form of his poems. His determination to master the works of such writers of high modernity as Stéphane Mallarmé, whose poem *A Throw of the Dice Will Never Eliminate Chance* [*Un coup de dés jamais n'abolira le hasard*] is distinguished by fragmentation and *mise en page*, derives in part from his interest in poetic forms.

The quest for beauty beguiled Hayashi, for he found beauty in death and nihilism—a common phenomenon among the Romantics of both Europe and Japan. It is one thing to indulge in the aesthetics of nihilism in the abstract. But it is quite another to espouse such a view in the face of death. Tragically, these student pilots used Romanticism as a way to aestheticize their own deaths by adopting the aesthetics of nihilism and to convince themselves that there was beauty and meaning in their forced sacrifice at the height of their youth—a tortured rationalization indeed.

In his infrequent references to cherry blossoms, Hayashi clearly rejects the symbolic meanings assigned to them by the military. "I don't like that sort of 'purity' of falling without hesitation. A human should not die easily." On the other hand, they always contain an element of ephemerality. Thus, in a poem composed at the Miho Naval Base in 1945, he uses falling cherry blossoms as a metaphor for beautiful women, the shortness of life, and himself. In another poem he uses blooming cherry trees to represent his friend while he describes himself as a desolate wilderness. For Hayashi, cherry blossoms represent life, youth, and beauty; when they fall they symbolize evanescent beauty, life itself, and himself as he faces imminent death.

Hayashi stands out among the student soldiers in his determination to master the European languages. Soon after his entrance to the Third Higher School, he took a leave of absence, using health problems as an excuse, to study English, German, and French in order to read European publications in the original languages—a practice he kept up even on the base. He became so proficient in these languages that he found a Japanese translation of Etienne Gilson's *Esprit de la philosophie médiéval* (published in Japanese as *Humanism and Renaissance in the Medieval Period*) inadequate and switched to the original French text to contrast Gilson's and Dorson's views of Christianity.

Hayashi's poems and diary entries are replete with words in French, German, Italian, English, and Sanskrit. He did not do this to show off his learning. He explained that, even though he realized his death was imminent, his *Lebensprobleme* (lifelong assignment to himself) was to understand the relation between the European social sciences (*Sozialwissenschaft*) and European societies. He sought to identify that which was distinctively "European." The motivation for his long essay concerning the economic history of modern Europe, which begins by noting that Japan was facing a crisis, was to understand why and how Japan took a historical course heading toward self-destruction, while European imperial expansions took different paths. His obsession with reading and with quoting passages he remembered was also his way of coping with and escaping from his unbearable situation in the military and the desperate realization of his imminent death. Hayashi remained absorbed in learning European languages, literature, philosophy, and history in order to understand the historical trajectory of Japan and Europe and to create a mental and psychological space for himself on the military base, which daily tried to crush the spirit and individuality of every soldier.

Hayashi differs from Sasaki in not being attracted to sports, which was an important part of life at all the higher schools and universities at the time as a way of building youths' sense of masculine identity. He devoted himself to listening to Western classical music, which he pursued with determination, describing the process as *Bildung*. The term *Bildung* was made famous by Thomas Mann, who defined it as "personal cultivation." In a chapter titled "Unpolitical Individualism," Dumont (1994) elaborates on the significance of this concept for Mann and other German intellectuals, pointing out that "inwardness," expressed with this word, is the characteristic most flattering to Germans' self-esteem. Dumont also points out that Mann later struggled to reconcile the "incompatibility between

Bildung and Politics" (54). Hayashi's life, too, was a constant struggle between the Bildung with which he searched for beauty and disciplined himself to master European languages, culture, and social thought and his sense of obligation to Japan, his "ancestral land," which he loved even as it behaved in a manner he called "stupid."

Hayashi's feelings toward two women—his mother and his sweetheart—were at once tender and reverent, without a tinge of machismo. He remained attached to his mother throughout his life. He saw himself as someone who was protecting her. Although he repeatedly struggled with sexual desire and longed for the sensuality of "the dark-skinned woman Dorothée," when he found a sweetheart he praised her intelligence; he also admired the prerevolutionary Russian women who against all odds founded the first medical academy for women. His political view and attitude toward women were quite liberal and progressive, but the very target of his criticism—Japan's militarism and imperialism—took his young life away, preventing him from fulfilling his intellectual and personal goals.

A PARTIAL LIST OF HAYASHI TADAO'S READING

Philosophy, politics, and economics—Classical: Aristotle, St. Augustine (Aurelius Augustinus), Augustus, Julius Caesar, Plato, Zeno of Citium; *French:* Réne Descartes, Blaise Pascal, Voltaire; *German:* Martin Heidegger, Karl Marx, Friedrich Nietzsche, Leopold von Ranke; *English:* John Bagnell Bury, Christopher Dawson, Harold Laski, John Stuart Mill; *Russian:* Nikolai Berdyaev.

Literature—French: Honoré de Balzac, Gustave Flaubert, Anatole France, André Gide, Pierre Loti, Martin du Gard, Guy de Maupassant, Prosper Mérimée, Romain Rolland, Henri Beyle Stendhal; *German:* Johann Wolfgang von Goethe, Hermann Hesse, Thomas Mann, Erich Maria Remarque, Rainer Maria Rilke; *English:* James Joyce; *Russian:* Fyodor Dostoevsky, Ivan Turgenev; *Japanese:* Izumi Kyōka, Kawai Eijirō, Kurata Momozō, Natsume Sōseki, Tanigawa Tetsuzō.

Romanticism is the flower for eternity that blooms at night.

January 1, 1940

Blue night—small waves gather large golden shells on the
shore.

One drop of water cracks a shell, without a sound. . . .

A graveyard without voice. . . .

Romanticism is withering away.

Good-bye, Romanticism.

July 15, 1940

The idea that one is patriotic and thus would sacrifice oneself is
a thought for the stupid masses.

July 28, 1940

Born in March 1921 in Fukuoka, Kyūshū, Takushima Norimitsu
was drafted into the Imperial Navy in September 1943 from
Keiō University, one of the two top private universities in the
country. Of the 4,726 students who were drafted at the time,
1,563, or one in three, died (Yasuda 1967, 267). Takushima perished on April 9, 1945, at the age of twenty-four, as a lieutenant.
He flew a land-based attack bomber as the captain of the ten-
member crew, which was involved in the last-minute Japanese
effort to save the country, although not officially a part of the
tokkōtai operation. His plane disappeared off Kinkazan only a
few months before the end of the war. His father, Takushima
Norijirō, who edited his diary (Takushima 1967) sixteen years

later, wrote that he had attempted to justify his son's death in terms of the duty to serve one's country, yet he never became reconciled to it. During all those years he kept running to the front door, imagining that he heard his son's voice saying, "I am back home, Father," only to gaze at a plaque posted at the gate bearing these words: "The home of the survivors of the late Navy pilot Takushima Norimitsu, Lieutenant."

Takushima Norijirō's brief foreword to his son's diary ends with a poem that the father composed (5):

> How lonely it is to see the flower without a voice
> > beaten under the rain
> The flower my son loved so much.

In Japanese, the Cape jasmine (*Gardenia jasminoides*) is called the "flower without a mouth" or "without a voice" (*kuchinashi-no-hana*) because its fruit never opens. Takushima Norijirō titled his son's diary *The Writings Left Behind: Cape Jasmine—for the Beloved People of My Homeland* (*Kuchinashi-no-hana: Aisuru Sokoku no Hito-e*). He chose the Cape jasmine because it was his son's favorite flower and interpreted it as a metaphor for the Japanese people, who could not openly express their thoughts in wartime but had to keep them private, some articulating them only in their diaries. As is evident in the pages of his diary, for Takushima Norimitsu the flower was a metaphor for his mother, who died on October 27, 1943, shortly after he was drafted. She used the flower to communicate her deep affection to her son.

Takushima's father was a well-to-do businessman who owned an automobile manufacturing company in Fukushima, a metropolis in Kyūshū. His mother, who came from Yamada, the mountainous area of the province, was devoted to her family, which included six sons and two daughters as well as her mother-in-law. Takushima's diary frequently expresses his tender feelings for his mother, who in his eyes embodied tenderness, selflessness, and the purity of nature in the mountains from which she came. Takushima took leave from the navy to return home when his mother was critically ill, and she died two days before the end of his leave. He wanted to stay for the funeral, but the family sent him back to the base, warning him of the military's strict rules (Yasuda 1967, 269). After his father remarried, Takushima struggled to prevent his intense love for his mother from negatively influencing his feelings toward his stepmother.

Cape Jasmine comprises 278 pages and consists of three parts: "The Flower without a Voice (Diary from the Navy Days)"; "To My Beloved (Collection of Letters)"; and "Diary during the Keiō University Days." A short foreword by his father and a brief essay by his friend Yasuda Takeshi frame Takushima's writings. I present these materials in chronological sequence, starting with the earliest diary entries, written when he was at Keiō University in 1940. The entries from January 1941 are sporadic, and they end entirely on February 11, 1941. Another set of diary entries begins on March 12, 1944. No diary was found for the intervening three years. Takushima may have kept a diary that was burnt when the Mi'e Naval Air Base was bombed, but Yasuda suggests that he deliberately gave up writing the diary during these years (Yasuda 1967, 268–69). The extant letters that Takushima wrote while he was stationed at Mi'e, Demizu, and Miyazaki Naval Air Bases are addressed primarily to family members. Every letter in *Cape Jasmine* bears the stamp "Inspection Done." The letters run from July 1943 to January 25, 1945. There is no surviving record of his thoughts during the months just before his death.

The diary and the letters enable us to trace Takushima's transformation from an idealistic youth proclaiming Romanticism as his religion to a young man facing his country's turn to total war, trying to convince himself to accept his fate, and finally reaching a state of resignation. The entries for July 1940 are pivotal in this regard. Lengthy descriptions of imagined encounters with women, with Don Juan as his alter ego, are filled with strikingly sensuous eroticism. He describes a woman with whom he fell desperately in love. Yet even these quests for young women, love, and beauty are haunted by a shadow of death. (Takushima Norimitsu is introduced briefly in Nihon Senbotsu Gakusei Kinenkai [1988] 1995, 28–40.)

DIARY ENTRIES WRITTEN AT KEIŌ UNIVERSITY, 1940

From January 1940 to February 1941, Takushima's diary is filled with Romanticism, as it swept through Japan at that time, profoundly influencing young intellectuals. His Romanticism takes the form of art for art's sake, or, more precisely, aesthetic for the sake of aesthetic. He sees love, beauty, and truth in nature as well as in art. Novalis (Friedrich von Hardenberg) had by far the most powerful influence of any writer on Takushima, who quotes Novalis as saying that "to become a human being is a form of art" and that "the beauty of nature transcends all the arts created by humans" (August 15, 1940). Takushima also read widely in French and English as well as German. His writings allude to many themes, images, and artists from European high culture, ranging from the figure of Beatrice in Dante's *Divine Comedy* to the forests depicted in Camille Corot's paintings. Many figures from Greek mythology appear in descriptions of his own imaginings and reveries. He also frequently uses the term *Vita Nouva* [*sic*] (New Life), likely from Dante's *La Vita Nuova*, as a declaration of a new life.

Painters and schools of painting he discussed include Botticelli, Leonardo da Vinci, Degas, Matisse, Picasso, Rubens, Van Gogh, Millet, and Gauguin; Fauvism, Cubism, Surrealism, and abstract art.

Takushima's reading resembles that of other student soldiers discussed in this book, but he took a special interest in the visual arts; he painted, visited art galleries, and commented in his diary on European painters. He discussed some unusual literary and philosophical works as well, including those of Stefan Zweig, a neo-Romantic poet of Jewish descent and a strong pacifist, Charles Fourier, a utopian socialist, Rawa Murtis, an Indian intellectual and political leader, and François Hemsterhuis, a Dutch philosopher of aesthetics. Takushima also played the violin and sang chansons in the original French. Occasionally, he wrote some sentences in English.

January 1, 1940

Takushima recalls the declaration in 1872 by the Meiji government that the imperial line had lasted for twenty-six hundred years, apparently accepting this nationalistic myth-history invented by the government to bolster the notion of the antiquity of Japan as a nation-state.

> I must begin a new stage for life and aim at self-improvement. When I was born, my father had a dream in which a goddess was casting light on a fading star in the dark blue sky at night. My father put the character for "light" in my name.

His personal name, Norimitsu, consists of two characters, *nori* (virtue) and *mitsu* (light).

> Thus, since birth, I have breathed my father's dream and nurtured Romanticism in my heart. Hopefully, I remain free from illnesses. . . . And I pray for a beautiful coexistence of reason and emotion.

He continues: "I am permitted to stroll in the world of reverie and abstraction just as ancient poets did. Following these sagacious poets, I will write down [what happens in] my imagination." He titles the work "Don Juan":

> I rode on a covered wagon which was drawn by one horse without a sound. Inside it was dark and I could not see the color of the horse, but I was quite certain that it was a white horse, since I always rode in the same wagon.

There was no rider, but the horse knew the road well enough to go on its own. As I entered a low entranceway covered with roses, beautiful maidens with blonde hair took my hand and led me inside. All the maidens were wearing skirts with layers at the hems and tight corsets. Underneath our feet lay flowers celebrating eternal life and beauty. Even when we lay on them, stems did not get broken. This is where Corot's forests often dance. Of course, they were barefoot. When I went to the bathing room, a crimson ray shone on the elfish body of Venus of the Medici family, who became very shy, bending her knees and looking down. Gingerly I approached her and offered gentle words. When I touched her shoulder, she uttered a small cry and looked the other way, like Daphne, who tried to get away from the arms of the sun god Apollo. The maidens, joyously laughing among themselves, were waiting for me at the entrance to the bathing room. Soon I was led to a bedroom. A large, bright chandelier was hanging in the center of the room. I realized that it was the bedroom for Marie Antoinette. I learned that she was away. I was told that I would be sleeping with Psyche.

After this musing, he continues: "When I engage in my imagination, my thoughts and feelings move according to a slow melody or a famous European painting, which emerges in my mind as three-dimensional." He concludes: "Romanticism is the flower for eternity that blooms at night." (149–51)

January 2, 1940

Continuing his reverie, he writes:

I was awoken by pleasant sunshine and beautiful fragrance. I heard a loud voice from the next room. Fragrance of the taste of a peach. I clapped my hands and called the blonde maiden. "Who occupies the next room?" "It is Don Juan. He has lived there for a long time. He is nice to everyone. Wouldn't you like to meet him?" I suppressed my rage and said, "A nice person? You must be joking—that hypocrite." Suddenly the door swung open and Don Juan appeared. He said, "You too are an escapee from this world." His loud voice had a wide range. A tall and well-built body, clad in medieval armor.

Don Juan tells him:

You might as well go back [to the real world]. Coming here clad in the clothes from this world is like asking for disappointment. Look, Don Juan is clad in a medieval armor, that is, he is wearing the past. You are wearing reality, the present.

As Don Juan guessed, Takushima came looking for an ideal woman. But Takushima tells Don Juan that there was another reason:

> You, who do not wear reality, may not understand. But, our reality is very dark. The only freedom allowed to us is to visit here every now and then in order to forget reality. . . .
>
> Lunch was served in the great hall. Surrounding the round table were Don Juan, Marie Antoinette, who returned this morning, Beatrice, blonde maidens, elves from the forest.

Takushima found a piece of paper on the floor on which a poem dedicated to "Beloved Antoinette" was written:

> Vowing not to love anyone
> I try not to look at the smile
> of white lily blooming in the river valley
> Though I closed the door to my heart
> Love quietly keeps coming back to gnaw at my heart.
> (151–56)

January 3, 1940; January 5, 1940

"Death is an inevitable absolute order." This, the first sentence in the diary of January 5, reveals the real meaning of his reverie involving Don Juan, which was written over the course of two days. On one hand, it indicates that he felt the imminence of death as early as 1940. On the other, it expresses the influence of Romanticism, as is evident in the one-sentence entry for January 5: "If one loves art and nature, he is extremely fortunate." (156–57; 158)

January 6, 1940

The power of the unconscious—what Gide called "the God's territory." Belief in the unconscious gave birth to Surrealism and, earlier, the basis for Dadaism.

Reflections on a summer night on Shiga Island: The sunshine at dusk in summer made both the lights of a distant city and the moon in the sky just white but not beautiful. The golden rays are caressing a motionless cloud with their hands. Apollo's chariot is sinking over the horizon. The golden rays turn increasingly red, and eventually purple. A fishing boat appears and approaches the port beneath my feet with a low, humming sound. The lamp

on the mast casts its light with eternal melancholy and a faint smile. Nature, as I perceive in my heart, stands for absolute beauty, fairness and goodness. Such overwhelming beauty makes me forget critical eyes, and I throw myself onto the pleasure of indulgence. White sand on the vast beach is a path to my imagination, and it continues for a long time until it finally melts into the shadows of distant pine trees. The moon goddess is in charge of night. Pleasant rustles of a breeze are like the whispering of a lovelorn maiden's breathing against my ear. The heavy night wind descends from a hill through the trees in the shrine compound and sinks into the sea. At this absolute standstill, my heart pulsates with imagination.
(158–59)

January 12, 1940

"Reverie"

In my reverie, a woman quietly crept into my room. Her black hair, bundled together, pressed against my shoulder, her half-open lips burning with flames for indolent pleasure, and the ray of love took residence in the utter oblivion of all things. Her beautiful eyes were moist with eternal life. Ah, a woman in my reverie. Whence have you come? . . . The night is over. Your reverie has disappeared and the loneliness of reality grips my empty heart.
(159–63)

January 14, 1940

Referring to Montaigne, he declares: "The heart without love is empty. Love teaches beauty and fills the heart." (165–66)

January 15, 1940

On a cold winter night, I think of Gauguin's paintings—the southern island filled with strong brown rhythm, naked people, indigo sea, burning hot sun.

My notes on Baudelaire: (1) Love is a hobby for prostitution. Even the loftiest of pleasure can be reduced to prostitution; (2) What is art? It is prostitution. . . . Baudelaire's view of love is Freudian and there is some truth to it.

Baudelaire appears in the diaries of other student soldiers, indicating the powerful influence of this leading figure of High Modernism upon young intellectuals at the time. (166–67)

January 22, 1940

Oh, beauty. The object of my adoration is beauty. But, how rarely can we discover beauty when we search for it through the lens of reality. (170)

February 7, 1940

The month of January has passed. I feel a new emotion in my heart. Romanticism, which used to be the spring of my heart, has started to raise its head again. It is a spring in the stillness of the night. It never becomes empty no matter how much we draw water. Halfway through, I returned to reality, since reality was a new world to me. But my own nature did not allow me to stay there. I will now return to the garden of a distant dream, but will keep my clothes of reality on. (170–71)

February 9, 1940

When I close my eyes, I see a lonely village I love. It is night. Lights flicker in the village, which sleeps under the blue shadows of stars. All music stops. Only silence creates the slow sound waves. Resting on the slope of a small hill, I search for the mystery of the white lily. "A shy princess set off in quest for her love"—thus spake the white lily. The white lily still blooms on the hill in search of her love.

A dream of Novalis. (171)

February 12, 1940

Not only did he pursue beauty on his own and through literature, but he also read various scholars of aesthetics.

I find the definition of beauty by Hemsterhuis interesting. He said: "Beauty brings about the greatest pleasure. The greatest pleasure teaches us the greatest number of concepts in the shortest time. The pleasure of beauty gives the greatest number of concepts and thus it is the highest form of cognition for humans." (173)

February 14, 1940

After reading Abe Jirō's *Aesthetics* (*Bigaku*) and *Fundamental Problems of Ethics* (*Rinrigaku no Konpon Mondai*), he comments: "An intimate relationship between aesthetics and ethics." (174)

February 15, 1940

I have been able to transform my personal quest for love into an intellectual pursuit of beauty. Although philosophers may not like it, I will call it a romantic search for truth. My love is no longer a maiden on this earth, but a maiden wrapped in eternal mystery. She smiles at suitors who fall at her feet with her smile as their only consolation. I might join the ranks and become a martyr. People lose their mind over the mysterious smile of Mona Lisa. . . .

It looks like Romanticism is my religion. (174–76)

February 16, 1940

Botticelli's paintings feel like shining apples. Van Gogh's are constantly and rapidly turning. Da Vinci was able to represent God. Raphael has feminine sensitivities, and as for Degas, the dancing girls! Millet expressed warm peace. (176–78)

February 23, 1940

Beautiful night. While the curtain of mystery offers a glimpse of an eternal smile, the moon kisses a treetop. . . . Why do not people love the night and peace? . . . Words of Emerson: "The ones who are able to embrace nature are those blessed by the God of Poetry, and not by Miller, Manning, or Locke." The goddess in my reverie is sobbing in the infinite vastness of the sky. Faraway stars are the tears of this goddess rolling down her breast. I can see her eyes. I am a knight of Romanticism kneeling before her. (178–79)

February 25, 1940

Communism was born as a type of idealism based on the dialectic. Totalitarianism was born as a national policy with realistic purposes. (181–82)

March 4, 1940

When the goddess of winter, covered in a gray veil, goes by, the goddess of spring arrives, clad in brocade. No longer are silence and solitude painful. . . . On spring afternoons you sense the sound of bees busily collecting honey among flowers in a far-off garden. . . . Well-developed breast—an expression of spring. . . . Vita Nuova of Romanticism. (185)

Late March and April 1940

A section of the diary written on this day is titled "Romanticism, Sentiments, Love" (March 29). He admonishes himself: "The homework for me is to get out of *Chagrin d'amour*" (March 30). Even when he returns home, he feels lonely and remembers the poems by Rimbaud (March 31). He then resolves (April 3) to "pray for the great spirit of Vita Nuova. I shall turn my gaze toward the beauty of great and lofty nature. Listen to the sound of a bell tolling for the blessed. Listen to the sound of the feathers of white doves flying in the sky. Then, the garden of happiness and love will be open to you. Free yourself from the shackles and pray for eternal freedom."

Having read *Fragments* [*Fragmenten*] by Novalis on his way home, he refers to two statements from it (April 4). The first, "Dusk is a sad period of time, in contrast to dawn, which is the time full of pleasant expectations," struck a chord in his heart. It recurs in his later diary entries (for example, July 5, 1940). Second, he points to Novalis's statement that "an excessive self-reflection will result in dulling of the sense toward the self and will prevent healthy understanding of the self." (189–96)

May 20, 1940

My feeling, which I thought was love, is gone, it seems. I am, after all, alone. I cannot be proud of the past and cannot believe in the present. Only hope for the future is shining over my head like a star with infinite truth and passion. Baudelaire declared love secular and base. . . . As Rousseau said, "I feel before I think." I trust and respect intuition.

Rawa Murtis changed my view of India and Indians completely. He is the intellectual who saved India from British domination and helped establish a new India with absolute independence.
(201–3)

Late June and Early July 1940

On June 27, Takushima notes that he is ill; his pleura and left lung are swollen. He plans to return home to "the bosom for rest and peace." After returning home, on July 3, he writes:

I feel lonely without the Cape jasmine (flower without voice). Mother cut a white Cape jasmine blossom and put it near my pillow in a vase. Sweet fragrance of a story lingers. The rose-colored sky. All natural phenomena are ready to wind down from the day's vigorous activities to a quiet time. It is dusk—something similar to a majestic ceremony. (204–10)

July 8, 1940

The Cape jasmine flower is withering, like the posture of a little girl in deep thought. Dusk again today. Golden rays and the fragrance of roses begin to permeate the air.

Pure white flowers, green calyces
Exquisite fragrance, hidden deeply
Alone at my bedside, consoles me
The blue sky after the lights [are] turned off
Stars cast bright chilly light,
Flickering in the shadows of trembling leaves.
(211–12)

July 15, 1940

This entry begins with an address to a woman, perhaps his sweetheart. "I am now writing my thoughts in response to your letter. Your letter was a poem with beautiful rhymes. As Novalis said, 'A true letter is basically a poem.'"

Passing of Romanticism

Blue night—small waves gather large golden shells on the shore. One drop of water cracks a shell, without a sound. A white dove flies—up and up to the sky.
Along a spiral line from a poor shell to the sky, there is a graveyard.
A graveyard without voice.
The white feathers of the dove turned black.
Romanticism is withering away.
Good-bye, Romanticism.
(212–15)

This poem is a dirge for Romanticism, whose space was being squeezed out as Japan's militarism and totalitarianism were rapidly taking control of the nation.

July 27, 1940

Although Takushima does not mention his sweetheart, Yayeko, by name, he writes a lengthy description of their first meeting. The description suggests that someone, perhaps his parents, arranged for them to meet.

> I had great expectations on meeting her, since she was said to be from a good intellectual family. I was impressed by her fresh thoughts, although her penmanship was not quite as good. While men (maybe only myself) have been unaware, women have attained a high intellectual level. . . . As long as women continue to rebel against men, their beauty will remain forever. (217–21)

Late July through August 1940

As he meets Yayeko and falls in love, Takushima repeatedly expresses his opposition to nationalism. These declarations are accompanied by an increasing sense of despair as he realizes that he must give up on Romanticism and all it stands for.

> I cannot think of my country before I think about myself, because I am not such a purist or a patriot. (July 27)

> The Japanese are very sentimental. It is quite convenient for the dictators. The idea that one is patriotic and thus would sacrifice oneself is a thought for the stupid masses. It is a type of narcissistic mania. . . . I advocate free contacts and exchange among the peoples of the world. I hate the rise of nationalism. . . . According to my view, the nation takes second place to individuals, but in reality individuals are completely ignored. The nation now takes absolute control over individuals. Turning around 180 degrees from the Romantic to the Realist, I am looking at the moon and smiling. (July 28)

Takushima likens militaristic sentiment to *shōchū*, a popular alcoholic beverage that used to be associated with the lower class:

> The right-wing spirit is like shōchū. Their excitement is like the shouting of a drunk. (July 31)

> Young people's thought processes are based on the celebration, hope, and anger of youth. Therefore, we are allowed to have a vision which is divorced

from reality. When the youthful imagination is coldly destroyed, youth must face reality. Then, our memory becomes painful. (August 5)

I made a mistake in being born in this century. All my principles are being expelled. Culture prospers only under liberalism, whereas totalitarianism simplifies it. (August 7)

Love—so far away. It sounds like an illusion from the past. Perhaps when I encounter beauty, I may be reminded of it again. (August 9)

With the rise of nationalism, people start to emphasize their superiority. The Germans do so. There is no way to judge the superiority of one people. That is nothing but self-deception or self-indulgence. (August 13)

Myth of Nazism
Myth of the "Japanese spirit"
Order for total mobilization
Totalitarianism.
(217–34)

August 18, 1940

Tonight the full moon is laughing in the sky, unaware that it will be hidden [by the clouds]. It is a chilling reminder, because I love culture and peace. But is my life dedicated to struggle against the current in which we witness the rise of nationalism, which promises the utmost happiness? Although I am not in principle opposed to any current, I find myself dissatisfied with the "national spirit," which completely lacks logic.

Oh, France. The friend of culture. I won't even extend my sympathy for your military defeat. I send my praise for the great culture which military power cannot destroy. The French—you have been loved as the friend of cosmopolitanism. (234–35)

August 21, 1940

Gazing at the sky in the quiet dusk, while listening to the sparrows gather in a large tree, I was reminded of Coppée's essay titled "Sunset." The last chorus of the day was perhaps the prayer to the setting sun. The dusk, the time for withering, as Novalis said, is approaching. It is indeed peaceful. But it is also a very lonely sunset.

Takushima's reference to François Coppée is quite significant, although he does not elaborate on his knowledge of or interpretation of the French writer. This Parnassian poet, whose work lies beyond that of the mainstream Romantics, emphasized a commitment to social values and plebeian life. In quoting him, Takushima shows that his commitment to lofty idealism is coupled with social concern. He is aware of the plight of the poor and of minorities within Japan and of civilian casualties resulting from Japanese colonialism.

After this passage, Takushima describes how his father has spoken about hardships that resulted from the war, such as high taxes and the devaluation of real estate. (236–37)

August 27, 1940

I told my mother about my stomachache. She gently rubbed my back for a long time. I told her that she had done so long enough, but she said, "Don't worry. Try to fall asleep as soon as possible." She kept rubbing my back gently. I dislike sentimentalism, but I was very touched by her love. I could not fall asleep. The clock struck 2:00 A.M. I lay still and mother left quietly, thinking I was asleep. I wanted to see her very badly and opened my eyes very slightly to see her leave the room. Mother lived only to raise her eight children. (239–40)

October 18, 1940

Individualism, egotism, amoral and demonic principles, the hypocritical/anti-emotion principle, the rational principle, antinationalism, utilitarianism—if people know how to skillfully combine them all, they will be great people in the world. The Jews and overseas Chinese have no country [nation]. They have strategically used these principles and succeeded in their effort; they should receive universal respect. (251–53)

January 23, 1941

"The twentieth century is the age of Romanticism"—what a lovely sound this statement has. This is the century of warfare, and most of us must find comfort in being told that the purpose of the war is couched in the language of beautiful Romanticism. The feeling involved in self-sacrifice for one's dream, ideal, and beauty is akin to the longing for a maiden at far distance.

The twentieth century is the century we should love. Before one caresses the hair, eyes, and lips of a maiden, one falls in love with her image in its entirety. We should first fall in love with the image of a nation.

These statements seem tortured, indicating that Takushima is trying to convince himself that he should accept the war effort his nation was engaged in, as borne out in the following diary entry. (255–56)

January 27, 1941

The Vow I Made at Night

Unwittingly, I stepped into a void in my thought. I had been fearing it. And I had tried to escape from this condition. Yet I feel that I am losing the battle. Meaninglessly, I am painting my life with hypocrisy. I feel that I am moving away from my own self, no longer being able to feel myself. It is now certain that I am a young man who is left behind by the times only to die like a shriveled-up leaf.

I must live. Strong and vigorously. And I must respect my emotions. But, alas, I no longer feel emotions. I have reached the end—only a step before the final collapse of rationality, gasping for air to regain hope for life. Tonight I chain my neck in order to remind myself of my own vow. Since I do not believe in God, I vow to myself.
(256–57)

ON ENTERING THE MILITARY, 1943

July 20, 1943

This letter to his father, Takushima Norijirō, shows his concern about his mother's health. At that time he was not sure whether he would be drafted and thus he was searching for an alternative to military service by applying for a particular position with the railroad. As mandated, he took an examination for the navy, hoping for a noncombatant position as an accountant. Unfortunately, the examination showed him to be qualified to be a pilot. At this point, Takushima becomes quite worried about the future, but his fate has not been determined.

I just received two letters from you, Father. Thank you. . . . How is mother? Since it is very hot, I am very concerned about her condition. . . . I went to the branch of the Western Railroad in order to take the examination for the job, but no one showed up. But I know that I would get the job without taking the examination. . . . No report from the navy. But, judging from the report to our friend Yoshizaki, . . . I suspect that I would not get the accounting job at the navy. I had no intention of applying for the pilot's position. But the examinations for the accountant and the pilot were combined, and they marked me as qualified for flying.

During the past year, or only within the past couple of months, I have had to face being drafted and to search for a job at the same time, and I feel the strong currents of this period. . . . At times I feel that whatever I do is only half-baked. Perhaps by joining in the war, I would feel more decisive both in my action and thoughts. My best to my mother.

THE DIARY AND LETTERS FROM THE TIME IN THE NAVY, 1943–44

The following poem, written while Takushima was stationed at the Demizu Naval Air Base, expresses his grief at the death of his mother. It is undated.

The Flower without a Voice (Cape Jasmine)

Day by day, the color of autumn is deepening.
Mother's illness became grave as the days went by.
Gazing at her children, she withered like a leaf under frost and passed away.
Sadness belongs to the past, and joy will return to life—I tried to convince myself.
But the sadness of the past haunts me today.

The poem cited above is followed by a copy of a letter from his mother that he had received the previous year, when the fragrance of summer filled the air:

This is the season for the hydrangea, telling us that your visit home is approaching. Your grandmother and I are anxiously waiting for you. As I am writing this letter, I glance at the yard and notice that the flower clusters of the hydrangea are bending down to the ground. I put on clogs and hurry to the flower. I am reminded of you when you were little. When you were three or four, I cut a white cluster for you. When you got up the next morning, you found that the petals had turned purple, and some petals had fallen. You began to cry as if you had caught on fire; you thought someone had exchanged the hydrangea with some other flower. I was at my wits' end and did not know what to do at the time. Now, as I look at the yard, all the petals have changed color to form purple clouds. I realized how intriguing this flower is. (92–93; 11–13)

March 20, 1944, at the Demizu Naval Air Base

Today is my birthday. I had forgotten it completely. What did I do on my last birthday? Mother was still healthy. At that time, Mother was looking forward to her planned trip to Tokyo to see me. Indeed, "Year after year the same flowers bloom, whereas people are not the same." For my birthday, Mother always prepared something special, such as my favorite sweets (*an'man*) or rice with beans. Remembering the past birthdays, I feel so lonely. Her tender feelings—no one else has such love. Why did I not take care of her better? I am filled with deep regrets. I feel sorry for my little brothers, who are unable to have the splendid childhood I had. My mother never leaves my mind, whenever I remember anything of my past. Mother, Mother, Mother. No matter how old one gets, the most important figure in life is one's mother. (16–17)

Letter to "His Beloved," March 21, 1944

In this letter to Yayeko, Takushima deliberately suppresses his feelings for her, as he usually did.

Last evening, I received your letter, in which you sounded in very good spirits. I was very pleased to receive the letter. . . . In my present life, I should not leave room for thoughts of such matters as love. In my daily life, filled with tension, any romantic thoughts or emotions are jettisoned like dirt scattered in all directions by rapidly turning wheels. The only time I can communicate with you is when I write my diary. I once promised you that I would leave my innermost thoughts with you. I have not had psychological room to do so. But, do believe my sincerity—I have not forgotten my promise to you.

. . . Now the only way to express my feelings to you is to write them down in my diary. My future is utterly uncertain. As André Gide said, the future belongs to God's jurisdiction. I cannot predict my own future. I am I, and yet I am no longer I. Since you are so bright, I believe you understand what I say. I love you, but my love at present must extend beyond you to Japan and to the Japanese people, including you.

Despite these words, I am far from falling into the trap of jingoism. I have simply transformed my concerns for my country during the university days into love of my country. I think I told you this. Perhaps I will not see you again—perhaps, never.

I am pleased that I ask you to choose Cape jasmine as the offering [to me after death]. My mother loved that flower, too. . . .

Around the time when the large white flowers of the homestead cherry [a type of cherry with large petals forming multiple layers] bloom, I will be going to the front. I will then, or even before, not be able to write my diary. (17–18)

March 21, 1944

Takushima wrote frequently to his two youngest brothers, who remained at home with their father and older sisters. This letter is labeled "To my darling little brothers."

The lawn grass which endured the cold winter is now beginning to bud with green leaves. The fragrance of green leaves symbolizes hope and youth. Your mother loved the color green. The warm sweaters she bought for me were often green. The color of green always reminds me of Mother.

When you two grow up and wish to recall fond memories of Mother, gaze at green leaves covering the trees.

Let me write down for you how Mother loved you. In a strict household, she never had a moment to relax. I remember Mother was always working very hard, doing innumerable household chores. This type of life is a tradition in Kyūshū. Given the shackles of old feudalistic customs that honor men and look down on women, it was rare that she ate dinner with us. I am quite disappointed that I cannot recall a happy family gathering with her over dinner. Even though she had to do so many things around the house, she never ever made you wear torn clothes or underwear or damaged shoes. Tears well up in my eyes when I think how she bought all the supplies of clothing for you two, even after her illness progressed, so that you would not be in trouble [after her death]. (20–21)

In other letters, using kana syllables—one of the phonetic writing systems with which children begin learning to write—he asked his younger brothers to accompany their father on a visit to him (September 22, 1943, 99; February 12 and 23, 1944, 127, 130–31). When Noriharu, his younger brother, entered elementary school, Takushima told him to study hard so as to rank first in his class (April 24, 1944, 138).

March 22, 1944

Camellia, camellia, camellia, on the fences of farmers' houses. Blooming in blazing crimson, they usher in spring. Their gorgeous blossoms are mirrored in a quiet stream. It is all so quiet. . . .

Camellias are not as cheerful as cherry blossoms. Nor are they as delicate as cherry blossoms. But far more than cherries, they insist on their own powerful presence. I like this flower. Once I knew a person who was like red camellia, egocentric and clever.

When I visited Mother's homestead, camellia was in full bloom. Mother was healthy at that time, and for me spring was the most joyful season. When I climbed up a little hill, I saw the far distant cities over the hedge of camellia. The stream too was beautiful. I once collected nectar from camellia blossoms, walking from one blossom to the next. The nectar was lightly sweet. It tasted of "youth." When Mother was around, evening dinners were peaceful times. (21–22)

Letter to Yayeko, March 30, 1944

Thank you for your response. I am pleased to learn that you are in good spirits. It sounds like Tokyo has changed a great deal. Many changes in society necessitated by the war on which our nation's fate depends are now acutely felt. We, the soldiers, and you, too, must march toward this single goal. At times like this, concepts and other abstract thoughts are almost meaningless to us. They are like a beautiful, expensive plate which makes food visually appealing; food of one hundred calories is still only one hundred calories, even on a beautiful plate.

It is lonely to think that scholarship, which should be respected, is no longer useful for us. But, truly, study is no longer necessary.

If it becomes possible for you to live in peace, indeed my life may be sacrificed. . . . I am just a very average person and do not hope to achieve honor through my death. . . . If my action contributes to building your happy and peaceful life, I can find meaning in all the unhappiness that I am enduring now. (26–29)

April 2, 1944

I spent a lovely spring day in a detached house on an old farm. Camellias, cherry trees, peach trees are all donning their beautiful spring attire, offering visual pleasure to people. . . .

Mother used to call me whenever she encountered beautiful scenery: "Why don't you come out? It is just beautiful." I just felt as if she called me, as she used to.

Even after she married my father and lived in the city, Mother never lost the innocence of a farmer. I remember the time when I was a little child and went with my mother to my mother's house, just as quiet but even more isolated than this one. At night, it was unbelievably scary, with the gushing sound of a mountain torrent hitting rocks and the sound of owls howling. My mother's bosom was the place for my escape. A shooting star went over the river. It was a cold, pale star.

The world around me is going through drastic changes. I try to suppress egotism and uphold my principles.

Last night's rain stopped and a strong wind, which I feared would blow off the cherry blossoms, subsided. It blows hard only now and then. Even that is becoming rare, indicating the end of the storm. Those little violets must have shivered. A large red sun peeks through dark clouds that are still hanging around. Truly beautiful, indeed. In the midst of golden silence, the mountains to the east are getting dark, in sharp contrast to the gorgeous beauty on the west side. (29–33)

April 2, 1944

Takushima wrote to his youngest brothers, Noriharu and Norimasa, offering some advice, expressing his own grief at the loss of their mother, and expressing concern about their future.

Last Sunday Setsuyo and Kazu'e [his sisters] came to visit me. I am pleased and relieved to hear that they are really working hard, taking care of the household. According to them Noriharu is quite rambunctious. It is good for a boy to be so. I hope the two of you grow up free of worries. I heard that Norimasa has not forgotten the practice of folding his clothes every night before he goes to bed. You are a good boy. A very good boy. Do not ever forget your mother's teachings on good upbringing.

I am truly in sympathy with your feelings when you felt that the new mother had to be the same as the one in the photo [their deceased mother]. I feel for you. I don't know if I can ever go home again. How helpless I feel that I can only pray for good luck for your future. (32–33)

April 27, 1944

It is difficult to hope for the glory of returning from the battlefield. Believing that a shortcut to eternity is to perish as a dew drop on the battlefield, and not having any guarantee of being alive the next day, it is only too human to take some drink, become intoxicated, and sing songs with passion. No one could laugh at such behavior. (37–38)

May 7, 1944

A Scene at Demizu

The sun is like a sunflower.
After a wagtail left for the bamboo bush along the river,
A calf took a nap on the bed of Chinese milk vetch.
Late blossoms of camellia, looking sad.
(42–43)

May 11, 1944

Golden dusk after the rain. Grape-colored mountain peaks in late spring are clothed in white clouds. When she was still alive, whenever I longed for my mother, I used to overcome the feeling by envisioning my mother. I cannot bear the thought that she will never return no matter how much I call for her and want to be spoiled by her. The only time when I want to believe in the soul of a deceased person is when I dream of her. With my father's remarriage getting closer, I pray that my mother's soul will be left undisturbed, without the knowledge of what is happening. (43–44)

Letter to His Younger Sister, June 8, 1944

Kazu'e, I feel sorry that you, when you are so young, must worry about so many things. I am sure you are worrying about me. Although I have not told anyone, when I go to the war, I am prepared not to return alive. I will forget all my thoughts from the past and join my mother without incurring disgrace. (46–48)

June 11, 1944

New seedlings of rice plants have come out and cover the water in the paddy, creating beautiful reflections in the sunset. A peaceful scene. Children called for me from a distance—so far away that I could not really see their faces. When I turned around to look for them, they all bowed down toward me [in respect to a soldier heading for the front]. How innocent they are! I cannot be moved to patriotism without a very realistic motivation. But, yes, for these children.

If the Germans lose faith, even slightly, in the new religion of Nazism, Germany will fall. It is a matter of time.
(48–50)

June 12, 1944

Yesterday I encountered a most delightful event. The white flower of Cape jasmine! I remember the time when I was sick at the height of summer. Every day Mother brought the flower to my bedside. I was sick for a long time—two months. And last year, when my mother was sick, I put the white flower in a vase at her bedside. The flower faithfully kept its fragrance for some time. This year, in this southern region far away from home, the flower is blooming for me. (50–52)

Letter to Yayeko, June 13, 1944

You must be anxiously waiting for my letter. I have been feeling a heavy responsibility to answer your letter. Let me tell you for sure—I loved you. And I still love you now. Yet today something more important than you alone occupies my mind, that is, the country where gentle maidens like you live. I was immensely moved by the children who called to me from afar in the quiet dusk in the paddy field. They bowed toward me, and I cannot forget them. If you realized that this feeling is stronger than my love toward you, you would be quite upset. No, I don't think you would be. You would understand my feeling. For those innocent children, I would not mind sacrificing my life. (52–53)

June 16, 1944

The spiritual life underlies all human existence. It is the realm where even the loftiest rationality cannot reach. This is so for all peoples. Even the Americans and British, whose lives are governed by materialism, have a spiritual life which involves patriotism and other useful spirits, even though the nature of their patriotism may be different from our patriotism or the way of the emperor. Since the spirit expresses itself in the form of social behavior, I consider it an entity.

After discussing Hobbes and Hegel, Takushima begins to write as if addressing Yayeko:

For our nation, enormously poor in material resources, the last [form of] capital is the body. When I think in this way, I forget about you. It must make you feel quite unhappy that my thoughts are so involved in this way, rather than focusing on you. I have no confidence that I can make you happy in the future. I replaced my love for you with my love for my country.

Strolling in the dusk with my comrades, we dream of beautiful pastures and orchards. It is marvelous that I can dream of a beautiful utopia when the world is going through vertigoes. I am happy to consider myself to be fighting to achieve the harmony of this universe. I am pleased and happy to provide good and beautiful reasons for my action—our sacrifice.

In this passage, Takushima is again trying to suppress his love for Yayeko and to convince himself of the official line: that for Japan without material superiority, its soldiers' sacrifice is the only means left for them. (54–55)

June 30, 1944

The other day, Lieutenant (Junior Grade) Nakayama and seven others on the reconnaissance plane disappeared. I pray these seven souls may rest in peace. Today another plane with seven soldiers went up in smoke right after they took off. All except one survived. Several mechanical problems were involved, although the direct cause was the loss of speed.

This passage reveals how Japan was no longer capable of manufacturing airplanes that functioned properly, resulting in a large number of casualties (see also the diary entry for August 1).

The Japanese imperial government declared that it will not deal with the Chinese government in Chungking [the wartime capital of China, to which Chiang Kai-shek was forced to move]. I feel a heavy weight in my heart. Today the Japanese people are not allowed freedom of speech and we cannot publicly express our criticism. However, I must say that the statement is quite stupid; it is embarrassing for a nation to issue such a statement. But no one would venture to voice his opinion. The Japanese people do not even have access to enough information to know the facts, since we have been forced to accept the suppression of public opinion with patience and resignation. This is just one example of the routines and demagoguery that have become the moving forces of our society. It is the sin committed by journalism, which should have supported public opinion. It is also the sin committed by the state authority, which has suppressed freedom of speech.

We must understand the basics of democracy. We Japanese have not been able to master individualism (not egotism).

As long as a religion holds the people together in *Gemeinschaft,* it will foster a passionate sense of collectivity. When it dissolves, it renders individuals helpless, without common beliefs binding them together. The people's rights, which occupied a prominent place in the Meiji constitution, were thrown out as the political parties became powerless. We need a new political education. Alas, however, it is too late now. I hope the statement by the government will not be accompanied by military action.

Let me state it once more. We are going to meet our fate led by the cold will of the government. I shall not lose my pride until the end. I will not lose my passion and hope until the end. . . . There is one ideal—freedom. (56–61)

July 18, 1944

At the end of the diary entry for this day is a long letter to Yayeko.

Mass suicide [*gyokusai*, which means "to scatter like a shattered crystal ball"] on Saipan. Some predicted it. Now we see it as a fact.

To Yayeko: I am not surprised by the way we are losing the war. I had anticipated it ever since my university days. I fully expected the American forces to come very close to us. The Japanese have overestimated their own strength and underestimated that of the Americans.

Where is Japan going? Is it going to be a clever fox, rather than a wild boar recklessly dashing forward? Now survival is the main problem, rather than loyalty to the country. Diplomatic negotiations would perhaps take place day and night.

If so, why must we fight? We no longer have any purpose for fighting. I do not hesitate to sacrifice my life for the country. What is most painful is to think about the future of my beloved ones. When I heard the news of Saipan, I felt pain in my heart at having to face the cold reality. No matter what happens, I must prevent you people from another tragedy like the one on Saipan.
(62–66)

July 23, 1944

Norikazu [his younger brother] was supposed to visit me but did not come. I spent the morning at Inomata's home and then spent the afternoon at the Ōtas, where they held a farewell party for me. I was very envious of the happy family atmosphere, although I was disappointed that their mother did not join us. I suppose that is what happens in old feudalistic families. I was reminded of our household when Mother was alive. I feel sad thinking of my mother's absence from the dinner table, following the old custom.
(66–67)

Addressed to Yayeko

This letter to his sweetheart, following the diary dated July 24, 1944, was written less than a year after his mother's death.

I have been thinking of you quite frequently. I dreamt of you walking by, wearing a pale blue dress, carrying a parasol. At these times my mind starts to wander searching for the lost times.

But the cold and cruel will [of the government] immediately erases my dreams. . . . I pray that my beliefs and predictions prove to be wrong. I hope to confirm my conviction that the ultimate victory is won by spiritual strength, not by material goods. . . . When cherished memories and passionate love are both gone, I still feel the pain of loneliness for not having someone to call "Mother." Forgive me, Yayeko—when I think of my mother, I forget about you. (67–68)

August 1, 1944, at the Matsushima Naval Air Base

At ten in the morning, we are told to go to Matsushima. Although we began to fly on plane no. 361, the plane had suffered enormous damage and at first the engine did not start. . . . One plane returned to the base due to malfunctions. (70–71)

August 17, 1944

I received your letter, I think, yesterday. You had told me that you would not write to me any more. . . . You tell me that you wish to come here to visit me. But, I prefer being left alone as I am now. If you came I could not forget you, or I fear that you might find me not as good as you think. I prefer leaving everything as it is and hope no stone will be cast into a peaceful spring. I live in my imagination and fondly recall you in your pale blue dress. (73–74)

September 5, 1944

Takushima broke his leg and could not go on leave. He did not even feel like reading. He describes a dream.

It was a deserted hospital in the countryside. I don't know why I went there. I met my mother. I was shocked but pleased to find my mother alive there. I could not believe it. I got close to my mother and asked, "Are you alive?" Mother replied, "Look at me. I am alive." Mother had lost some weight. I lay next to her and was able feel her soft skin. I thought to myself: "It is not true that she is sick; look, her body is so warm, soft and beautiful." Mother thought I was not feeling well and made some medicine for me. Alas, it was a dream. But it is all right, since I was able to see her again. (75–76)

October 14, 1944

We leave Taiwan and head for the Philippines. . . . Our fighting spirit was intensified by the news that two comrades, Haga and Ochiai, were shot down by enemy planes. (78–80)

October 15, 1944

The last entry in Takushima's diary begins with this observation:

The news of the death of my comrade Shōda was a great blow to my heart. . . . He was idealistic and more patriotic than most of us. He still lives in my heart. His navy uniform and other personal belonging he entrusted to me are still in my room. I had kept hoping that he might have drifted onto an island in the South Pacific. But the news that his plane was shot down terminated that dream. Lieutenant Yuta, too, died when his plane plunged into a mountain [it is not clear whether it was an accident or an intentional act]. I am very sorry to have lost these two close comrades. But to have met the proper death must have been quite satisfactory for them as males.

This passage is the only one written with a brush and is the last entry in his diary, expressing his deep sorrow about his friends' deaths (Yasuda 1967, 278) and also about his realization that his turn was to come very shortly. (80–84)

Poems, 1944

Thirteen poems, also written with a brush, follow this diary entry. Several poems, such as the following, voice his desperate search for a rationale to lend meaning to his death.

To the other world where my mother lives all alone,
I shall bring the honor from the battlefield.

Another poem voices his longing for his beloved Yayeko, who lives near the Tama River, and likens her to the cherry blossom; "Yaye" in her name means "double petals" of the flower.

How I long for the double-petaled cherry blossom along the Tama River.
It blooms with fragrance, without, however, bearing a fruit.
(81–84)

CONCLUSION

Takushima's diary shows four stages in the development of his thought. First, when he was a student at Keiō University, he declared that Romanticism was his religion and ardently pursued his quest for beauty, while suppressing an increasing awareness of the encroachment of authoritarianism. Then, beginning in late July 1940, he openly opposed the rise of nationalism and expressed his determination not to succumb to it. By the beginning of 1941, however, he saw fighting in the war as his unavoidable fate and started trying to justify it by contemplating the beauty of sacrifice. Finally, by March 1944, when he was at the Demizu Naval Air Base, he became totally resigned to his fate and struggled to find a rationalization for his death.

Takushima was a political liberal who condemned the right wing, comparing its supporters to drunks shouting slogans. He declared that the notion of sacrifice as a patriotic act was an idea that only the stupid masses would believe. At the time of the Nazi persecution of the Jews and the Japanese invasion of China, he admired the overseas Chinese and the Jews, who live in a diaspora, without a nation, and thought them worthy of respect from the peoples of the world. He read Stefan Zweig, who advocated humanism and pacifism. At this stage, he repeatedly declared that he could not put his nation before himself.

Takushima's early years at the university were filled with his longing for a woman, intensely erotic and sensual in nature but all in his imagination. Then he met and fell in love with Yayeko. He respected her intellect as much as he admired her beauty. But as his death became imminent, he started to suppress his feelings for her, telling her—and, more importantly, himself—that he should not think of her or of such matters as love, since he was now fully committed to serving his beloved country in its crisis. His mother's death intensified his awareness of the end he felt was fast approaching. He found consolation only in his memories of her loving care, which was the sustaining moral force throughout his life. Takushima repeatedly criticized the feudal custom that prevented her from joining the family at the dinner table. In reference to his sweetheart, he praised women who challenge men.

A poet, painter, violinist, and singer during his university days, Takushima became a devoted follower of German Romanticism (*Romantik*).

He refers often to Novalis, who attended Jena University, the birthplace of Romanticism, and later Leipzig University and was closely associated with other major figures of the German Romantik school, including Schiller and Schlegel, as well as Fichte and Kant. Novalis was the creator of the blue flower (*die blaue Blume*), an important emblem of the movement. Takushima's obsession with Cape jasmine and other flowers may have been influenced in part by Novalis. Novalis's favorite themes, especially death and dusk as the time for death, appear frequently in Takushima's poems and essays.

Yet from the very beginning of the diary, Takushima acknowledged that his reveries were escapes from reality, which he felt was becoming darker and darker. In his imaginary encounter with Don Juan, who notices that he was fleeing from the present rather than living in the past, he admits that he is seeking to forget a reality that is "very dark." A careful reading of his diary during this early period leaves the painful impression that Takushima was seeking to escape the grim reality that was closing in around him by searching for imaginary experiences of erotic sensuality and inner freedom. Rather than the overflowing spirit of youth, he celebrated the haunting and ephemeral beauty of the dusk, the sunset, and the lily of the valley.

Seen from this perspective, his devotion to Romanticism takes on complexity. It may have started as an influence on the youthful Takushima. But it could have been the other way around: perhaps he sought refuge in Romanticism precisely because his world began to collapse and then shatter. Over a romantic youth's love of dusk purely for the sake of its melancholy beauty hung a thinly disguised anguish over his death, which was quietly but steadily approaching.

Toward the end of July 1940, he filled his diary with expressions of his anger at and frustration with the ever-increasing pressure of the government's demand for patriotism. The entry for July 28, 1940, is especially revealing. The bold assertions that "I hate the rise of nationalism" and that "according to my view, the nation takes second place to individuals" are followed by the recognition that "in reality individuals are completely ignored" as "the nation now takes complete control over individuals." This outburst ends with a sarcastic statement: "Turning around 180 degrees from the Romantic to the Realist, I am looking at the moon and smiling."

Yet less than a year later, by the beginning of 1941, this "turning around" ceased to be the sarcastic statement of a nonbeliever and became a description of Takushima's own course as he began to justify the inevitable. This devoted follower of Romanticism, who disdained nationalism, tried to transform his attitude to make fighting for his country into the moral equivalent of service to a higher ideal. On January 23, 1941, he remarked: "This is the century of warfare, and most of us must find comfort in finding that the purpose of the war is couched in the language of beautiful Romanticism. The feeling involved in self-sacrifice to one's dream, ideal, and beauty is akin to the longing for a maiden at a far distance." This whole entry has an ambivalent tone, half sarcastic and yet with a hint of trying to convince himself of the duty for all Japanese under the circumstances. This tortured twisting to rationalize his fate was not unique to Takushima; the same tendency is apparent in other student soldiers' diaries. Most important or, in fact, scary is that he began to use the wartime rhetoric of the government that the last capital for the Japanese is their body—the very ideological rationale for the tokkōtai operation—against Americans, whose material resources are too vast for the Japanese to compete with.

The rationale for self-sacrifice that Takushima began to entertain never took the form of dying for the emperor. As reflected in the subtitle of the diary, *For the Beloved People in My Homeland,* he imagined himself dying to protect the children who bowed to him in the rice paddy and for women like Yayeko. Above all, it was his family, his beloved, the natural landscape, and the people of Japan whom he loved. These all remained stubbornly particular, even as he linked them to abstract ideals that justified his coming death. Thus Takushima tells us in a most concrete way what has become increasingly clear in recent years from the writings of soldiers in various wars: that soldiers need to convert an abstract idea, such as love of the king/president/country, into something personally meaningful, such as protection of loved ones. It is for this reason that patriotism becomes intensified when "homeland invasion" and similar happenings threaten their loved ones.

Takushima's symbolic use of flower imagery is complex, with layers of influence ranging from his mother to Romanticism. The Cape jasmine was the most important flower for him because it was his mother's favorite. He also associated the camellia with his mother, because her home in the mountains was full of camellia blossoms in the spring. He especially enjoyed it because, he said, the flower knows how to assert itself. In this respect, the camellia is unlike the Cape jasmine. Takushima mentions cherry blossoms throughout his diary, including the two poems written in brush strokes in its last entry. In one, introduced below, the flower symbolizes himself, as he falls like a petal without leaving offspring. In another, cited above, a double-petaled cherry blossom without a fruit to bear—a possible child of his and Yayeko's—is a metaphor for her. For Takushima, the cherry blossom represents beauty without hope for life, a sad flower indeed.

We find parallels with other student soldiers in two significant respects. First, Takushima accepted his imminent death as given: as early as January

3, 1940, he noted that "death is an absolute order that cannot be evaded." Major military setbacks, especially the mass suicides at Attu and Saipan, had an enormous impact on these young men, because according to the government reports they signaled the "Homeland Invasion" by American military forces. These youths recognized clearly that Japan's defeat was inevitable, yet they resolved to sacrifice their lives in the hope of preventing an invasion of their homeland. The comradeship that they experienced at school and especially on the base made them more willing to embrace their fate, even as they recognized the stupid, arbitrary, and soul-deadening rule of the military. As they watched their comrades perish on a daily basis, these young soldiers felt compelled to carry on the mission.

Tragically, when Japan's defeat became imminent and their sacrifice ceased to be meaningful, nationalism gained the upper hand by fanning young men's patriotism in defense of their homeland. This took place at the very time when Japan no longer had functioning airplanes, yet soldiers were put into airplanes by the military only to be killed in accidents. Takushima's description of his resolve to fight to protect innocent children tells us how far the government's propaganda had penetrated into the minds of small children and, in turn, how powerful an influence that had on soldiers. Children came to worship soldiers, and, sadly, their trusting veneration motivated young men to fight at a time when Japan was heading for its ultimate destruction.

Takushima's last diary entry, written on October 15, 1944, expresses in a poem his extreme loneliness and his desire to visit Yamada, where his mother was born and where his father moved to avoid bombing in the city during the war.

> When lonely, I will visit the scarecrow
> Along the river at Yamada in Tsukushi.

> Although I am to fall [like a cherry petal], I wish to have a son, who is
> Even better than a treasure made of silver, to continue on to the next
> generation and to succeed [me in] the family.

Tsukushi is an older name for Kyūshū, lending the poem a nostalgic tone. A scarecrow is a lone figure guarding a rice paddy, eloquently expressing Takushima's feeling of being all alone in the vast emptiness. It may also express the feeling of loneliness of a soldier helplessly fighting in a losing war. But the scarecrow in the poem is also a particular scarecrow—it stands for his mother's homestead in Yamada. Used as a place name *Yamada* refers to her home, but the same word used as a common noun denotes a rice field surrounded by mountains; it appears in a children's song, "The One-Legged Scarecrow in the Rice Paddy in the Mountains." It has been an enormously popular song, originally created in 1911 for second graders (Horiuchi and Inoue 1958, 258–59). The song touches the hearts of many Japanese with nostalgia for their childhood and for a rural Japan that has been constructed to embody the primordial "purity" of the Japanese (Ohnuki-Tierney 1993a, 1993b). For Takushima, the image represented a fond and vivid memory of his visit to Yamada with his mother, who held him in her bosom when he was scared by the gushing sound of a mountain torrent. The scarecrow at Yamada fuses his utter loneliness with his longing for the warmth, nurturance, and safety that his mother offered. Above all, this poem expresses a deep sadness, voicing his unfulfilled desire to leave the world with a son—a fruit of his love for Yayeko—to succeed him in the family and his distress at departing the world without any continuing ties to it. This utter sense of loneliness at the thought of a permanent disappearance into the vast emptiness is shared by almost by every student soldier whose diary is introduced in this book. The final diary entry and poems were written with a brush, rather than a pen; Yasuda says that was a deliberate way of indicating that this was his final entry (Yasuda 1967, 278).

A PARTIAL LIST OF TAKUSHIMA'S READING

French: Honoré de Balzac, Charles-Pierre Baudelaire, Paul Bourget, L. Boyer, François Coppée, Charles Fourier, André Gide, André Maurois, Michel de Montaigne, Arthur Rimbaud, Jean-Jacques Rousseau, George Sand; *Italian:* Dante Alighieri, Toni Rossi; *Spanish:* Miguel de Cervantes (Saavedra); *English:* Thomas Carlyle, John Dryden, Thomas Hobbes, John Keats, Dante Gabriele Rossetti; *Dutch:* François Hemsterhuis; *German:* Georg Harsdoerfer, Georg Wilhelm Friedrich Hegel, Karl Marx, Friedrich Nietzsche, Novalis (Friedrich von Hardenberg), Theodor Storm; *Austrian:* Stefan Zweig; *Russian:* Leo Tolstoy; *Indian:* Rawa Murtis; *Japanese:* Abe Jirō, a prominent scholar of aesthetics.

I sleep intoxicated by the beauty of amber-colored wine
An illusion of peace—no, we must not laugh. . . .

> Matsunaga Shigeo

Thinking it too painful
for my heart to bear
  I parted from her,
So why through the years
Do I still miss her face?

> Teika

Failing
To die from longing
  I have passed these years,
in my stubborn hope
of living to see you yet.

> Teika

"A Beautiful Illusion" (the first epigraph), a poem written by
Matsunaga Shigeo in 1938 while he was stationed with the
Japanese Army in China, captures the painful feelings of many
student soldiers and is quoted in a well-known collection
of writings by soldiers who died during World War II.[1] The
Matsunaga brothers, Shigeo and his younger brother Tatsuki,
were not involved in the tokkōtai operation, but they were
drafted as students and were forced to fight and die. Their writings were compiled and published in 1968 as *War, Literature,*

and Love: Writings Left Behind by Two Brothers Who Were Student Soldiers by Izumi Aki, who attended the same university as they did but did not know them personally. The volume starts with the younger brother's "Diary in Poems," which expresses his longing for his older brother after his death. The rest consists of diaries written by both. Their writings chronicle the painful experience of being torn between social pressure and their idealism.

The Matsunaga brothers came from a family that enjoyed a high status in society. They wrote in an exquisitely refined form of language used only by the upper class. Their father, who was very strict at home, was a high-ranking officer in the Japanese Navy. Their biological mother, who died when the brothers were very young, was a well-educated Christian. She was exceptionally talented in literature and art. In her family's retrospective view, her brilliance and refined sensitivity made it difficult for her to cope with the day-to-day realities of life, and her sufferings led to or hastened her early death. She left an enduring imprint on her sons; their bond rested to a significant degree on their shared pain at the loss of their mother. Their father remarried; his wife was also refined and very kind to the brothers. Using a polite form of address, "okāsama," they refer to their mother as "Midori Okāsama" and to their father's second wife as "Yoshiko Okāsama." Their life was filled with cultural activities such as piano concerts in their home. The family frequented the best restaurants and hotels.

The brothers both studied at Kokugakuin University, a special university established in 1882 that became the most important institution in the nation for research on Japanese history, law, and literature. The most prominent scholars in the field, including Orikuchi Shinobu and Kindaichi Kyōsuke, taught there. On the whole it was more conservative than other universities, where both liberals and conservatives were represented on the faculty. The Matsunaga brothers studied with distinguished professors, and by the time they were drafted the brothers had been recognized as younger peers by these giants in the field of Japanese studies. Both published their poems and essays in prestigious venues. After their deaths, with money donated by the family, the Research Institute for Japanese Literature, at the suggestion of Professor Orikuchi, bought a complete set of the definitive books about Buddhism and housed it in a case together with photographs of the brothers. The brothers were remarkably well accepted by their teachers, although both held liberal, perhaps radical antiwar and antinationalist views.

Despite their social and educational background and their father's position in the navy, both were drafted into the army, where conditions were far more miserable than in the navy. The younger brother's diary offers us an opportunity to follow his transformation from a severe critic of the military and of Japanese aggression and a man deeply in love with a woman whom he married into an officer who dedicated his life to the education of conscripts as thinking human beings, preventing them from being slaves for the military, and who decisively gave up the hope of returning to Japan to be with his wife. The brothers shared many experiences with their fellow student soldiers and articulated their views with unparalleled clarity and poignancy.

Because both Matsunaga brothers were steeped in Japanese literature, their diaries contain extensive discussions of Japanese scholars and authors. Only very small portions of those discussions are included here, since extensive, in-depth knowledge of Japanese literature and debates in the field would be required in order to follow their arguments and reflections. The entries are selected in order to show them as human beings and also to portray their views of the increasing militarization of Japan and their predicament as soldiers.

MATSUNAGA SHIGEO (1913–38)

Matsunaga Shigeo was born in 1913. He entered the First Higher School in 1931 as a science major. In 1935 he took a job teaching literature to elementary schoolchildren at Hanaoka Gakuin, a private school with a liberal curriculum. At that time he also began his literary career, publishing eight issues of the famous *Yumehiko,* a literary magazine, and a number of poems, essays, and works of literary criticism. In 1936 he entered Kokugakuin University. He was drafted into the army in 1937 and sent to China, where he attained the rank of corporal. The following year he contracted amoebic dysentery and died at the age of twenty-five on November 28, 1938. Some of Matsunaga Shigeo's writings were edited and published privately by Matsunaga Tatsuki, his younger brother, in a volume titled *Handwritten Notes of a Student Soldier.*[2] Although Shigeo died before World War II began, his younger brother was profoundly influenced by his views and by the writing he left behind.

The essays about Japanese history and culture included in the first section of *Handwritten Notes* contain candid denunciations of ultranationalists, including the nativist scholars Motoori Norinaga and Watsuji Tetsurō, and Yasuda Yojūrō, the founder and leader of Japan's Romantic School, which disguised its far-right ideology under the name "Romanticism" (Ohnuki-Tierney 2002, 265–68).

HANDWRITTEN NOTES OF A STUDENT SOLDIER

The diary entries are not dated, but they were written between October 15, 1937, when he entered the army, and November 28, 1938, when he died.

> While the summer heat is still on the street, we hear "Banzai" (Hail) on the street every day. "You must be anxious to go [to war]" people [say]. I remain silent, with a faint smile. (Matsunaga and Matsunaga 1968, 52)

> Cheap sentimentalism, spur-of-the-moment heroism, and blind patriotism—these are taboo for student soldiers. (52)

> A warrior cannot leave the warrior's way while drinking a cup of tea. Student soldiers may not leave intellectual pursuits even in the rain of machine guns. (53)

> I consider religion only as the government's strategy. Accepting the sincerity of those who contributed to the thousand-knot sash, I burned it to ashes before going to the front. The only "amulet" for student soldiers is their soul, ever aspiring to learn. (53)

The "thousand-knot sash" (*sen'ninbari*) to which Matsunaga refers was a white sash on which one thousand red knots, each tied by a woman, were sewn. These knots were often gathered at street corners from women who passed by. Claiming that the knotted sash would protect the soldier from bullets, the government used the project to create a bond between women at home and soldiers at the front.

> Students are apostles of truth. Students' patriotism is to uphold the truth of the nation. The souls of students seek truth without nation, rather than a nation without truth. (54)

> Look at Zola of the Dreyfus affair. The rebellious spirit of students, like burning fire, shines for eternity. (54)

> Students are neither nihilists nor anarchists, because they love truth and never doubt rationality even for a moment. (54)

> We should crush both liberalism and egotism. They are products of the leisurely upper class, which ignores the necessity of life. (56)

> Remember a student soldier [referring to himself] who recites the poems from *Shin-Kokinshū* under a shower of heavy cannonballs. (58)

Practical reason rules the [other] soldiers. In order to protect themselves and their famil[ies], they obey the authority of the imperial nation. (64)

We see in these statements that Matsunaga rejects the upper class, from which he comes, by accusing it of "liberalism," which often transforms individualism into egotism. He also criticizes fellow soldiers who are simply "pragmatic," protecting themselves and their families, without working for higher moral goals. In contrast, he positions himself as upholding the dignity of spiritual and intellectual pursuits by means of a deep appreciation of the Japanese classics. The *Shin-Kokinshū,* a collection of poems from the tenth century, became Matsunaga's spiritual citadel, and he wanted to write a major work about it. This twenty-volume collection, compiled between the years 905 and 915, contains eleven hundred poems. Many anonymous poems are included, as well as pieces by the most famous and revered poets of the time.

Democracy fell apart and autocracy raised its head. Some politicians seek the ideology of Japanese reform in the ideology of the National Socialists of Nazi Germany. (69)

The course Germany took may teach some things to Japan. But I am against the idea of Japan following the path of Germany. (69)

Matsunaga expresses his opposition to Nazism at a time when some Japanese were trying to imitate Germany in their effort to build their country in the turbulent years 1937–38.

POEMS

Matsunaga Shigeo included many poems in his letters to friends. A few poems reflecting on war are translated here.

Guynemer and Manfred

At the bottom of the people's heart
Runs the instinctive struggle between love and fighting.
Guynemer was a bright youth.
War is another name for murder,
Thus thought Guynemer.
However, he took up the weapon
Because he loved his country.

As he killed an enemy,
He realized that he committed a murder.

Manfred was a carefree lad.
He fought because he loved his country.
Tragedies and fear of death
Never entered his mind.
For him, the war was a sport.
When he killed an enemy, he felt no pain.
He only felt the joy of having served his country.

Both died eventually.
But the war went on.
Their death had no impact
Either on the war or on their country.
Should I bear the pain of Guynemer,
Or should I go along like a sunny Manfred?
Either way, there is little difference [between the two paths one might take]
To myself or to humanity at large.

"Guynemer and Manfred" (74–75) was composed in 1936 during Japan's invasion of China, when Matsunaga was not yet in the army. Guynemer is Georges Marie Ludovic Jules Guynemer, the French ace fighter pilot during World War I. Manfred is Manfred Albrecht von Richthofen, the famous German ace pilot, referred to by the British as the Red Baron, also during World War I. It is not clear why Matsunaga Shigeo characterized Guynemer and Manfred as opposites.

The last two lines of the poem express Matsunaga's nihilism—nothing an individual does makes a difference in life and war. This nihilism is also expressed in the following poem, composed in 1938, when Matsunaga was in the army in China.

Odyssey

Due to some fate, we foolish soldiers are
Fighting an eternal war without a name.
For us, without a map, is it glory or shame
Waiting at the end of our road?

Dire difficulties and a severe shortage of supplies
Paralyze the intellect.

Exposed are thinly disguised lies.
Soldiers realize they are but clowns.

Those who lost trust in the ancestral land
have no spiritual home.
They are left only with nostalgia which has no place for anchoring.

Those who, even then, love Japan are fortunate.
But, poor souls; it is the happiness of a wild goose.
It is the fake blue bird whose color fades away under light.

A Farewell Song to the Young Chinese Boy

Farewell, my dear friend; we enjoyed each other for three days.
Although I wish to stay with you forever,
Autumn is calling me.

Tomorrow we will likely go up the river.
I will sing in my heart, again and again, the song of the little lambs that
you taught me.
Come to think of it, our encounter was fortuitous
Just like the one in the poem by Po Chu-I.
But our parting was even more painful than Po Chu-I's.
Let us remain friends, forever and forever.
(78)

Matsunaga composed this "Farewell Song" (79–80) in 1938. Po Chu-I (772–846) was a famous Chinese poet of the Tang dynasty. (His name is spelled variously in English, for example, Bai Juyi, Bo Juyi.) He wrote poems about nature as well as about ordinary people and quotidian life. While exiled from the capital, Po Chu-I met a well-known female entertainer who sang her life story while playing a *pipa* (a lute). Listening to her narrative, which resonated with his own experience in exile, Po Chu-I wrote a poem. Matsunaga makes an analogy between his meeting with the Chinese boy and that of Po Chu-I with the female entertainer, emphasizing the fortuitous nature of the encounter and the pain of parting shared by these two couples.

MATSUNAGA TATSUKI (1916–1944)

Born in 1916, Matsunaga Tatsuki graduated from Kokugakuin University in 1941 and married a woman named Ayako in September of the same year. Two months later, he failed the physical examination for the Navy Reserve Unit. He was drafted by the army at the beginning of 1942 and sent to China via Korea within a week. After being promoted to the rank of first lieutenant, he died on the battlefield in 1944 at the age of twenty-eight.

Matsunaga Tatsuki left a detailed record of the painful torment of a man who was passionately in love with his wife but had to choose death on the battlefield, expressing the agony and loneliness felt by many soldiers who had to leave their sweethearts and wives. Equally important, his writings document his transformation from a cynic who disdained the military into an officer who dedicated himself to training new conscripts. After he was forced to take the examination to qualify him as an officer, and passed it, as his superiors had planned, Matsunaga Tatsuki re-created himself, giving up his resistance to serving in the army. But he still challenged the military system by teaching new conscripts to use their intellect rather than simply obey orders blindly. He went to his death in passionate devotion to this project of his own making. Matsunaga's transformation was not a matter of moving to the left or the right. Rather, he retained his idealism and found a new way to act on it within the military. Being forced to become an officer was a decisive event for him; he gave up any hope of returning to his young wife and prepared himself to die. He rejected the army's sacrifice of his life as meaningless but gave meaning to his life and death through his devotion to his ideal of soldiers who act mindfully and in solidarity with the conscripts for whom, he maintained, officers should risk their lives. Matsunaga arrived at this tortured rationalization when he realized that there was no escape from death and that he had to make the best of his life in an army he detested.

Matsunaga's view of women was quite progressive, a characteristic he shared with several student soldiers whose diaries are introduced in this book. The "new feminism" was being discussed at the time. Matsunaga and his friends advocated women's education and their full realization as human beings, but they did not support women's political movements, in part because, like women, they themselves had renounced fame and success outside their family life. Like Takushima Norimitsu, Matsunaga Tatsuki wanted his wife to be an independent and even rebellious spirit. He wanted her to "grow intellectually" during their separation. His feelings toward his wife were extremely tender and passionate. He was enormously attracted to her physically but restrained his sexual desires out of respect for her, even on the night before he left for the army.

Nakao Takenori (front row, fourth from left), with his hands on the drum, after the dormitory festival at Fukuoka Higher School. The character on the white banner on the left stands for "dormitory" (*ryō*). Courtesy of Nakao Yoshitaka.

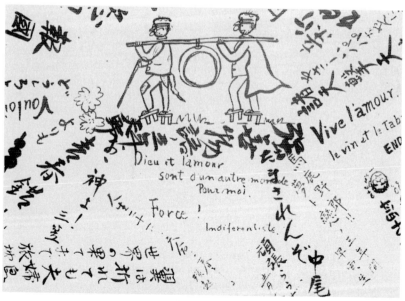

Creating a *yosegaki*, a collection of impromptu writings on a piece of paper, a fan, a flag, and so on by members of a social group was a common practice. This *yosegaki* was written at the time of their graduation from Fukuoka Higher School by Nakao Takenori and his classmates, all nineteen years old, in 1942. Nakao Takenori wrote: "I shan't be fooled." Courtesy of Nakao Yoshitaka.

Left to right: Sasaki Taizō, Sasaki Jūsuke, Mrs. Noma, and Sasaki Hachirō. Sasaki Taizō is Sasaki Hachirō's younger brother. Sasaki Jūsuke is the brothers' cousin; in 1944, at thirty-nine, he was killed in battle on Mindanao. Mrs. Noma was a neighbor who took lessons in *utai* (singing accompanying the noh play) with their mother and was a frequent guest in the Sasaki household. This photo was taken by their father in April or May 1942, the year Sasaki Hachirō entered the Imperial University of Tokyo and Taizō entered the First Higher School. Courtesy of Sasaki Taizō.

The cover of *A Picture Scroll of Yasukuni* (*Yasukuni no Emaki*) by Tōjō Hideki, published on the occasion of the Spring Grand Ceremony at the Yasukuni National Shrine. Copies were given to survivors of fallen soldiers. Published in 1944 and edited by the army and navy, the booklet starts with a drawing of "Spring in the Sacred Realm"—a painting of a part of the Yasukuni National Shrine compound with cherry blossoms. The painter is Fujita Tsuguharu, a well-known artist who studied in Paris and introduced the artistic tradition of the École de Paris to Japan. The rest of the booklet contains twenty-six paintings accompanied by narratives describing Japan's wartime struggles and military victories. Courtesy of R. Kenji Tierney.

The famous "grand send-off parade" at the Meiji Shrine Outer Garden Stadium on October 21, 1943, in the rain. Those drafted were from seventy-seven universities, higher schools, and vocational schools from metropolitan Tokyo and from Kanagawa, Saitama, and Chiba Prefectures near Tokyo. The twenty-five thousand students, some female, marched in front of Education Minister Okabe Nagakage. The University of Tokyo students led the parade, with a white flag on which only "University" (*daigaku*) instead of the "Imperial University of Tokyo" was written. They were the first students to be drafted for World War II. At this time Japan had already begun losing the war. Courtesy of the Mainichi Shinbunsha Photo Bank.

A medal given to the survivors of fallen soldiers. It is in the shape of a cherry blossom with a tasseled cord in purple, the color of the royal family. "A medal of the survivors of a soldier" is inscribed on the back. Courtesy of R. Kenji Tierney.

Bills issued during the war. Both had a value of fifty sen (a sen is one-hundredth of a yen) and bore the imperial crest of the chrysanthemum with sixteen petals. The top bill, with four sets of cherry blossoms and the rays of the rising sun over Mt. Fuji, was issued in 1938, which is indicated on the left as year 13 of the reign of Emperor Shōwa, and on the right as year 2598 from the mythical origin of the enthronement of the legendary first emperor.

The lower one was issued in 1943, which is indicated on the right as the eighteenth year of Emperor Shōwa. It shows the torii entrance to the Yasukuni National Shrine. In addition to the seven single cherry blossoms, a phoenix is shown flying into the shrine. Ever since the middle of the Heian period (794–1185) the imperial palanquin was called *hōren*, or the "phoenix palanquin," and the phoenix has been an important emblem of the emperor. Since the beginning of Japan's military period the government deployed the motif of the phoenix, putting it, for example, on military and regular currency.

Government-produced cigarettes were given to soldiers on the battlefields, often as *onshi no tabako*, "cigarettes given by the emperor." The packages usually had very colorful designs and bore legends such as "Celebration of Victorious Returns," "Battle Field Victory," and "The Rising Sun." Although foreign words were taboo during this period, some English words were printed. This package depicts cherry blossoms and a soldier celebrating a victory, although the cigarettes were issued in commemoration of army grand maneuvers that perhaps took place in Hokkaido, a map of which forms the background for the soldier's image.

Umezawa Kazuyo, a tokkōtai "boy pilot," with cherry branches on his uniform. Courtesy of Umezawa Shōzō.

A tokkōtai plane with a single cherry blossom painted on its side, housed in the Exhibit Hall of the Yasukuni National Shrine. Photo by R. Kenji Tierney.

Female students from Chiran High School, waving blooming cherry branches as the tokkōtai (Shinbutai corps) planes take off, April 1945. Courtesy of the Mainichi Shinbunsha Photo Bank.

Nakao Takenori wearing his pilot's goggles. Courtesy of Nakao Yoshitaka.

DIARY WRITTEN WHILE AT UNIVERSITY, 1940-42

January-August 1940

Resolution: There are two years before I enter the military. No matter what people say, the entrance into the military represents a type of death. I have to live now as best as I can. (82-83)

Rediscovery of *Shin-Kokinshū*: The first collection of poems I read was not *Manyōshū* but *Shin-Kokinshū*. As a young boy who was in pursuit of passionate but pure love, I was not satisfied with the poems in the collection which did not express their feelings directly and openly. . . . But I was touched by the love sung in those poems. Although I could not follow their mode of expression, the collection became the bedrock of my literary quest. (83)

Finally, I discovered what sublimity is—as you find in the graceful ink paintings. . . . I fell deeply in love. (84)

In the meanwhile, my learning led me to seek something beyond poetry— society and culture in general, in which poems are composed. (This is the period when I was devouring Durkheim and works about him.) Poems of a small group of people, removed from reality, were of no interest to me. A number of disturbing events threw me out of society psychologically [he became alienated from society]. I spent my days idling in a world in which I had no more interest. At that time, I rediscovered the *Shin-Kokinshū*, while enjoying reading Dostoevsky and Shestóv. (85)

Lev Isaákovich Shvártsman Shestóv was a Russian Jewish philosopher and critic.

At the time of the French Revolution, England without revolution gave birth to the poems of Shelly and Keats. The *Shin-Kokinshū* had to be born among the courtiers who became completely alienated from politics at the time when the Genji and Heike clans were competing to gain hegemony. The two thousand poems of the *Shin-Kokinshū* are the literature of pain, suppressed pain, or, more accurately, pain transcended. (85-86)

April-November 1941

Matsunaga Tatsuki's diary entries for 1941 reveal how close the Matsunaga brothers were to the most prominent scholars of Japanese history and literature. Orikuchi Shinobu was one of the two founders of Japanese ethnology who approached ancient texts as ethnographic material. Saigō Nobutsuna was an authority on ancient Japanese literature, especially *Kojiki,* the eighth-century myth-history and the first written text of Japan. Kazamaki Keijirō's scholarship centered on ancient and medieval literature, including *The Tale of Genji.* Tsumura Nobuo was a novelist and poet; Hori Tatsuo was a novelist. Kadokawa Gen'yoshi, who studied at the Kokugakuin University, as the brothers did, was the founder and the first president of Kadokawa Shoten, a major publishing house in postwar Japan. Kadokawa Gen'yoshi believed that the best way to rebuild Japan after the war was to develop publishing houses, and he opened his own in the living room of his house in Tokyo. His first publication was the collected essays of Hori Tatsuo, and when he began the famous Kadokawa paperback series, the first book was a translation of Dostoevsky's *Crime and Punishment.* All these figures, who were already established when the brothers were alive or became established later, were close friends of the Matsunaga brothers; they lived within an intellectually exciting circle.

> Mother has been working very hard to find me a "little wife." There are many hints that Father and Mother are putting a great deal of thought into it. I wait to see how things develop without interfering. Recently Father ceased to be strict. He no longer scolds me if I sleep late or return home late. It is overwhelming to think of his love and concern for me. I also understand how concerned Mother is. I only wish Teichan were with us. (90)

Teichan was an affectionate name for his deceased elder brother.

> Father returned. I was so impressed by his accounts of Thailand and French Indochina. I wish I could go there, too. How such a trip would enlarge the horizon of my scholarship and worldview, not just theoretically but in my body and my feelings, so that I become at least pan-Asian, if not cosmopolitan. . . . I would rather be a cosmopolitan than a narrow-minded country hick, even if people may laugh at me today. I wish to be familiar with international air travel, learn the mentality of the people of the South Pacific, and learn about Africa and Algeria, which will make a difference in our view. (August 1, 95)

> Yesterday as well as today, I wanted to talk to Kofumi [a woman at a café]. She said three times, "You must be afraid of the war," but I did not answer. Indeed I am afraid of wars. But, above all, I am opposed to the war Japan is engaged in now. I don't agree with their policy. There is something basically wrong with the government's policy and the army's military strategy. (96)

Even if the solitude of a beautiful spirit is violated, I shall try not to commit suicide. (97)

On the war—I feel aversion or disgust, even in a physical sense, more than fear. (August 9, 97)

This entry is not the only one among his 1941 diaries to mention suicide. He also discusses it on July 19 (93–94), but that entry is written in such an oblique way that it is impossible to guess the reasons for his bleak mood. Because of the war, Matsunaga Tatsuki considered but resolved not to commit suicide. His reasoning is not recorded directly, but he seems to have considered the act as a way of preserving the inviolability of his spirit under the conditions of wartime and then rejected it as a futile act.

I reread *Tonio Kröger* [by Thomas Mann]—an entirely different reading from the one I did when I was a young boy. The struggle between life and the spirit and the bewilderment of a humble citizen really struck a chord with me. This novel most succinctly demonstrates how literature is tragedy. I now reappraise this literary piece from the perspective of an art critic. The female painter *qua* art critic as she narrates to Tonio Kröger is the central theme of this literary work. . . . The spirit of tragedy appears in the form of an artist who loves life. Is a philosophy of tragedy possible? . . . I keep thinking of Shestóv, who considered tragedy to be the essence of life, while Mann thought it could be understood only by special individuals. (August 10, 98–99)

The dark mood he felt during this year, however, lifted as he fell in love with and married Ayako, a well-educated young woman. In his imagination he had been longing intensely for a woman, whom he called Yukari after a young woman in *The Tale of Genji*. She was now replaced by Ayako, whom he affectionately calls "Ayapin," "A-ko," and "my Yukari."

For the first time I visit A-ko. Accompanied by Mother. I think she is too good for me. She deserves someone like Hans Hansen in *Tonio Kröger*, who is happy and enjoying life. That she will accompany me throughout my life—it is like a dream. I declare—from today, I affirm life. What a lovely sound in the phrase "to live." ...[I] just think of A-ko, and I feel warmth in my heart. For the past few days, not a second has gone by without thinking of A-ko. . . . I used to say that love and marriage are different; the former is romantic and the latter is pragmatic. But it has changed 180 degrees.

I declare—I am in love. A-ko—I love you and I will love you even more in the days to come. (August 11, 99)

We talked about our church. . . . Midnight. Beautiful and gentle rain. I love rain. I wonder what you are thinking now. Is she thinking of me, I hope? (August 11, 100)

In modern Japan, so-called arranged marriage usually starts with the mother looking for a suitable marriage partner for her daughter or son. The first stage is a "paper screening," the exchange between the prospects of documents containing the relevant information—where their parents came from, information about the rest of the family, and their life history, including education, details of employment (the positions held, the name of the company), and hobbies or special interests—together with a photograph. The parents of each party inspect the prospect's background, at times traveling to the other family's place of origin to make sure the family has no skeleton in the closet. In this instance, Matsunaga's mother and stepmother and Ayako and her family were all Christians, which meant that they had a common set of values.They were from the same social circle, although they may not have known each other in person. Many Christians in Japan belong to a particular segment of the upper class that places emphasis on education and high culture, both European and Japanese. After the prospects pass the preliminary screening, the two young people meet, accompanied by both sets of parents. If they both like what they see, then "dating," a period of courtship in which the young people get to know each another, begins. At any time, either party can say no without any negative repercussions, at least until one refuses too many prospective spouses. If all goes well, the couple agrees to marry; as in the case of Matsunaga Tatsuki, one or both may fall in love.

At night again at Suikōsha [a restaurant]. We spent some time in the garden. . . . I feel that I am loved. I won't say a word. I just watch her. Just the two of us. . . . I restrained myself and did not ask when I can see her next, which I regret[ted] in the following days. (August 16, 103)

I no longer need literature. . . . I already have Yukari. Ayapin—when can we talk again forever! I wish I could see her tonight, but I am restraining myself. Shall I call her tomorrow? Why did I not ask her when I could see her again? From now on I should always make certain when our next date is. I waited all evening hoping she would call me on the phone, but no call. (August 18, 104)

I love her more and more every day. . . . It is painful to control my passion. How I wish to embrace and kiss her. Words are of little use. Words are for teachers and friends. When we sit silently together and talk quietly—we need both. (August 20, 105)

A splendid day. Blue sky. Not a single drop of rain. In the morning I talked with Professor Orikuchi. What a marvelous teacher he is! . . . In the afternoon, I had a most inspirational talk with Mr.Tokimasa. My life work begins! I must read Croce's *Philosophy of the Spirit* and Kant's *Critique of Judgment* [*Kritik der Urteilskraft*]. (August 25, 108–9)

Today I raise my white flag [of surrender to Ayako]. At 2 o'clock in the afternoon, you came with my father. Just the two of us spent the time in the room upstairs, first in the back of it and then mov[ing] toward the veranda, where until sunset we talked, feeling the autumn breeze, looking at the clouds in the sky. What a pleasure to be reassured of your youthful and rebellious character. We spent some time with Mother. Then Father called. We looked at the crimson sky over the vegetable garden. And, dinner together. Then, holding hands, we talked as I accompanied you back over the dark road. Then, I was invited into your house for a beer. Enough said. My love toward you is being intensified every moment. Perfect happiness.

I call you "*mon* [*sic*] *petite femme.*" Or, shall I use "*Frau*"? Or, *femme dame*? Or, *épouse*? What are you going to call me? I would like it best if you call me *anata* [a polite form of "you" in Japanese]. Perhaps you won't be able to call me *kimi* [a colloquial masculine second-person pronoun, which can be used humorously by women]. Or, would you be able to use *du* or *tu*? As a reference term, you might refer me as *mon mari*. Although it sounds too gentle, I much prefer it to "hus" [the Japanese abbreviation of *husband*]. French is a beautiful language—"*mari.*" (September 7, 108–9)

Ah, everything is beautiful and serene. I am confident that I can say on the day I die that the world I have seen was beautiful. Ayapin—it is you who gave me this beautiful world. . . . I wonder what you are thinking tonight. Are you feeling sorrow? Are you having intense feelings about leaving your maidenhood? Knowing your personality, I expect that you will brave through this threshold almost unconsciously. . . . I hope you will be able to spend tonight peacefully. I will try my best to do so, too. . . . Tomorrow, and the day after. What is waiting for us? A long (or very short) life together. What fate [is] waiting for us? . . . Ayapin—good night, sleep peacefully. So that you are not tired tomorrow. I too will bid farewell to my life alone and think about it in bed. (111–12)

> Through the process of preparation, I began to have a very unusual love to-
> ward Mother Yoshiko. I loved her before, but I began to have a deep respect
> toward her. The feeling is like that of a friendship. Mothers of this kind must
> be few and far between. I close this part of my diary with deep gratitude for
> Mother Yoshiko. When can I repay all that Father and Mother have done for
> me? (112)

There are no entries in his diary from their wedding day until September 27. On September 13, the day before his wedding, (109–12), Matsunaga Tatsuki is feeling contemplative, looking forward to marital happiness but also considering the meaning of life in the face of death. He and Ayako were married on September 14, 1941. Wartime was an uncertain moment to marry.

When the diary resumes, Matsunaga is continuing his studies but is increasingly aware of the expansion of the war.

> I finished reading *Fyodor Dostoevsky* by Murray. Of all the books I read this
> year, I read this book most passionately. Where is the harmonious point
> of meeting between the despair of Dostoevsky (philosophy of tragedy) and
> Murray's sunny humanism? That is the focal point of interest for me; I am an
> ordinary person who discovered a genius and who discovered tragedy in life.
> I must write an essay on Dostoevsky. I will read Kobayashi Hideo's work on
> Dostoevsky and Murray's *The Life of Jesus Christ*. (November 23, 116)

The first work to which Matsunaga refers is John Middleton Murray's *Dostoevsky: Letters and Reminiscences;* the last is possibly *The Betrayal of Christ by the Church.*

> The annual meeting of the Society for National Literature, which was also
> meant to be a farewell party for me. . . . The passion of Yasuda is directed
> toward himself, and not to the classics. (November 24, 117)

This remark about Yasuda Yojūrō, the far-right figure who led the Romantic School in Japan, shows that Matsunaga sided with the antimilitarists among scholars of Japanese culture.

> What is leading Japan today? It is the military. What thought process is lead-
> ing Japan today? It is the military ideology. What is military ideology? Let
> me start with the agrarian problem, since it is the agrarian problem that is
> the most important factor determining the future of Japan. Today's leaders
> emphasize the agrarian problem in a loud voice. They say that Japan has

been an agrarian nation throughout its history for three thousand years. They claim that agriculture is the [bed]rock of Japan and despise cities and city dwellers. They resort to history to back up their claim, but it is just an excuse. The real problem is the shortage of food for the Japanese people. . . . They emphasize that self-sufficiency in food is necessary when we enter a war. . . . But there is no reason to think we can ever achieve self-sufficiency. We have to import foreign rice. . . . We cannot live on the land of the Japanese archipelago. . . . We must keep trading with Manchuria, China, and French Indochina. If we can rely on these countries, there is no need to emphasize agricultural self-sufficiency. We should tackle more important matters. So, then, why does the military keep insisting on the importance of rural agricultural land? They are looking at rural villages not as land for the production of food, but for the production of people. Most soldiers come from rural Japan. Rural Japan produces the best soldiers. . . . That is why the government is not encouraging the improvement of productivity through science and technology. They want to keep the status quo so that they produce people suitable for military duties—strong in body, hard-working like oxen, and with an uncritical attitude which produces absolute obedience. (November 27, 118–23)

PREPARING HIMSELF FOR WAR: DECEMBER 1941 TO JANUARY 1942

On December 8, he wrote only "Sensō no Hajimatta Hi" (The Day War Began) in roman letters (125).

> I failed the [physical] examination for the Navy. When I think of my father's disappointment, I feel like blaming my body. (December 21, 130)

No details about the examination are given.

> Every day, a beautiful clear winter sky. The war is going on intensely. There is no celebration of Christmas or New Year. . . . I finished reading a few books: [José] Ortega [y Gasset]'s discussion of the problems of modernity and his observation of love; *Nahoko* [a novel by Hori Tatsuo], the very best among Hori's work; *Yamato Koji* (*Ancient Temples in Nara*) by Inoue Masatsugu. After reading Ortega, I began to hope to write my aphorism about Dostoevsky and others. I am gaining more confidence [in my ability] to write an essay on Stendhal and Dostoevsky. . . . I wish to write on beauty, life, love, and sunny dispositions. I wish to write an essay weaving in Middleton Murray, Ortega,

Valéry, and Stevens. Others can write academic articles and epic poems. I will write something in between the two, in which lightness and darkness are woven like in a tapestry with the tone of [Rainer Maria] Rilke and [Hans] Carossa but without that German-style straight line; mine will be music of prose, poetry of concepts. (December 30, 132–35)

The following passage from January 8, 1942 (137–39), constitutes an imaginary exchange with a friend considering death in the military.

"Why don't you let your imagination run wild? If you want to be alive and healthy by being a model soldier and feel happy being buried among fruits in the southern Pacific, so be it. If you want to put up a protest, be hit [by your superior] and die, so be it. The end of the story." How about this as my speech for being drafted?

Professor Orikuchi Shinobu treated us [members of the literary circle] to dinner. . . . It was a rare occasion to talk about women. . . . His opinion on women and marriage was interesting and had good insight. But, after all, his own complex about his bachelorhood kept interfering with the free flow of our conversation on the topic.

A quiet Sunday. The result of the examination for the navy reserve was posted. Everyone tries not to notice it [the fact that he failed]. . . . I feel relieved—it signals a longer time to enjoy freedom. I am no longer a nineteen-year-old youth who knows nothing about death. (January 11, 139–40)

On January 15 (140–47), he wrote a long essay titled "On Literature—Record of My Favorite Readings: Autobiography of My Soul."

Most people between twenty and forty years of age who talk about literature find their point of departure in the novels of the Meiji and Taishō periods [1868–1912 and 1912–1926, respectively], such as [those of] Natsume Sōseki, Shimazaki Tōson, Tanizaki Junichirō, Shiga Naoya, and Yokomitsu Ri'ichi. For me, my starting point was very different. . . . I did not need those novels and I feel resistance to them. The reading I enjoyed most was "Christmas Hen" and "David"—children's books that are beautiful. Perhaps my interest was somewhat religious. I did not care for those who purposely focused on adults and the ugly aspects of life.

After I graduated from "Little Princess Seira" and "Nina," I read with passion Little Women and the rest of the stories by Louisa May Alcott. . . . Then I moved to Peter Pan [a play by J. M. Barrie] and A Child's Garden of

Verses [by Robert Louis Stevenson]. I always carried them in my pocket. A random reading of foreign novels in Japanese translation led me to books for young people represented by Hans Christian Andersen's works. His *Picture Book without Pictures* and *Improvisatoren* [*The Improvisatore, or, Life in Italy*]—they are really like works of Mori Ōgai [a Japanese novelist]; among all the Japanese literary figures, I share the most affinity with Ōgai.

Tolstoy's *Boyhood* opened the door for me to the literature for adults. My reading of Maurice Maeterlinck, August Strindberg, and Fyodor K. Sologub led me back to unfulfilled nostalgia for lost childhood and dark despair. Of Japanese novels in the same genre, I read Tokutomi Roka's *Memoire* (*Omoide no Ki*), Nakamura Seiko's *Boyhood* (*Shōnenkō*), Naka Kansuke's *Silver Spoon* (*Gin no Saji*).

I modeled my very first literary piece after *Silver Spoon*. . . . At that time I identified my work as belonging to the art for art's sake school and sentimentalism. I felt my utmost sentimentalism was pushing me toward the darkness and an emptiness verging on nihilism that had become my world.

Then I began reading Tolstoy's *Anna Karenina* and *War and Peace,* which I thought was the most beautiful novel in the world. I became drawn to Russian literature, especially Dostoevsky—*The Brothers Karamazov*. Spiritual struggles in life I had never entered were in his work. *Crime and Punishment, The Idiot, The Possessed,* and, of course, *The Brothers Karamazov*—they depict the dark tragic beauty of human beings. Our age must begin with Dostoevsky.

I began to seek something even more beautiful and turned to poetry. . . . [A lengthy discussion of various Japanese poets follows.] Miyazawa Kenji is not my type of literature. But I came to realize that there are other types of literature than my own genre of art for art's sake.

At that time, I could not forget the literature for the young. Duvivier's *Poil de carotte* [*Carrot Hair* by Julien Duvivier, a film based on Jules Renard's book and play about child abuse]. . . . I could not feel quite comfortable with its darkness. . . . I finally discovered *The Red Bird* (*Akai Tori*) [a collection of children's stories from various historical periods by Suzuki Mi'ekichi] and met a marvelous girl in [Louisa May Alcott's] *Rose in Bloom* (*Bara wa Ikiteiru*).

Psychology—no one has surpassed Wilhelm Wundt. The psychology of words makes me go back to the Japanese classics, since contemporary literature is too crude [with words]. My youthful sentimentalism found its home in the literature written by women of the ancient court. *Kagerō Nikki* [a tenth-century, three-volume diary by the wife of Fujiwara no Michitsuna, a prominent politician, detailing her agony of jealousy and other struggles as a wife, her awakening to art, and her intense experience as mother], *The Tale of*

Genji, and *Shin-Kokin Wakashū* . . . cannot be compared with with contemporary writers such as Shimazaki Tōson or Tanizaki Junichirō. Nihilism and romanticism in classics have far more depth and sublimity than those in contemporary literature.

I sought concerns with social issues in modern Western literature and found the ultimate in André Gide, *Straight Is the Gate* [*La Porte étroite*], *The Pastoral Symphony* [*La Symphonie pastorale*], *The Counterfeiters* [*Les Faux-Monnoyeurs*], and *The Fruit of the Earth* [*Les Nourritures terrestres*]; Raymond Radiguet, *Count d'Orgel's Ball* [*Le Bal du comte d'Orgel*]; and Roger Martin du Gard, *The World of the Thibaults* [*Les Thibault*]. . . . I felt as if *Les Thibault* was written for me. . . . The religious inclination of my childhood drew me toward Katherine Mansfield, Gottfried Keller's *People of Seldwyla* [*Die Leute von Seldwyla*], and George Sand. . . . My foray into literary history led me to Shakespeare and Goethe. *Hamlet* and *The Sorrow of Young Werther* [*Die Leiden des jungen Werthers*] trained me in philosophy and love. My quest for a psychological approach led me to Hori Tatsuo, the only Japanese novelist I love. Subsequently, I felt the medieval sublimity of [Rainer Maria] Rilke, whose work reminds me of the classics. Dostoevsky reminds me of the ultimate of philosophy of the individual. I found in Thomas Mann (*Tonio Kröger, Death in Venice* [*Tod in Venedig*], *The Magic* Mountain [*Der Zauberberg*]) my painful longing for death since my boyhood. In a somewhat opposite way, I found the same pain in Romain Rolland. . . . *The Magic Mountain* and [Rolland's] *Jean-Christophe* are the Bible today. (140–47)

On January 20 (147–50), he made a visit to the tomb of his birth mother, whom he called "Mother Midori," with his stepmother, a male friend, and his wife. It is customary in Japan to visit the tomb of the deceased on the anniversary of the day they died, and Matsunaga knew that he would not be able to visit her after going into the military.

This is the last day for Mother Midori. After going to school early, Mother, Akio, and we [my wife and I] went to her tomb. We offered daffodils, sweet-peas, and lily—all very gentle flowers. Afterwards we had lunch at Senbikiya, but things did not go well. Later I went to Zensenza to see Julien Duvivier's "The Great Waltz." . . . It was not as good as I had anticipated. (148)

The fact that "things did not go well" prompts him to write the following passage, addressed to his birth mother:

That evening [the day she died] makes me tremble even now. There still was some snow on the ground that evening, too; the wind was piercing the body, and in the night sky stars looked as if they were falling. I had never before felt such powerful light from stars. That night, Shigeo and I embraced each other while crying. Until today, I thought I could comfort you most by keeping the home with Father and new Mother in beautiful harmony. I have believed that you did not want me to be a great man but a family man whom people love. But because of my shortcomings, I have caused sufferings to Father, Mother, and Ayapin, whom you, Mother, would love dearly if you were alive. Last night and today—the last time for nihilism and pessimism, I vow. Mother Yoshiko and Ayapin inherited your struggle. But it was you who suffered most. Your suffering was hard to bear even for me, although I was very young. But you kept going. Your will for love and peace supported your worn-out body. . . . My first task is to prevent Mother and Ayako from the same sufferings. Our family must transcend that stage. (148–49)

Father's return was very late and you [Ayako] were really tired. Mother noticed it and told us that you could go to bed without waiting for Father. You told me how you went to sleep dead tired and felt quite sleepy and tired with a headache the next day. But there is very little I can do. (149–50)

The allusions to his mother's suffering, his stepmother's sorrows, his own difficulties, and the family's troubles are never explained, although they occur frequently in the diary and he vows that his wife will not suffer the same way his mothers did. Izumi Aki, the editor of *War, Literature and Love*, suggests that the father, a high-ranking navy officer, was perhaps quite strict and patriarchal (Izumi 1968, 3). It is likely that before their marriage these women were quite talented and pursued their own intellectual and cultural activities, for example, composing poems and going to symphony orchestra performances and piano recitals as well as playing piano themselves. When such a woman marries, the weight of her responsibilities as the wife of a prominent man becomes overwhelming; she must follow proper protocol in order not to damage the family reputation, look after children to make sure they are properly raised, and in most cases manage a large household with a number of servants and other domestic employees. In addition, wives were expected to wait up until their husband returned, no matter how late. The Matsunaga brothers' antimilitarism and their antiestablishment stance of refusing to pursue social, financial, and political success at all costs may very well have come from their personally witnessing the negative consequences of what it took to be successful in Japanese society at the time: the suffering of women. We recall that Takushima's enormously tender and protective feeling toward his mother derived in part from his daily observation of her suffering because of feudal customs—she, who could not sit at the family dinner table once, was forced to be a flower without a voice.

The following entry, written on January 24 with the awareness that their time together was coming to an end, is addressed to Ayako:

> Later in the afternoon, you wore a kimono. I bought for you a band for your watch at Hattori [a famous store on Ginza, the most fashionable shopping district even today] and a purse at Kuwabara. They are perhaps the last presents for you. I hope you love them and use them for a long time. You wanted a pair of shoes. I wanted to buy them for you, but I was not certain if I had enough money. Then we went to Emura [a restaurant]. . . . I was ecstatic. . . . What a warm and beautiful night. This should be the farewell party for me. I am too happy to write down [my thoughts]. (January 24, 150–51)

> At noon, I paid my last visits to my teachers at school. . . . In the afternoon, I finally had a very good dialogue with Mother at Minamichō. We talked about Christianity, death, and friends. (January 26, 151)

> Then you played ballades by Shimizu followed by Mozart's sonata. How beautiful it was. Our large guest parlor without heat. Two of us alone. Beautiful and well played melody. Your hands on the piano keyboard that produce such beautiful music. Mysterious serenity of composure in my mind. Today you understand me completely. Is there such a marvelous feeling? Perfection I had not known before. Happiness—quiet and beautiful. (January 26, 151–53)

> In the evening, I invited two friends and we discussed various topics, including "new feminism." We talked about men's role in enabling women to achieve full realization as human beings. We are not interested in politics, enlightenment movements, revolution, etc., but we wish to find our place in the home, seeing to it that our wives and children get a good education. (January 27, 152–53)

> With tears in your eyes, you could not say a word as I left you at home. . . . I went to school, resigned from the post of assistant professor, and handed over all the work to my successor. . . . At 10:00 P.M., finally we two could be alone. . . . Recently, you have stopped laughing, and it makes me feel lonely. (January 28, 153–54)

He and his wife continued to prepare for his entry into the military.

> In the afternoon, I went to a concert with an invitation from Shimizu. . . . Music with poesy. Musicality. . . . I am reading your letter. Thank you for

writing it. I won't say anything now. I will leave you [for the military] quietly. . . . You said five years. But it is a long time, and I hope you keep maturing. Do grow intellectually. . . . It is important to be feminine, but I want you to be as intellectual as a man. I will return as I am now, since for five years my intellectual activity will be stopped. (January 29, 154–56)

I finished the third chapter of my *Research on the Development of Shin-Kokin Waka-shū*. . . . In the afternoon, I went to school to hand over my writing. . . . Perhaps it was better that I did not see Professor Orikuchi. When I returned home, there were so many people [who had come to bid him farewell]. . . . Finally we were alone at night. We squeezed our bodies together. You fell asleep—quiet and pure. Of course I did think "once more," but I restrained myself. (January 30, 157)

The final entry in this diary is for January 31, 1942:

I woke up on the last day—a beautiful dawn. (158)

RECORD OF LIFE IN THE ARMY (JŪGUN TECHŌ), PART 1 (1943)

On February 1, 1943, Matsunaga Tatsuki organized the notes he had written during the previous year while he was stationed with the army in China, calling the notes part 1 of *Record of Life in the Army* (159–75). He used *Handwritten Notes of a Student Soldier* as the framework for his own writing, responding to his deceased brother's views and even having mental dialogues with him about such questions as the sacrifice of soldiers. The headings ("New conscript," etc.) are Matsunaga's, but no dates are given for specific entries. A retrospective poem stands as the prologue (159–60):

We spent all of last year on the battlefield.
I confess
I did nothing the whole year.
My spirit was locked by the key [of the military].
My body only followed orders.

The military must change its organization and atmosphere
From the very bottom.
If the Japanese army is to achieve its glory
I as a soldier

Must shoulder responsibility well beyond what is assigned to me as a soldier.

Matsunaga was quickly sent to Korea and on to China.

"New conscript"

My pride would not allow me to write down the details of our daily life. A blasphemy against the sanctity of the Imperial Army is the way. . . . The army is the citadel of the feudal spirit. . . . Duties mean impossibilities and irrationalities. The military rules are products of deceptions and conveniences. For new soldiers, there is no human life to lead. (163)

"Combat with the enemy"—as mindless acts

Early summer in north China is unexpectedly green. Wheat and acacia are growing, while the air is filled with the songs of Chinese cuckoos. . . . Bullets are pleasant. At least they stir excitement, which pulls me taut, even with my completely exhausted nerves. Soldiers unite, leaving all other things aside. . . . The glory of winning a war, and the misery of losing one. As we retreat at night, we put our wounded soldiers on our shoulder and try to follow a road in the dark. We stop, even when we want to go forward. We sleep while walking. Suddenly, we fall down on the road. I find myself at least not allowing my gun to touch the dirt. Why so? But there is no time to even think why. We march forward, throwing all our soul and body into it. (164–165)

"Duties on the base"—and momentary pleasures

Newly drafted soldiers are all right. All they have is appetite. Let me jot down the truth about life on the base in north China. Daily life at our post consists of drinking and talking about their longing for home—every day. Officers spend all night visiting prostitutes and playing mahjong. Enlisted men seek momentary pleasures, while counting the days [before they are] released from the army. . . . Does the threat to life the next day make them so? . . . During the past year, there have been a series of punishments resulting from attacks on commanders, disobeying orders, and an increasing number of defectors to the Chinese side. (166–67)

With strict censorship and tight control of news media, such information as given in this entry was unavailable to the Japanese people at the time.

"Letters"—and the impossibility of writing true feelings

Until I can assert myself openly, I won't write my true feelings, which will offend my superiors. Without raising fundamental questions, I won't be able to write about our lives here. (167)

"Soldiers"—and their dreams

To return home is the only wish the soldiers have. They just want to go home, as if peace and pleasure still exist at home. . . .But come the day of battle, they meet their death instantly. Then suddenly all become Japanese "deities.". . . With such ease they believe that they are brave soldiers to protect their country. They pride themselves in believing "No ancestral land without us." It is just cheap sentimentalism. . . . By comforting themselves in this way, they are spared from regretting the waste of their youth. (169–70)

Matsunaga Tatsuki sees the apotheosis that the government promised to fallen soldiers as ideological manipulation and, like his elder brother Shigeo, deplores the waste of young lives.

"Passionlessness"—becoming desensitized

But why have I lost my passion altogether? Since I entered the army a year ago, there has been nothing that moves me. . . . It was an amazingly eventful year. Suicides of my comrades, showers of bullets, questioning with torture, finally smearing my gun and sword with blood—yet I remained completely insensitive, as if I am a fool. What I write here is what I should be ashamed of. They all feel like things of another world. . . . This has been true since that dreadful day in the fall of 1938—the day my brother died. Since that time I have been living on another planet and I lost all interest in life. . . . In truth, here [on the base] the world of the dead is much closer than the homeland. I increasingly lost interest in this world and began to brush with death and risk encounters with the dead. . . . What nihilism! I trained myself to wear a mask. But in order to reach this state, I had to battle my self-hatred. (171–74)

By "smearing my sword and gun with blood" Matsunaga evidently means that he killed an enemy soldier. But he still dissents from the war, and he identifies more closely with his dead brother than with the battle or with life itself.

"Mission"—on the meaning of loyalty

The word *loyalty*, identification with the emperor, dedication to the nation and society—somehow my way of being loyal is blasphemous to the basic policy of the army. (175)

Matsunaga believes that true loyalty to his country is to challenge the military.

RECORD OF LIFE IN THE ARMY (JŪGUN TECHŌ), PART 2 (1943)

Between May and September 1943, while stationed in China, Matsunaga Tatsuki organized the rest of the notes from the previous year and called the result part 2 of *Record of Life in the Army*.

"Officer"—assuming responsibility

It has been a month since I was made a probationary officer. . . . I want to make myself clear here in case I fall [die]—as advice for those who succeed me after I fall. I was forced without choice to go through the examination to be a candidate to be an officer. . . . Yet, the official line is that I volunteered. (170)

In the army, there is an absolute line between enlisted men and officers. . . . Now I am required to change my policy. I have to establish my position in the army and must work to contribute to this society called "Army." Until now, I did my best "not to kill." From now on, I must strive to "kill." I used to think I wanted to return alive no matter what. . . . Now I must die. . . . It is not forgivable for officers to survive when enlisted men die. Now I won't expect to return alive. Of course, I thought so at the time I was drafted, but it was more passive. Today I [actively] seek my death, never to return alive. (176–77)

There is no other pleasure, except if I can make the army more scientific and modern, and transform soldiers into citizens who uphold modern individualism. (179)

"Testament"

Now the testament I wrote to Yukari is no longer sufficient. I must now convince her that she will not see me ever again and establish her daily life accordingly. I must have her give up the hope of my return. . . . If I can convince her now, rather than waiting until I die, I will feel I succeeded. If I die—No, I will die. You will no longer have me. Now I no longer belong to you. You only had me as I was before February of last year. . . . Your life with Father and Mother no longer has any connection with my life on the Asian continent. (179–80)

Matsunaga recognizes the responsibility that has been forced on him as an officer and realigns his vision of the future. His legacy will now lie in helping to transform Japanese soldiers into thinking beings. He views himself as already dead to his wife, who, after his death, continued to live with his parents in Japan.

"Teika"—the poet

Matsunaga Tatsuki devoted much time to a long discussion of Fujiwara no Teika (1162–1241), or Fujiwara no Sadaie, known as Teika, one of the greatest poets of all time. His poems were included in the *Shin-Kokin Wakashū* and *Shūi Gusō,* which Matsunaga had taken as the object of his life's work. In the diary, he quotes several of Teika's poems and exclaims: "Teika understood my thoughts." Except for one poem from *Shin-Kokin Wakashū,* all are drawn from *Shūi Gusō,* an early twelfth-century collection of poems in four volumes selected by Teika. I present, in H. M. Horton's translation, only some of the poems quoted by Matsunaga.[3]

According to Horton, the following poem expresses Teika's sorrow over his mother's death, which occurred on the last day of spring. The clouds remind him of the smoke from her cremation, and the departing spring reminds him of her departure. In mourning his mother's death, Matsunaga identifies himself with the twelfth-century poet. (181)

> She is parted from me,
>   and at evening
>   the clouds fade away;
> in everything
> I resent the passing of spring.
>   *Shūi Gusō,* no. 2615

Matsunaga uses the three poems by Teika that follow to express his pain concerning Ayako, with whom he felt united but who he already knew would be left alone after his death. (185)

I wish to forget,
so do not tell me uselessly
    that she pines for me,
autumn wind on the peaks
    of pine-clad Inaba Mountain.
                    Shin Kokin Wakashū, no. 968

Thinking it too painful
for my heart to bear
    I parted from her,
    So why through the years
    do I still miss her face?
                    Shūi Gusō, no. 2452

        Failing
to die from longing
    I have passed these years,
in my stubborn hope
of living to see you yet.
                    Shūi Gusō, no. 2440

Shirochidori (White Plover)

Matsunaga Tatsuki intended to publish a series of his brother's writings under the title *Shirochidori,* or "White Plover." Now that it is too late, he contemplates the meaning of this unfinished task.

I should have published *Shirochidori,* the writings left by my elder brother Shigeo. I spent a great deal of time and energy, but was able to finish only the first volume before I was drafted. It was because I tried too hard to be objective and not to have my subjectivity and feelings interfere. . . . In retrospect, it was the first and most important task I should have carried out. He [Shigeo] had social concerns and leadership qualities. It must have been quite painful for him to leave the unfinished work. To compile and edit Shigeo's literary creations and academic articles and to write his biography—the immense scope of the work, and my love and respect for him, and the sorrow [I felt] prevented me from doing it; I did not have confidence. . . . Now that I will die, I hope this is done, not for him or for me. Leave the dead to bury their dead [Matthew 8:22]. Publication of Shigeo's writings and a biography is not for remembrance or sentimentalism. . . . It is our obligation to the next generation, our historical mission for the next generation and for the nation, that we inform young people how the young buds were cut short by the war. (185–86)

"German soldiers"—war letters

In *German Students' War Letters* [*Kriegsbriefe gefallener Studenten*] there is a letter in which a soldier says, "The most important thing is the spirit of sacrifice and it is not a question of for what one sacrifices." Well, I think this is very romantic. Shigeo would have said that he was "a victim of a vice called sacrifice."

The second letter from the same German soldier reads: "What I am afraid is the loneliness in my heart. I am afraid of losing faith in human beings, myself, and all that is good in life. I dread this happening far more than physical pain. The most unbearable thing is the unbelievable sense of abandonment that governs the soldiers here. Even if we are spared bullets and grenades, how can we save ourselves if our mind is ruined? If only someone had told me of this before [I joined the army]."

Our army is just like this. I cannot read the last sentence without crying. Even during the war, with strict control of speech, it is not right that an individual's real feelings cannot be conveyed. The same sentiment about speech censorship is expressed in Shigeo's *Handwritten Notes of a Student Soldier.*

In the third letter by this German student soldier, which was written just before his death, he claims that what he had written in his earlier letter was simply an expression of unhappiness among the soldiers. He says that everything was fine then. Judging from my own experience and from Shigeo's *Handwritten Notes of a Student Soldier,* I would say that finally the power of intense and cruel intellect took over his thought.

Intellect forces deception and a distortion of reality, suppressing one's feelings and simply celebrating the victory of the will. (187–88)

"Epilogue"

The third part of this *Record of Life in the Army* should be the most important of all, because it describes the process of being educated to be a probationary officer, participating in two major battles, being promoted to first lieutenant, and teaching newly drafted soldiers. Having become an officer, I unlocked everything, resulting in numerous confrontations, and my life was ridden with tension. Because of it, my spirit was awakened and filled with vigor, and I began to feel myself as I lived in tension. The only problem was that I hardly had time to write down my notes. But a rich sensitivity, like what I felt as a young man, returned to me, and I shed tears for the first time after entering the army two years ago. I am spending my life with gratitude and excitement. (189–90)

Although he became an officer against his will, Matsunaga created a challenge for himself—to train new soldiers to think for themselves, rather than mindlessly obey orders—which engaged all his ideas and his emotions. In his struggle against the prevailing order within the military, he found the vitality that he had not felt in the struggle against the enemy.

"New Conscripts"

My distrust in the rigid army education and my own judgment have made me adopt a unique educational method. I am almost obsessed with my own way of teaching. Succeed or fail? Intellect wins over the body? What sort of difference would result if the new conscripts were educated to use their intellect, compared to other soldiers? That will determine my worth. (190)

This is the very first task in my life. It is the task into which I pour my entire energy and spirit. In this for the first time I have discovered my passion for life. (190)

It is easy to talk about death in the abstract, as the ancient philosophers discussed. But it is real death I fear, and I don't know if I can overcome the fear.

Even for a short life, there are many memories. For someone who had a good life, it is very difficult to part with it. But I reached a point of no return. I must plunge into an enemy vessel.

To be honest, I cannot say that the wish to die for the emperor is genuine, coming from my heart. However, it is decided for me that I die for the emperor.

Hayashi Ichizō was born on February 6, 1922, in Fukuoka, Kyūshū. A graduate of the Imperial University of Kyoto, he was drafted as a student soldier on November 10, 1943, and assigned to be a tokkōtai pilot on February 22, 1945. He died on April 12, 1945, off Okinawa, with the rank of navy ensign, at the age of twenty-three.

A Sun and Shield: Diary and Letters to Mother, Writings Left by Hayashi Ichizō (1995) includes his diary and his letters to his mother, other family members, and friends. Hayashi told his mother not to show these items to other people. But because Hayashi also wrote that he wanted to make a difference in the lives of the people, his sister, Kaga Hiroko, decided to edit and publish his writings in order to contribute to public understanding of this tragedy. This collection is much shorter than the diaries of other student soldiers, because his sister's purpose in editing the book was to portray Hayashi's extraordinarily close relationship with his mother.[1] The biographical details presented below are based on his sister's essay (Kaga 1995a) and postscript (Kaga 1995b), which are eloquent as well as informative.

FAMILY AND UPBRINGING

Hayashi Ichizō was born into a well-educated Christian family. He was the oldest male child. He had two older sisters, Hiroko and Chiyoko, and a younger brother, Makio. His father, Hayashi Shunzō, firmly believed in the Meiji motto "Enlightenment and Civilization" and taught young people to become teachers of agriculture. He had become a devout Christian under the influence of Uchimura Kanzō, perhaps the most important Meiji Christian, who defied the imperial system and refused to bow toward the emperor's signature on the Imperial Rescript on Education when, on January 9, 1891, the First Higher School celebrated its issuance (see Ohnuki-Tierney 2002, 92–93). Hayashi Shunzō was appointed assistant professor in the Department of Agriculture at the University of Tokyo. Right after arriving at the university, he wrote to his daughter, addressing her as "Hiroko-sama"; this polite form of address is quite unusual for a father to use with his daughter, and it expresses his principle of egalitarianism. The letter reported his delight with his new laboratory: "Here if I stretch my right hand, water runs, and on my left, I can start fire right away. So, I can study very hard." He told his wife and children that he would come home soon and bring them all to Tokyo so that they could visit Enoshima for a holiday.

The family received news of Hayashi Shunzō's sudden death in Tokyo on June 15, 1924. Ichizō was then two years old. His father's brother came from Tokyo and held Ichizō, clad in the crested kimono and hakama, in his arms since Ichizō, as the oldest son, was the person nominally in charge of the funeral.

Ichizō's mother, Hayashi Matsue, struggled to support herself and her children. Sharing her husband's belief in enlightenment and civilization, she devoted herself to teaching farm girls at the local elementary school. At that time, most people thought there was no need to educate peasants, let alone peasant girls. Ichizō's mother told others that she was determined to give them an education equivalent to the one at the girls' high school. Given her very busy schedule, her children were entrusted to her mother, who was living with her son and his family. According to Hiroko, Ichizō's older sister, their uncle and aunt provided the children with a secure home. Their aunt was enormously generous and always gave food to them despite the shortage of food. Their son was a gentle soul, but at times he quarreled with Ichizō. Ichizō's siblings fought on his side against their cousin, who had no one to come to his aid. The aunt laughed and said, "Quarrels help children grow." Once Ichizō's mother felt embarrassed by their quarrelling and put Ichizō in the storage house. The grandmother felt sorry for Ichizō and came to get him out. But Ichizō refused to come out, insisting that the person who put him there must come to get him out. His sister's account implies that, for Ichizō, no one could substitute for his mother or overrule her thoughts and feelings, so he stubbornly awaited her decision. Despite the hardships that followed his father's death, Ichizō spent a happy childhood in the countryside, especially since, as the heir of the Hayashi family, he was pampered.

Ichizō's mother Matsue, who had converted to Christianity because of her husband, remained a devout Christian after his death, despite his mother's opposition. The local pastor was an important source of moral support for her. Tormented by her husband's premature and sudden demise, she begged her minister to explain why her husband had to die. Following her late husband's wishes, she was determined to raise her children as Christians. Although Hayashi Matsue did not spend a great deal of time with her children, all of them had profound respect and love for her. The Bible united the family spiritually, keeping the children close to their mother.

Hayashi Ichizō began writing his diary on January 9, 1945, while stationed in Korea. The title he chose reflects his Christian faith: the phrase "a sun and shield" is taken from Psalm 84:10–11.

For a day in thy courts is better than a thousand elsewhere.
I would rather be a doorkeeper in the house of my God than dwell in the tents of wickedness.
For the Lord God is a sun and shield; he bestows favor and honor.[2]

It was customary for family members, friends, and others to write their wishes and messages on a national flag and send it to a soldier, so when the Hayashi family sent Ichizō a national flag, his mother wrote a passage from the Bible on it (Kaga 1995a, 183): "A thousand may fall at your side, ten thousand at your right hand; but it will not come near you" (Psalm 91:7). His sister Kaga Hiroko also wrote a passage from Psalms (84:6). No explanation was given for their choice of these specific passages. Although Hayashi's mother was always opposed to the war, it does not seem that she wrote the passage as an expression of protest against the military; it is more likely that she trusted in her Christian God to protect her beloved son. On the other hand, before Ichizō's death, his mother and Hiroko went to Kudan in Tokyo, where the Yasukuni National Shrine is located, but the mother told her daughter to go to the shrine alone, while she waited at the bottom of the slope below (Kaga 1995b, 205). Her refusal to go up to the shrine was clearly an act of protest against the war and the state ideology.

Hayashi's older sister recalled that in the early spring of 1944 she accompanied her mother to a shrine in Sasebo to pray for good luck on the battlefield. Her mother purchased an amulet there. In a letter to his mother, Hayashi said he would carry this amulet with him at the time he plunged into a vessel. His sister was puzzled but understood that their mother, a Christian, would pray at a Shinto shrine and purchase an amulet because she had heard that an amulet from the shrine would protect a soldier from bullets (201–4). Her fervent wish that her son would be protected led her to seek out a Shinto amulet as well as to inscribe a Christian text on the Japanese flag.

These incidents demonstrate the open nature of Japanese religious beliefs. In Japan, institutionally separate religions such as Shintoism and Buddhism do not require exclusive allegiance, as Western Christianity and Islam do. Instead, these religious traditions have become a part of daily life. All Japanese go through Shinto rituals for births and weddings, but almost all funerals are Buddhist. So-called ancestor worship, at the core of Japanese religiosity, is also Buddhist, since Buddhism governs matters related to death (Ohnuki-Tierney 1984, 145–66). Hayashi Ichizō was quite concerned about how he would be remembered after death and told his mother in advance that the memorial service should be on April 10. The most important ritual, after the funeral, is the monthly commemoration of the day of a family member's death. A monk recites a sutra as the relatives gather and listen in front of the ancestral alcove in their home. Hayashi spoke repeatedly about a Christian heaven, yet he assumed that the Buddhist ritual of commemoration would be held, as was always done in his family.

Hayashi's mother dreamed of the day when her son would become a family man and asked him several times in her letters to consider getting married. He replied only that he was destined to die and thus could not consider marriage. She still hoped for a future for him, while he faced his fate.

On the day the war ended, according to Hanada Chiyo, Hayashi's other sister, their mother bitterly complained that death in the tokkōtai operation was "the death of a dog (*inujini*)," a meaningless death (Hanada 1995, 124). Hanada Chiyo was quite shocked by the strength in her mother's voice when she shouted that its inventor, Vice Admiral Ōnishi, "must die," because ever since Hayashi's death Matsue had become visibly weakened (Ebina 1983, 311). Hayashi Matsue died on September 19, 1981, at the age of eighty-eight (Hayashi 1995, 12). The poems she wrote indicate that, as she prepared to join her husband and son in heaven, she still protested the military that sent her son to his death. Here I translate only a few of the thirteen short poems (119–22), which are collectively titled "My Son Has Fallen [like cherry blossoms]" (*Wagako wa Chiriniki*).

When the word "loyalty" governs all,
　　How sad it is to be born in the era.

Believing that it is the way to save the one million Japanese,[3]
　　You left your mother behind and went to the war.

Knowing that crying is against my son's wish,
　　It is unbearably lonely not to cry.

When I look at the clouds in the southern sky,
　　I see you in the clouds.

Be at peace, my children. I eagerly go
　　To Heaven where my husband and my son are waiting.

The last poem was written shortly before her death.

　　Kaga Hiroko thinks that their mother believed and fulfilled the sayings that "parents would die for their child" and "no one is more precious than one's own mother." In her later years, when Hayashi Matsue was no longer physically active, whenever her grandchildren visited her, she kept talking about her husband. But around the same time she told Hiroko that she had dreamed of Ichizō and reminisced about the visits by her grandchildren. She had refitted her bridal kimono to wear for her long journey to heaven (Kaga 1995a, 199).

HAYASHI'S EDUCATION AND ENTRY INTO THE MILITARY

When he was young, Hayashi did not mention that he wanted to be a soldier. Unlike other children in wartime Japan, he never sang "I Love Soldiers [*gunjin*] Very Much," which was quite popular at that time. Instead, he and his friends went to a nearby air base to dissuade young boys from volunteering to be pilots, telling them that they could not win the war by such means. His mother and sister interpreted this act as a result of his being a Christian because many Christians in Japan advocated peace (Ebina 1983, 305).

Hayashi enjoyed a successful academic career at the Fukuoka Higher School and the Imperial University of Kyoto. He wanted to major in philosophy, but pragmatic concerns, particularly the need to support his widowed mother and sisters, made him choose economics. His philosophical, cultural, and aesthetic concerns were not forgotten, however; while a university student in Japan's ancient cultural capital, he took tea ceremony lessons in a kimono (169).

When university students were called into the military, his mother and sisters begged him not to enlist in the navy, because his mother believed that the navy would send him outside Japan into an arena of active combat. However, at that time many university students thought that Japan was controlled by the army, which was notorious for its feudalistic system and its brutality. They viewed the navy as Japan's internal "West"—an intriguing metaphor, indeed—that was out of reach of the army's control. As Hayashi put it, to enlist in the navy was like "a domestic exile." He explained to his mother and sisters: "If I did not volunteer in the navy, I would be enlisted in the army, in which case I might commit suicide since I would not be able to tolerate the bullying by the army" (Ebina 1983, 304–5). Later, when his active military role in the navy became a reality, he repeatedly apologized to his mother for going against her wishes. After being chosen as a tokkōtai pilot, he wrote: "Perhaps I should have followed your advice" (57).

In order to understand Hayashi, we must understand his love for his mother, his Christianity, and his patriotism, which were closely interrelated. His diary and letters are unique in the degree of openness with which he expresses his feelings toward his mother.

DIARY WRITTEN ON THE NAVAL BASE (1945)

The published portions of Hayashi's diary cover the period from January 9 to March 21, 1945, when he was stationed on the Wŏn-san Naval Base in Korea.

January 9, 1945

To my surprise, I was given a new notebook. So, I start writing my diary. . . . Even though it is our goal to fight, it is frustrating that we are just waiting. . . . Today we again cannot go on the plane. . . . On the Wǒn-san Base I won't be able to go to the front even after cherry blossoms are gone and new leaves come out on the trees. (16–17)

January 16, 1945

No letter again. (20)

He is awaiting a letter from his mother.

January 29, 1945

I have not replied to my mother's letter yet. Her mention of my marriage feels like something remote, although it makes me feel good. I am definitely going to die. Of course I can marry, but I am definitely going to die. Marriage is all right as long as it does not benefit only one party and does not take advantage of the woman. (20–21)

At that time, a fair number of men, already drafted or destined to be drafted, got married. Hayashi is critical of this practice, since it only benefits men and uses women as a "tool" for men.

February 22, 1945

On this day, he is assigned to the tokkōtai unit.

We should follow the expression "As His Majesty's assignment." We are assigned the location of our death. We should simply plunge. . . . Human beings are endowed with an ability to forget. (25)

Hayashi often uses the phrase "to die beside His Majesty" (*Ōkimi no soba de shinu*) and states that he and others will die for the emperor (25, 27, 31, 40–41, 108, 110). This phrase, originally in a long poem by Ōtomono Yakamochi in the *Manyōshū* (vol. 18, no. 4094), was adopted in a song, "When you go to the sea [*Umi yukaba*]," which surpassed the national anthem in its importance as a propaganda tool during the war. A recording of it was played at every departure of tokkōtai planes. The song, or the section of the poem, reads:

In the sea, waterlogged corpses,
In the mountains, those corpses with grasses growing on them,
But my desire to die next to our emperor unflinching,
I shall not look back.

By "plunge" Hayashi means to plunge into an enemy vessel in the tokkōtai operation. The next day's diary entry, which is unusually long, demonstrates how strenuously he is trying to believe and follow the emperor-centered state ideology while agonizing over its meaning.

February 23, 1945

It looks like our life will last only about three months. I have dreaded death so much. And yet, it is already decided for us. . . . My environment in the past was beautiful. So, I feel I can die dreaming. But when I think of my mother, I cannot help but cry. When I think of my mother struggling over twenty years, relying on me who was her hope, and when I think how capable and talented she is and how beautiful she is, I cling to my life. How I wish that we spent happy days together. I am sure people will try to console her [after I die]. But, I know there is no way to ease her pain. . . . There is some pleasure in receiving praise from people [such as his mother will receive after his death]. There must be some consolation in dying beside His Majesty. But, for my mother, my death is final. I cry as I think of my mother. . . .

How fortunate I am that I believe in God, whom my mother believes in. My mind is at ease when I think that God takes care of everything. God would not make my mother or myself sad. I am sure God will bestow happiness upon us. Even [though] I will die, I dream of our lives together. . . . I know my country is beautiful. . . . My earnest hope is that our country will overcome this crisis and prosper. I can't bear the thought of our nation being stampeded by the dirty enemy. I must avenge [it] with my own life.

To be honest, I cannot say that the wish to die for the emperor is genuine, coming from my heart. However, it is decided for me that I die for the emperor. . . .

I shall not be afraid of the moment of my death. But I am afraid of how the fear of death will perturb my life. (25–29)

The phrases "there must be" rather than "there is," and "it is decided" rather than "I have decided," reveal that Hayashi did not choose to become a pilot or volunteer for the tokkōtai operation. He regarded this as the fate that was chosen for him and faced the end with agony, wrestling with doubt and seeking religious reassurance without success.

March 2, 1945

I dreamed of my death in a fierce battle. My only wish is to die for the emperor. How consoling it is to know that you would be honored upon death.

At least people would remember me. When I think how I would live in their mind, I feel pleased. (31–33)

March 4, 1945

Hayashi never mentions suicide with reference to his death as a tokkōtai pilot. But he considers it in a discussion of Kierkegaard, using the Japanese term for *suicide* twice:

> I just remembered the time when I was contemplating suicide. It was a time when I had given up on myself. I had to forgo the thought of happiness and dedication. Today, death is given to me. Although it has been given to me for some time, I am now acutely feeling its immediacy. . . . The reason why I am reminded of suicide is that a battlefield death means a complete annihilation of myself, preventing me from making contributions [to society] and engaging in enterprises. It is easy to talk about death in the abstract, as the ancient philosophers discussed. But, it is real death I fear, and I don't know if I can overcome the fear. I am drawn to the notion of the battlefield death, but it is an escape for me. Although death is given to me, I will hold onto life. It is better not to think of death, but to think of life precisely because death is given to me. I shall live! I will try to find an eternal life. (33–35)

Hayashi contrasts suicide, which arises from despair within oneself, with death on the battlefield, which is caused by an external event, rendering one's death meaningless.

March 5, 1945

A person who daydreams is a person clearly in despair. If my ideal is a person who is not in despair, who is able to pull himself out of the midst of "the sickness unto death," then it is critical that one get out of daydreaming. The things that I find difficult to part with [at my death] are: my mother, women, beautiful people, scenery, and honor (people's accolades for me). (36)

March 19, 1945

I have a wish to make a difference in the world. [The idiomatic Japanese expression is "to throw a stone."] I cannot deny that one element of that is my wish that people recognize my existence. But, above all, it derives from the emptiness I feel in myself and my rage over the so-called leaders who are incapable of recognizing problems even I can identify. Within two or three months, I will die. If my death is a glorious battlefield death, then, I will welcome my fighting. . . . Our ancestors' wish was to die beside the emperor. Loyal individuals wished to do so. . . .

The military personnel who hold important positions are committing a sin which should not be excused; they are killing infants and innocent civilians in China. . . .

There is no more time for me to escape. . . . This time I shall not try to escape. (39–41)

March 21, 1945

Even for a short life, there are many memories. For someone who had a good life, it is very difficult to part with it. But I reached a point of no return. I must plunge into an enemy vessel. As the preparation for the takeoff [for the final flight] nears, I feel a heavy pressure on me. I don't think I can stare at death. . . . I tried my best to escape in vain. So, now that I don't have a choice, I must go valiantly. . . .

Despair, despair is a sin.

I waited for my mother's letter but it has not arrived. Even now I cannot forget the happy family life I had. How I wish to see her once more. There is very little time left for me. (41–43)

LETTERS TO HIS MOTHER FROM THE WŎN-SAN NAVAL BASE (1945)

There are four letters to his mother that are not individually dated but were written between January 9 and April 3, 1945. Selections from two of them are given here. They are addressed to both his mother and his elder sister, but in the first (47–51) he responds to his mother's recent letters, and in the second (55–56) he speaks directly to his mother.

Thank you for your letter. I am reading it over and over again. Although I don't know how to express my thoughts, such a subject matter [her urging that he marry] feels remote to me. . . . But I really appreciate Mother's thought. I am reading over and over again the three letters you sent me this year. Is it all right to keep the photos? I much enjoyed the photo of you, mother, elder sister Chiyoko, and elder sister Hiroko's daughters, Junko, and Yōko. Junko really has grown. I wish I could see you all.

. . . Enemies are frequently bombing Osaka. How is elder sister Hiroko [who lives in Osaka]?''

. . . It has gotten warm at Wŏn-san. . . . I am waiting for cherry blossoms to bloom. Are they in full bloom in Fukuoka? Enemies are approaching, so we have to be on guard. . . .

I enclose a money order for four hundred yen. I have no need for it. . . . Please buy something for [a list of the names of his nieces and a nephew follows]. . . . I cannot send anything from Korea.

This letter ends by citing a poem from the *Manyōshū* which laments that one cannot forget the person left behind.

Hayashi wrote to his mother and elder sister on what he believed was the last day before his final sortie. He says that he hopes to fly over Hakata, where his mother was at that time, and look down at his home. Hayashi begins by addressing his mother as *okāsan,* a form of address used by adults. In the middle of the letter, however, as he begins expressing the pain he feels at his realization that his death is imminent, he switches to *kāchan,* a form used by children, which I render as "Mommy."

Mother, finally the time to write a very sad letter has arrived. My thoughts echo the following poem: "Parents' thought is deeper than children's thought of them. How would they take today's news."

I have been truly fortunate. I did whatever I wanted to do. Please forgive me; it was because I was relying on your indulgent love. I am happy to go as a tokkōtai pilot. But I begin to cry when I think of you. When I think how Mommy struggled so hard to raise me, I find it so hard to leave you behind without ever having given you pleasure or peace of mind. . . . I still want to be spoiled by you. There is nothing that pleases me than your letters. I wish I could see you once more. I want to be held in your arms and sleep. . . . I am writing this letter when my final flight is the day after tomorrow. By chance I might be able to fly over Hakata on my way.

Mommy, Mommy—I went against your advice and had to reach this destination. I wish I could say that I am pleased to have my wish fulfilled. But I should have followed your advice.

Mother, I am a man. All men born in Japan are destined to die fighting for the country. You have done a splendid job raising me to become an honorable man [*rippana otoko*]. . . . I will do a splendid job sinking an enemy aircraft carrier. Do brag about me.

My wish to return to you haunts me. But this is not good. Do you remember that I was told to die at the time of baptism? . . . All is in God's hands. Life and death in this world are of no importance. . . . I read the Bible every day. When I am reading the Bible, I feel I am next to you. I shall bring the Bible and the book of hymns on my plane and sortie. And also the mission medal which the school principal gave me. And the amulet Mother gave me.

Mother, you are a person who commands great respect. I have always thought that I would not measure up to you. . . . Tomorrow is our day to fly. I find it hard to concentrate, but I wanted to leave my words to tell you that I want to be spoiled by you.

Cherry blossoms must be at their peak. . . . I imagine horsetails are growing in the schoolyard. I fondly recall the spring vacation. Please send my best to Teacher Hagio, the principal, and [a list of teachers and relatives follows].

I am going to have Umeno, a close friend and navy comrade, come and we will chart the course for flying. I shall fly over Hakata and Munakata. I shall bid farewell as I look from a distance at the cherry blossoms in Nishi Park.

Mother, please be pleased that someone like me [using a phrase expressing humbleness] was chosen to be a tokkōtai pilot. I will die with dignity as a soldier. We are Christians. Nevertheless, Mother, I am sad. When you are sad, please cry. I too will cry; let us cry together to our hearts' content. I will sing a hymn as I dive onto an enemy vessel. I have a great deal more to say, but I stop here. . . .

The day before the final sortie. Good-bye.

LETTERS TO HIS MOTHER FROM THE KANOYA BASE (1945)

Hayashi's final flight was postponed because of a malfunction in the plane. He wrote three more "last" letters to his mother from another air base between April 5 and 12, 1945.

The first letter (66–74) opens: "I trust you are healthy. The name of my corps is: *Shinpū Shichishō Tokubetsu Kōgekitai.*" The word *shinpū* means "God's wind"; *shichishō* means "seven (or multiple) lives"; and *tokubetsu kōgekitai* is the long form of *tokkōtai*. By letting his mother know the name of his corps, Hayashi may be trying to make his death easier for her, since it is supposed to signify that the pilots will be reborn. But he knows very well the futility of his act.

Today about half of the corps plunged onto enemy vessels off Okinawa. We will do so in a couple of days. Perhaps on the day of the birth of Buddha? We have no light here. So, I am writing with light from a bonfire. As the news of success keeps coming in, we are really gearing up.

At dusk, I took a walk and lay down in the field of Chinese milk vetch. Coming from Korea to this southern spot, I was surprised to see that cherry blossoms have all fallen. But the green leaves are lovely, reminding me of home.

Mother, please don't feel lonely after I die. This is an honorable death, fighting for the glory of the imperial nation. As I came down here, I did not go over Hakata, but as I flew over Kyūshū, I sang to my heart's content. There is nothing more to say.

Do give my best to all. I no longer have the time to write to them. We are all going to plunge onto the enemy vessels. The attire for the tokkōtai pilots at the time of their final mission includes the rising sun headband and a pure white scarf around the neck. They look like the forty-seven loyal retainers.[4] For my last flight I will put on my body the rising sun flag on which you wrote, "A thousand may fall at your right side, ten thousand at your left. . . ." I will put your photo right on my chest. I shall be sure to sink an enemy vessel. When you hear over the radio of our success in sinking their vessels, please remember that one of them is the vessel I plunge into. I will have peace of mind, knowing that mother is watching me and praying for me." Then he adds humorously, "I will also bring the dried bonito Mrs. Tachi'ishi gave me as an amulet for protection, since in order to return to you, I must go through the sea.

It is like a dream. Tomorrow, I am no longer alive. Those who went on sortie yesterday are all dead?—I can't feel it as reality. I feel like they will suddenly return. You might feel the same way about me. But, please give it up. After all, "Leave the dead to bury their dead" [Matthew 8:22], right? . . . It's all right for you to cry. Please cry. But please do not be so sad.

The enemy's action is being dulled. Victory is for us. Our mission will be the last blow to the enemy. "For to me to live is Christ, and to die is gain" [Philippians 1:21].[5]

I will be going ahead of you. But, I wonder if I would be allowed to enter heaven. Mother, please pray for me. I cannot bear the thought of going to a place where you would not join me later.

The second letter (75–77) has an elegiac tone.

Last night I went out to a field of Chinese milk vetch [rengesō] and lay down, thinking about home. My friends told me that I smell of you, Mother. They think that they felt the mother-son bond in me. I have been fortunate. People have been so good to me.

Cherry blossoms of the Yoshino variety have fallen, but double-petaled cherry blossoms are blooming. Yellow rose [Kerria japonica] blooming on the fence is wet from rain. Every morning, as I wash my face in a brook, I think of our house in the country with blooming Hibiscus mutabilis and the little brook where daffodils bloom.

> Tomorrow, I shall plunge onto a group of enemy aircraft carriers. If you perform a memorial service, the date should be April 10.

> Thinking "today is it," eleven days have passed. The commander-in-chief of our combined squadron came to tell us to do our best. Mother, I have written all I wanted to say. Today, I went with my friends to a nearby school and sang hymns accompanied by an organ. (78–79)

This is the activity that always makes him feel close to his mother.

LETTERS ADDRESSED TO OTHERS

Letter to His Brother Makio from the Wŏn-san Base

Hayashi's younger brother, Makio, had just joined the Naval Reserve.

> I saw your photo and you look splendid [in your uniform]. Spring in the field of Tsukushi [an ancient designation for Kyūshū] must be marvelous with plum blossoms, then mustard green (*nanohana*) followed by cherry blossoms. With the enemy getting closer and closer, I am sure you are going through strenuous training. Do take care of yourself. Do try to send as many letters as possible to Mother. I am sure she is very lonely. At times she sends me interesting letters. (88–89)

Letter to His Brother Makio from the Kanoya Base

> I take it that you have been healthy, going through training. Cherry blossoms are blooming and it is time, finally, for me to sortie. "Seven lives"—I will try my best until I bring about a good battlefield victory. I am glad that I am born at the decisive time for our nation—whether to prosper or perish. . . . We had many fights, but quarrels between brothers were fun. (90–91)

To his brother he writes, as expected, to portray himself as a soldier ready to die for his country.

Letter to Yoshida Shōhachi from the Wŏn-san Base

Yoshida Shōhachi was a close friend with whom Hayashi went to Fukuoka Higher School and studied economics at the Imperial University of Kyoto. Yoshida's draft date was deferred because of illness. Six of the letters, some very long, sent by Hayashi to Yoshida are included in Hayashi (1995).

Hayashi addresses Yoshida as "Elder Brother" (*ani*), a customary form of address for friends, showing both respect and affection. This excerpt is typical of their tone.

> *His majesty's "ugly shield."* Yes, I pray that I will be one. I completed reading *The Sickness unto Death*. I find a fighting spirit surging in myself, when I have been avoiding [my destiny] ever since my Higher School days. . . . I bet you feel enraged about the air raid. (107–9)

It is not clear why *The Sickness unto Death* gave him a fighting spirit.

Letter to Tsuchi'i Kentarō from the Wŏn-san Base

Tsuchi'i was another of Hayashi's close friends from Fukuoka Higher School and the Economics Department of the Imperial University of Kyoto. He also joined the navy and was stationed with Hayashi at the Wŏn-san Base. During the last days before Hayashi's final sortie, Tsuchi'i was away for training in land combat. Hayashi went to his absent friend's room after the farewell party for those flying out the following day and wrote a letter in Tsuchi'i's notebook frequently using the Kyūshū dialect. Hayashi also referred to Tsuchi'i as "Elder Brother." He gave him an inscribed photograph of himself (110–11):

> The time has come. Elder Brother, I am sorry that I cannot see you. Elder Brother, do survive the war. How pleasant it is to die beside His Majesty.

He then appends:

> Please tell to my friends—how hard it is to terminate my life. [Written in English:] "For me to live is Christ. To die is also gain." This is for a memory of the time we drank sweet wine.

Hayashi draws a connection between the beauty of cherry blossoms and the spiritual beauty of his friend and reminisces about the past they shared.

> As long as you are alive, it is OK. You, my good friend, I enjoyed your friendship. The cherry blossoms in the schoolyard must be in full bloom. A beautiful friend of mine. The day when I fly my plane, I will sing hymns and the dormitory song. At the end of the clouds, fondly remembering my home. The farewell party was fun. I, the brave warrior, will definitely destroy our enemy, even if it takes seven lives. Hopefully, you won't forget about me

after I go. Since I am intoxicated, I don't know what I write. I am sure you understand. Forgive me if I said anything nasty to you. As long as you are alive, it is OK.

I am lonely.

CONCLUSION

Hayashi was a peace-loving Christian and a cosmopolitan humanist. As a child, he tried to dissuade young boys from volunteering to fight in the war. He repeatedly expressed how perturbed he was by the injustices committed by the military. For example, he was deeply concerned about the innocent civilians in China who were victimized by Japanese military aggression. Yet his diary and letters contain strong patriotic sentiments as well.

Hayashi's assertions of his complete devotion to the military defense of Japan are always contradicted by other thoughts and feelings. After I reread them several times, it became clear to me that he was painfully torn by two opposing forces in himself: patriotism, which meant his death, and his love for his mother, which demanded that he live. Although it is not possible to retrace the development of his thought in detail, the major stages are clear. First, he was drafted with the rest of the university students; he did not volunteer. He chose the navy instead of the army because the feudalistic system and the brutality used on soldiers in the army were well-known among young men at the time. Hayashi was reluctant to become a pilot in the first place, and by the time he was sent to train as a tokkōtai pilot he recognized clearly, with no attempt at evasion or rationalization, that he was allowed no choice about his role in combat even if it amounted to a death sentence. It is for this reason that he wrote in his diary innumerable times: "death is assigned to me." This is the statement not of a volunteer but of a person who faces a fate that has been decided for him.

Hayashi's patriotism, as expressed in the diary he began while on the base, derived from the immediate situation. He entered the navy relatively late in the war, and his final sortie took place when the Japanese mainland was being bombed by the Americans day and night. A remark he made to his close friend Yoshida offers one clue: "You must feel terribly angry about the bombing." This reaction to aerial bombardment of the civilian population is almost universal, as discussed in the introduction. But, for these young men, it still remained as a rationale—a last-ditch effort to convince themselves of the value or meaning of the dreaded sortie.

The opposite force within Hayashi, which is ultimately much stronger even though it could not save him, was his attachment to his mother, whom he deeply loved and respected. Every statement of his patriotism and forced resolution to ram into an American vessel is immediately followed by an expression of the anguish and agony of being separated from his mother forever.

In this conclusion, I tease out his complex thought processes by revisiting his thinking about three themes: the emperor-centered state ideology, his philosophy and his ideas about religion, including the Bible and Christianity, and his relationship with his mother.

The Emperor-Centered State Ideology

Like Nakao, who is introduced in chapter 6 of this book, Hayashi tries his best to embrace the emperor-centered ideology promulgated by the Meiji government in the late nineteenth century and propagated during the late 1930s and early 1940s by the increasingly militarist and imperialist Japanese state. His patriotic statements contain references to the *Manyōshū*. The ancient term for the emperor (*Ōkimi*) appears many more times in Hayashi's diary and letters than it does in any of the other diaries by student soldiers. This term comes from the *Manyōshū*, the oldest collection of poems in Japan, which consists of twenty volumes and contains poems composed during a period of four hundred years up to the middle of the eighth century. The section of the *Manyōshū* that became most important for the Meiji government contains ninety-nine poems composed by the ancient border guards, the *sakimori*. These peasant soldiers were summoned, especially from the eastern part of Japan (Azuma), which was known for producing good soldiers, to guard northern Kyūshū (Tsukushi) and Iki and Tsushima Islands and then the western frontier of Japan. This border guard system lasted from 664 to 826 C.E.; at its height, there were at most two thousand to three thousand border guards.

From these verses the Meiji government selected forms of address for and reference to the emperor, including the term *Ōkimi*, His Majesty, which Hayashi uses in referring to the emperor. The government also promulgated the terms that the sakimori used to speak of themselves. For example, the border guards used *masurao*, a word for young men that in later years foregrounded masculinity, and Hayashi and other pilots discussed in this book used this term to refer to themselves. Border guards metaphorically called themselves *shiko no mitate*, "ugly shields" to protect the emperor. Some scholars argue that the phrase refers to "the damned shield," expressing a disguised note of resistance (Horton forthcoming). This phrase, which appears six times in the *Manyōshū*, appears at least as often in Hayashi's writings. Fighting and dying "at the side of the emperor," a phrase Hayashi employed repeatedly, also originated in this collection.

These archaic terms and phrases from the *Manyōshū* were used in prayers offered at the Yasukuni shrine. More important, the state sought to propagate the emperor-centered nationalism by using these terms in school songs and popular songs, as well as textbooks. By taking these terms from ancient Japanese texts, the Meiji government constructed a magnificent metanarrative to portray the antiquity of the Japanese imperial system and, above all, to reinforce soldiers' unwavering fealty to the emperor. Absolute loyalty to the emperor was cast as the Japanese tradition from time immemorial. Yet, like the young men serving in World War II, the ancient border guards were forced to compose poems vowing their loyalty to the emperor while they also left poems expressing deep sorrow and agony on leaving their parents, wives, and children (Ohnuki-Tierney 2002, 74–77, 258). Governments since the Meiji period had used only the expressions that suited their ideological purposes, just as during World War II the military forced the pilots to leave testaments vowing to die happily for the emperor.

Perhaps most striking in this regard is Hayashi's use of the phrase "His Majesty's ugly shield." The term *shield* in the title of his diary refers to the Bible, not to any element of Japanese tradition. In the psalm that Hayashi quotes, it is God who becomes a shield protecting the people. But Hayashi calls himself the "ugly shield" of the emperor. This usage is taken directly from the *Manyōshū*. In other words, Hayashi couches his patriotism in the language of the *Manyōshū* and lets the meaning of *shield* given there override the meaning given in the Bible. Can we therefore conclude that Hayashi's case is an example of successful penetration of the state ideology? Not quite. To the very end he maintains that only God protects people and that he does not die for the emperor. Hayashi's writings make it especially clear that, no matter what these young soldiers said officially, they refused the meaning of their death that was offered by the state. As Hayashi put it: "To be honest, I cannot say that the wish to die for the emperor is genuine, coming from my heart. However, it is decided for me that I die for the emperor" (29).

Other evidence supports the suggestion that the partial imbrication of his patriotism and the state ideology was more superficial than deeply felt. First, his references to the terms in the *Manyōshū* derive from his love of the ancient poems in it. He memorized some and wrote them down in his diary and letters. Second, these terms are those of the border guards who were stationed in his part of Japan, Kyūshū. He was deeply attached to this place, as is evident in his frequent descriptions of its natural beauty and his fondness for using the local dialect in writing to close friends who were also from Kyūshū.

Another important register of the limited influence that the state ideology had on his thinking is Hayashi's use of the imagery of cherry blossoms. Descriptions of and symbolic references to nature are prominent features of most Japanese people's writings. Hayashi's diary and letters are suffused with his love of nature and full of references to flowers. He mentions cherry blossoms more frequently than he does any other aspect of nature, and images of them appear in others' letters to him as well. Cherry blossoms serve as a shared symbolic system by which Japanese people contemplate the transitory and fragile qualities of beauty and the ephemeral nature of life itself. Hayashi frequently employs images of cherry blossoms in precisely this way.

As Hayashi entered the military and struggled to come to terms with death, he came to identify himself with cherry blossoms. In a letter to his mother, he laments his fate: the cherry blossoms at the Wŏn-san Base in Korea, where he was stationed, have already fallen, and yet the time for his sortie has not come. To his younger brother he writes from the Kanoya Base: "Cherry blossoms are blooming and I am going" (90). Hayashi consciously draws an analogy between himself and the flowers; their falling signifies the time for his death.

Other people also used the metaphor of cherry blossoms to refer to Hayashi. A poem written by his mother after the end of the war contains the idiomatic expression the "falling of my son," applying the word conventionally used for the falling of cherry petals to the death of Ichizō (120). Hayashi's friend Hidemura Senzō laments that "Hayashi's youth is fallen," like cherry petals, but adds: "Peace arrived but not the peace you wished to bring through your sacrifice; it is only in the miserable aftermath of defeat." Hidemura concludes, "Beauty appears in a sensitive vessel and life is short" (143–47).

Despite all these implicit and explicit links between cherry blossoms that fall and soldiers who die, Hayashi's diary and letters contain not even a hint that he was aware of how the government had attempted to transform the meaning of cherry blossoms into a symbol of sacrificing one's life for the emperor in hopes of being reborn in the national shrine. And although writings by his surviving loved ones speak of him as a fallen blossom, they explicitly repudiate the meaning that the government tried to ascribe to the metaphor.

The government was successful in maintaining an analogy between these flowers and soldiers in Japanese tradition. Nonetheless, neither

Hayashi nor his loved ones accepted the militarized meaning that the government attributed to cherry blossoms. Instead, they used this metaphor in the ways that Japanese people had done long before the Meiji period and the war. This awareness became excruciatingly poignant when young soldiers fell like cherry blossoms, but it did not signify assent to the state's ideology. Indeed, the metaphor could be used to say that soldiers died tragically for nothing at all, or with ideals that differed profoundly from those held by the government that sent them to their deaths.

Philosophy and Religion

The two books that Hayashi discusses most fully in the diary entries that his sister selected for inclusion in the published volume are the Bible and Kierkegaard's *The Sickness unto Death*. He carried both books, along with his mother's picture, onto the plane for his final flight.

Kierkegaard's work, especially *The Sickness unto Death*, was widely read and discussed by Japanese intellectuals at that time. Other student soldiers also refer to Kierkegaard. Hayashi first read his works during the spring break in 1941. During his first year at Fukuoka Higher School, students formed a Bible reading group in the dormitory and read this work within the framework of Christian philosophy under the guidance of Professor Kōno, then an assistant professor of religion at the Imperial University of Kyūshū (149).

Over the next few years, as Hayashi faced his own death, his chronicle of agony was replete with concepts such as dread and fear that echo Kierkegaard's *The Concept of Dread*, although the writings included in the book do not specifically mention Kierkegaard in this context. Hayashi committed long portions of *The Sickness unto Death* to memory and referred to it frequently. Despair, in its relation to suicide, is the book's central theme. Hayashi found this work meaningful because he was so torn between his deep attachment to life and his equally deep sense of obligation to fight in defense of his homeland that he often reached a state of despair. Kierkegaard offered a language in which Hayashi could contemplate the self, life, and death within the framework of Christianity and, even more important, it offered him a route out of despair. Because in Kierkegaard's view despair leads to suicide, it is quite clear that this is an act that Hayashi absolutely and determinedly refused. His death in the tokkōtai operation is not a suicide in either the imperial or the religious sense. Rather, Hayashi seeks philosophical and religious perspectives that will lead him away from despair and self-destruction even as he faces death most directly.

His Mother

From the time Hayashi was assigned to be a tokkōtai pilot, he was consumed by agony about the impending separation from his mother, to whom he was very closely attached. Toward the end of Hayashi's life, his Christianity became blurred with his feelings toward his mother, who served as his exemplar of Christian devotion. He desperately wanted his mother to forgive him for joining the navy rather than the army in opposition to her wishes, a decision that ultimately led to his assignment to the tokkōtai operation. His Christianity was a way for him to be close to his mother psychologically as well as spiritually. His diary and letters are filled with expressions that attest to the conjunction between his fragile faith in God and his abiding love for his mother. For example, right after declaring, "Despair, despair is a sin," he remarks that he has not received a letter from his mother (43; see also 20), perhaps expressing his sense of despair in the language of Kierkegaard. In the long letter Hayashi writes to his mother from the Wŏnsan Base in Korea immediately after being selected as a tokkōtai pilot, he tells her that he derives strength from believing in the same God that she does. He longs to go to heaven and wait for her there, just as later she too would long to go there to join her son and husband.

Hayashi's diary attests to the real limits of the penetration of the emperor-centered and militaristic state ideology into the thinking of student soldiers, including tokkōtai pilots. Hayashi expresses his patriotism in the language of the state ideology and adopts the analogy between fallen cherry blossoms and fallen soldiers. Yet he confesses that the wish to die for the emperor is not his true feeling, and the idea of being reborn as cherry blossoms at the Yasukuni National Shrine never crosses his mind. As he grapples with the meaning of his life in the face of death, Hayashi turns instead to his family and homeland, Japan's cultural traditions, Christianity, and European and Japanese philosophy and literature.

> How lonely is the sound of the clock in the darkness of the
>   night.
> The sound of the clock brings back fond memories of my
>   childhood;
> Remembering those sleepless nights
> Unable to sleep for loneliness
> Many thoughts come to my mind as rain falls outside.

> I, who have come to know the depth of life and live that life,
> must sacrifice my life for our country since my life is destined
> to be given for the nation? . . . I painfully struggle in pursuit of
> truth.

Nakao Takenori was born on March 31, 1923. A graduate of
the University of Tokyo with a degree in law, he was drafted as
a student soldier in December 1943. He died on May 4, 1945,
as a tokkōtai pilot at the age of twenty-two. Those close to him
often called him "Butoku," another pronunciation of the two
characters for his first name.

Nakao's diary and letters were edited by his younger brother,
Nakao Yoshitaka, and published in 1997 as *The Record of a
Spiritual Quest: Handwritten Diary Left by Nakao Takenori,
a Student Who Perished in the War*. With more than seven
hundred pages of fine print, this is the longest of the diaries
introduced in this book. It also covers the longest period, from
January 1, 1934, when Nakao was in the fifth grade, until he
was drafted at the age of nineteen. He continued to keep a diary

throughout his time in the military, but it was destroyed when the Takuma Naval Air Base, where he had been stationed, was burned down in an air raid. *The Record of a Spiritual Quest* (Nakao 1977) covers this period by including letters he wrote to his parents, brothers, and friends from December 18, 1942, until April 28, 1945, less than a week before his death.[1]

Nakao was born in Fukuoka, Kyūshū. At the time of his death, his father, Nakao Kōzō, was the manager of a factory producing silk threads in Gifu, although the company had transferred him to factories in several locations. His mother was Nakao Somo. The diary says little about the family, but they were obviously fairly well off, given the father's position in the business. Nakao's elder brother, Mitsuaki, went to a technical high school specializing in silk thread production. His younger brother, Yoshitaka, became a painter as well as a professor at Seinan Gakuin University. Tokenori also had an elder sister; her name is not given in the book, but by 1945 she was married and living in Tokyo. On May 5, 1945, his parents went to the Takuma Base hoping to see him but were told that he was no longer there; they were not told that he had been killed in battle in Okinawa the previous day. His elder sister joined their parents in Gifu after her house in Tokyo was bombed, but the father's factory was bombed on July 9. All moved to a house along the upper reaches of the Nagara River in Gifu. His elder brother was in the army and his younger brother was in Kyoto. It was not until after the war, in August, that the family received notification of Nakao Takenori's death.

The title of the published volume, *The Record of a Spiritual Quest* (*Tankyūroku*), epitomizes the life of Nakao Takenori; his ardent quest for purity and the meaning of life is evident on every page. Like other student soldiers, he wanted to be "pure," free from materialism and egotism, although Nakao was definitely not a Marxist. He sought purity in his idealism and in his imaginary ideal woman. If ever there was a pure soul, it was Nakao's. It is all the more painful to read this diary because he was almost too innocent to see through the government's attempts to turn unselfish patriotism into support for its aggressive and destructive military policy. On the surface, Nakao believed the government propaganda that Japan had to defend itself against the threat of Western colonialism and that other Asian countries would benefit from its program, the Greater East Asia Co-Prosperity Sphere. The love of their country and commitment to its culture that student soldiers like Nakao shared with many other Japanese people were used to promote imperial expansion.

Nakao's writings posed the most difficult task for interpretation. In contrast to the writings of Sasaki Hachirō and Hayashi Tadao, who are explicit about their liberal stance, Nakao's diary and letters appear decidedly conservative at first glance. He records and repeats with evident approval some of the most reactionary statements made by the military government. But at the same time, his writings reveal that much more was going on in his mind. I strove to understand his thoughts by comparing diary entries made on different dates and comparing diary entries with letters to his parents. I began to see that Nakao was making a conscious effort to believe in the emperor-centered ideology of the time. Other passages, such as those concerning his passionate convictions about equality regardless of race and ethnicity, clearly indicate that he was not a true believer in the imperial ideology. Although he did not seem to have teased out all the implications of the imperial ideology, he was wrestling with doubts about the prospects for victory and the wisdom of the entire imperial project.

Nakao struggled to convince himself that his death in the war would have meaning, but all the while he desperately wanted to live, and sought meaning in an ideal of purity and truth that lay far beyond the state's imperial ambitions. *The Record of a Spiritual Quest* (Nakeo 1997), is, above all, a painful chronicle of Nakao's desire to live in the face of imminent death.

Nakao expressed his agony and reflected on the meanings of life and death in soliloquies as he read and commented on books that expressed his thoughts and feelings. He read a large number and wide variety of literary and philosophical works, both European and Japanese. At times his diary quotes from them verbatim, sometimes in the original European language in which he read these works. His commentaries on his readings are quite impressive as he compares one author and work with another across national and linguistic lines. For example, after reading Maupassant's *A Life* (*Une vie*), he notes that it explored themes he also saw in Mérimée, Gogol, Balzac, Chekhov, and Turgenev (May 27, 1940, 261).

Nakao read a vast amount of French literature, often in the original, and expressed a sense of satisfaction that the frequency with which he had to consult a dictionary decreased as he kept reading (June 20, 1940, 265). Romain Rolland's *Jean-Christophe* seems to have had the greatest influence on his thinking (229–30, 232, 238, 240, 242), although he read Rolland's *Beethoven* (*Beethoven the Creator,* or *Vie de Beethoven*) as well (444–45). He wanted to emulate Jean-Christophe and Beethoven, who both struggled against the odds to fulfill their goals. Nakao's interest in German works tended more toward philosophy than literature. In this respect, he differs from Hayashi Tadao, who also read widely in French literature but was heavily influenced by Thomas Mann. Nakao read more Greek and Latin philosophical writings than any other student soldier, especially as the time of his death approached. And he was deeply influenced by Chinese and Japanese philosophers. In particular, he read and considered the ideas of Dōgen, a Japanese Buddhist philosopher, as he contemplated the meaning of life.

Another characteristic that stands out in Nakao's reading is his interest in sociology and anthropology. While Sasaki read Weber and Simmel, Nakao read Simmel, Durkheim, Lévy-Bruhl, and Malinowski. He thought it was important to study not only the modern Western cultures that had been introduced to Japan since the Meiji but also the ancient Greek and Judaic cultures that had been the wellsprings for Western civilization. He considered that comparing Japanese culture with other cultures would bring out its special characteristics and facilitate the further development of the Japanese spirit (January 1, 1941, 331).

More than any other student soldier, Nakao filled his intellectual reservoir with classical Japanese literature, including the *Kojiki*, the "myth-history" of Japan dated c.e. 712, and *The Diary of Lady Shikibu* (*Shikibu Nikki*) by Murasaki Shikibu, who chronicled life at the imperial court between c.e. 1008 and 1010 and wrote the world classic *The Tale of Genji*. He devoted equal time to contemporary Japanese writers, including those who followed the art-for-art's-sake movement, such as Akutagawa Ryūnosuke, Hori Tatsuo, Izumi Kyōka, Kawabata Yasunari, Kunikida Doppo, and Mori Ōgai.

What distinguishes Nakao's reading from that of other student soldiers is his earnest quest to find a Japanese intellectual identity. It is for this reason that he was drawn to the philosophers who belonged to the Kyoto school of philosophy, including Nishida Kitarō, Tanabe Hajime, and Watsuji Tetsurō. These thinkers attempted to establish a Japanese philosophical tradition that was not simply a copy of Western philosophy. Although they engaged in intense dialogue with Western philosophers, especially Heidegger, they developed a set of ideas and approaches to major philosophical questions that they believed expressed the highest and most fundamental traditions of Japanese culture.

ELEMENTARY AND MIDDLE SCHOOL, 1934–39

These diary entries document the process by which the ideology of emperor-centered state nationalism was propagated through the school system and demonstrate how successful it was in making an imprint on very young minds like Nakao's.

The diary begins on January 1, 1934. During Nakao's elementary school years, the entries are relatively short; he wrote in the diary just before going to bed and detailed the day's activities, starting with the time he woke up. Nakao often described the lessons at school, including those in music (*shōka*), ethics (*shūshin*), and "national history" (*kokushi*). These were the three main subjects through which the government strove to disseminate its ideology.

The Propagation of the Emperor-Centered Militaristic Ideology

When the Meiji government, following the advice of Lorenz von Stein, elevated the previously powerless Japanese emperor to the position of powerful warrior king (commander in chief in the Meiji constitution) *qua* Almighty God, it instituted many ceremonies and commemorations (Ohnuki-Tierney 2002, 61–101). For example, a new holiday celebrated the supposed enthronement of Jimmu, the first emperor of Japan, previously regarded as a mythical figure. To instill belief in the new emperor in the minds of the people, the government utilized popular songs that extolled the virtue and benevolence of the emperor, on whom the welfare of the people was said to depend (ibid. 125–53). Nakao's diary records numerous emperor-centered exercises in music class, including the song "The Beginning of the Nation" (*Kigensetsu*) and the song "Celebration for the Birth of the Crown Prince" (*Kōtaishi Gotanjō*) (January 10, 1934, 11). The school observed the birthday of the emperor (April 29, 1936), the birthday of the empress (March 6, 1935), and the commemoration of the enthronement of the Meiji Emperor (August 27, 1935). In his national history class, Nakao learned how the emperor loved his people and said that he felt very grateful (February 8, 1935, 39). Nakao was also taught about the enthronement of the Shōwa Emperor in 1926. In his ethics class he was taught about the *Imperial Rescript to Soldiers* of 1882 (March 4, 11, 1935, 47, 49). When reading *The Realm Beyond* (*Onshū no Kanata ni*), a novel by Kikuchi Kan, a liberal but patriotic writer, Nakao was impressed by the effort of the monk Zenkai, whose twenty-one years of work bore fruit: the enemy became too impressed by his behavior to carry on the offensive (February 16, 1935, 42). On March 1, 1935, the school participated in the national commemoration of the establishment of Manchukuo, a puppet state created by the Japanese government in 1932. During the ceremony, when they sang Japan's national anthem, he felt as if his head naturally bowed down at the weight and dignity of the anthem (46). Elementary school students participated in the commemoration of military victories and the heroism of Japanese soldiers in the past—and the present (March 9, 1935, 48).

These nationalist celebrations of history were placed directly in the service of imperial aims and encouraged students to see themselves as future soldiers. When he was only thirteen, Nakao went very early in the morning to a nearby town to help send off the soldiers of the twelfth unit. He writes afterward that he hopes the soldiers were encouraged by the enthusiastic shouting of the people who came (April 10, 1936, 92). During an athletic event that same year, he participated in the "Three Human Bullets" (June 1, 1936, 100), which sounds like a simulation of the event celebrated as "The Three Brave Heroes as Human Bullets" (*nikudan sanyūshi*). On February 22, 1932, three privates carrying a three-meter bamboo tube packed with explosives dashed into a wire-fenced Chinese fortress in Shanghai so that the Japanese Army could advance. The army deified these three soldiers, statues of whom were raised all over Japan to remind people of this "beautiful story of the military nation" (*gunkoku bidan*). In 1939, when he was sixteen, Nakao commented that a classmate from the higher school who had exceptional ability in French and a promising future had "honorably" entered the military. People sent him off, shouting enthusiastically (May 18, 1939, 145–55).

A thoughtful youth as well as an attentive student, Nakao periodically records making resolutions about how to conduct his life. For example, at the age of eleven he pledges to take seriousness, perseverance, and hard work as his three mottoes. He affirms that he is determined to pursue the loftiest of goals, citing the poem by the Meiji Emperor: "If one wishes to climb up high mountain peaks thrusting into the sky, there always is a path to do so" (January 15, 1935, 30). Looking at plum trees blooming in the cold, he resolves to have a strong spirit like theirs (February 8, 1935, 39). After being told at school that students should study so hard that their parents have to scold them to go to sleep, he decides to study until eleven at night or even later (March 8, 1935, 48). In many other diary entries, he tells himself to work hard and even harder. Like Sasaki Hachirō and Hayashi Tadao, Nakao sets a strict daily schedule for himself at home: in the morning, he will rise at 5:30 A.M. and use the first hours for reading and morning prayer; after the day's schoolwork is concluded, he will exercise and gargle before going to bed at 10 or 10:30 P.M., saying the evening prayer, and writing the diary entry (January 26, 1936, 76).

Nakao expresses pleasure when he passes an entrance examination or receives special recognition for academic achievement, especially when he sees how pleased his mother is. But his aspirations do not always follow the direction that the government wants them to take. He resolves to aim for a Nobel prize in science, rather than the Kinshi Kunshō, a medal given for military valor by the Japanese government that his teacher told pupils to aspire to (August 12, 1937, 120). The Kinshi Kunshō, or Golden Kite Medal, was named after the *kinshi*, the golden kite that perched on top of the bow at the time the legendary first emperor of Japan was on the path of conquest of the "eastern barbarians." The elementary school program was designed to inculcate the emperor-centered ideology of an expansionist Japan. Nakao absorbed much of this belief system, yet still demonstrated some independence of thought.

FUKUOKA HIGHER SCHOOL AND THE IMPERIAL UNIVERSITY
OF TOKYO, 1939–42

Nakao's intellectual and personal development accelerated when he entered the prestigious Fukuoka Higher School in Kyūshū, which he attended from April 1939 to March 1942, and it continued steadily at the University of Tokyo, where he studied from April 1942 until he was drafted in December 1943. I trace his thoughts and feelings during this period, looking at his development over time in relation to specific themes.

Nakao's Higher School days were full of fun, as they were for other student soldiers. Nakao Yoshitaka sent me a number of photos (see gallery), for example, one showing his brother's smiling face, his hands on the drum after the dormitory festival. Another photo shows a collection of impromptu writings on a large sheet of paper (*yosegaki*) at the time of Nakao's graduation from Fukuoka Higher School. Nakao's writing with a brush states, "I shan't be fooled." Nakao Yoshitaka wrote me: "Who would have expected him to be 'fooled,' swept up in the war fervor, drafted as a university student, and then sent to the tokkōtai operation?" In the drawing, the two students in uniform with black cape and high wooden clogs are carrying a Japanese drum like the one in the photo for the festival. These youths' voracious appetite for intellectual development is shown in their attempts to write in French.

By the time Nakao went to the Fukuoka Higher School, however, Japan had already become a police state. Nakao details an incident that occurred on April 8, 1940, when the students were drinking heavily and carousing in a "storm," the institutionalized form of singing, drinking, and disorderly conduct at the dormitories of higher schools and universities. The police came in and arrested some students, while others begged them not to arrest their fellow students. Nakao himself cried at the contemptuous way in which the policemen behaved toward his friend. He regrets that he did not realize at the time what exactly was happening and did not have enough passion and sense of responsibility to challenge the policemen (248).

As we have seen in the cases of Sasaki Hachirō and Hayashi Tadao, Marxism appealed to many Japanese youths as a form of idealism, although its influence was waning by 1940. Nakao was never a Marxist; instead, he was a serious student of fascism and totalitarianism. But after reading Vilfredo Pareto, Giovanni Gentile, Alfred Rosenberg, Carl Schmitt, and others, he concludes that Nazism and fascism are the "totalitarian camp which rose against liberalism and materialism" (439–40). In other words, he interprets fascism and totalitarianism as antidotes to the materialism and ultraliberal individualism verging on egotism that characterize modernity. He is in sympathy with those who oppose the ills of modernity, as he quotes Anatole France: "We must pity the rich. Their property surrounds them but it never goes into them. They are empty inside. It is painful to watch how pitiful they are" (January 8, 1940, 214).

The Quest for an Aesthetic of Purity

Nakao's life was a self-conscious quest for an aesthetic of purity. This goal is expressed in a long entry he wrote in his diary shortly after entering Fukuoka Higher School (April 13, 1939, 32–33).

> Purity!! Look at the incense with its white head bowing down, while its smoke, white and faint, rises upward. It fills me with the feeling of mysterious purity. I love purity. But I am not one to turn my face from ugly evil. It is because ugly evil is a test for me to transform it into purity. I do not find purity in flowers blooming gaudily. Opening the window at night when spring rain is falling, I gaze at cherry blossoms in pale pink. I feel pathos like the rain itself and think of the [woman]. I taste the pleasure of satiating purity. I search for a woman with whom I can share purity throughout our lives. A thoughtful person. . . .
>
> There is nothing that holds the aesthetic of purity more than love tinged with pathos. Love. Human beings seek beauty. . . . I too love beauty. But the beauty I seek is not the one found in this ordinary world. Beauty must be accompanied by purity and sorrow. Without it, today beauty becomes a shallow and worthless thing, contaminated by a Western smell.

Nakao seeks an aesthetic of purity in his idealism and in his love for an ideal woman. Yet he denies himself all of this by locating it outside the ordinary world, perhaps because he knows his eventual fate.

Time and again, these young men's diaries voice their awareness that they are facing death; this real possibility looms forebodingly as early as 1939–40, before the outbreak of World War II. Nakao is well aware of conscription but unsure how soon he will be drafted. This awareness of approaching death threw these students' future into uncertainty, compelling them to wrestle with the questions of life and death.

Whereas, for other soldiers, cherry blossoms served as the flower to think about life and death, Nakao makes relatively few references to this flower. He uses cherry blossoms in spring rain as a metaphor for the purity and pathos of his ideal love, as cited above. On several occasions, he praises their beauty and then laments that the blossoms have all fallen. But Nakao never mentions falling cherry petals as sacrifices to the emperor or suggests that blooming flowers represent the souls of fallen soldiers. The complete absence of the political meaning that the state tried to impose on cherry blossoms is notable, especially because Nakao often expresses other aspects of the emperor-centered military ideology.

It seems that Nakao's quest for an aesthetic of purity was in part influenced by Baudelaire's search for beauty as expressed in his poem "Hymn to Beauty" ("Hymne à la beauté") in *The Flowers of Evil* (*Les Fleurs du mal*). He also must have been drawn toward Baudelaire's complex aesthetics of darkness, ugliness, and the fearful. Finding that a copy of the original French edition of *Les Fleurs du mal* was at the Yūbundō bookshop, he got up quite early to purchase it for the relatively steep price of five yen. He especially enjoyed reading the poems aloud in French (July 30, 1942, 478). Concerned that his thinking was becoming too simple and too healthy, he was determined to thoroughly understand *Les Fleurs du mal* in order to nip the flowers of "illness" in the bud—that illness, or "evil," which gnaws at and outlives the mortal human being.

The Penetration of State Nationalism

During his elementary and middle school years, Nakao was quite receptive to the state's emperor-centered ideology. This tendency continued during his higher school and university years. Yet over time Nakao's thought processes became more complex as his growing intellectual sophistication came into conflict with his desire to comply with the state ideology. His diary and letters reveal enormous tension between different tendencies in his thinking: for example, that between his passionate espousal of egalitarianism and humanitarianism, on one hand, and what he thinks he ought to think according to the state ideology, on the other. Furthermore, he begins to sense his destiny and becomes acutely aware of the implications of the state ideology for his own life. Although he shares the other student pilots' realization that death awaited them just around the corner, he does not engage in rationalization or denial by escaping into an aesthetic of nihilism, like Hayashi Tadao and Matsunaga Shigeo, or embracing a utopian Marxist vision of the destruction and renewal of the world, like Sasaki Hachirō and Hayashi Tadao.

In order to understand Nakao's thinking, it is necessary to tease out several facets of what appears on the surface to be adherence to the state's emperor-centered ideology. The diary for the year 1941 starts with the notation that the year is Kigen 2601, as measured from the supposed beginning of the imperial line (331).[2] Nakao praises key concepts of this ideology: loyalty to the emperor (kan'ō) as an expression of the warrior's way (bushidō) and the notion of the national body (kokutai), of which the emperor is the head. Nakao writes that respect for the national body is the cornerstone of the national spirit and that Japan is unsurpassed by other nations because of this respect (November 12, 1941, 408–9). After seeing a film titled The Shogun, the Staff, and a Soldier (Shogun to sanbō to hei), in which a shogun prays to the Sun Goddess, the presumed ancestress of the imperial family, asking for her help in bringing about victory on the battlefield, he was overcome with emotion. In his diary, he notes that he cried and says that Japanese soldiers, from shoguns to lowly foot soldiers, fight while dedicating their lives to worship of the imperial ancestress. This dedication, in Nakao's perspective, is the national spirit (June 20, 1942, 466–67).

Nakao's thinking was deeply influenced by Tanabe Hajime, a professor of philosophy at the Imperial University of Kyoto. His diary refers to Tanabe more often than do those of any of the other student pilots. Tanabe was one of the most influential philosophers at the time, and Nakao's diary testifies to his impact on young intellectuals. When Nakao reads Rekishiteki Genjitsu (Historical Reality), he realizes for the first time the significance of nation:

> Although it is a small book, it points to the historical nature of human existence. . . . It explains so well the relationship between the individual and the nation . . . not that I agree with everything he says, but he is right—because of the liberalism and idealism of the nineteenth century, I have been thinking only of the individual and humanity. The book clearly elucidated the importance of the nation. I had observed our nation and its reality, which is far from the ideal. I had not realized that the imperfection of the nation itself is the stage for us to work on. I was born as a member of a nation. . . . If we assume the position of a leader of a nation, we should actively identify the ills of a nation and try to get rid of them from the roots. (October 19, 1941, 361)

Reading Tanabe makes Nakao realize that he has previously thought only of the individual and of humanity as a whole, leaving out the collectivity of his nation, which mediates between the individual and the world. He begins to think that his criticism of Japanese society for falling short of its own ideals was misguided. He comes to believe that real leaders and, indeed, all persons dedicated to their country should not stand aside in contemplation but instead act to remedy the country's problems and work to fulfill the ideals their nation represents.

Nakao's diary refers to Tanabe quite often thereafter, suggesting that *Historical Reality* had a continuing influence as Nakao reread that work and discussed it with others. In addition to this book, he read at least a dozen of Tanabe's other works. Not all students shared his enthusiasm for Tanabe; for example, Sasaki read four of his works and Hayashi Tadao read only one, and both were quite skeptical of his philosophy.

In 1943, Nakao reiterates:

As Dr. Tanabe explains, the nation is not simply a stage on which we exist, but we must aggressively work on it. . . . We must act on historical reality. That is true history. (May 5, 1943, 569)

He compares Tanabe with Descartes to illuminate the importance of action, as distinct from mere contemplation:

I feel a great deal of difference between the times when Descartes lived and the present. He used the proof of *Ergo sum* in *Cogito* [a section of his *Discourse on the Method*]. But, for those who live today, rather than starting at an abstract level like his, we must start with our identity as a member of a collectivity—a nation or a people—that is centered on blood and love. Shouldn't we live with the feeling of dedication for our collectivity? (June 20, 1942, 466–67; July 27, 1942, 476–78)

After rereading *Historical Reality,* Nakao concludes:

Tanabe's argument is protected by dialectic armor to leave no room for fault. But, it lacks the vividness of "shedding blood." (May 3, 1943, 567)

In other words, he sees Tanabe thinking to be in pale abstractions. Nakao might have inferred that Tanabe could argue philosophically in the safe haven of the University of Kyoto while young men who carry out his philosophy are wounded and killed in the war.

It was Tanabe who made Nakao realize the importance of nationalism and the active contribution that a person could make as an engaged member of society. This philosophical framework represented a shift from the framework of the individual standing alone in relation to all of humanity that was the basis of nineteenth-century European liberalism and idealism. It certainly provided a foundation for Japanese nationalism. For Nakao, Tanabe's view of the nation also expressed his aspiration to transcend the egotism and materialism that he saw as corrupting his country. This critique of Western society and determination to address the contradictions of modernity to create a more progressive Japanese society was a view that Nakao shared with other student soldiers, although the nationalist element is more prominent in his writings than in theirs.

The Nationalist Response to the Threat of Western Imperialism

A strong component of Nakao's espousal of nationalism is a response to the government's call to fight against Western imperialism. Other student soldiers share this patriotic commitment to defend their country against a corrupt and threatening external adversary. The Meiji Restoration was carried out by ambitious individuals, most of them lower-class samurai, whose primary purpose was to overthrow the shogunate, which, they charged, was sleeping when Western colonial powers seized control of all the Asian countries except Japan. The return of the emperor system was in fact a façade for this purpose. Japan's program of modernization, since 1854 when Commodore Matthew Perry of the United States pried open its door, was driven by an effort to strengthen Japan politically and militarily in order to ward off the Western powers so that Japan would not become another Hong Kong, which was annexed by the British after the Opium War with such ease. Given this geopolitical situation, loyalty to the emperor was a corollary of protecting Japan from external forces.

Nakao's heroes are those who helped overthrow the shogunate to protect Japan against foreign threats. One of the heroes whom he and other student soldiers praise, Kusunoki Masashige (1294–1336), was a medieval warrior who fought against the shogunate government on the side of Emperor Godaigo (April 26, 1942, 454). Nakao describes Saigō Takamori (1827–1877), who played a critical role during the Meiji Restoration, as the person he most admires (September 22, 1942, 493–94; September 9, 1943, 601). Like Nakao, Saigō Takamori was from Kyūshū. In 1868 he managed to force the last shogun to relinquish Edo Castle without shedding blood. The castle was originally built and occupied in 1590 by Toyotomi Iyeyasu, the most powerful of all shoguns, and had been occupied by his descendants. It became the residence of the emperors and remains so at present. Nakao also reads *The Interpretation of the Constitution* (*Kempō Gikai*) by Itō Hirobumi, the major architect of the imperial system in the Meiji constitution (August 22, 1942, 483). Nakao's response to this work emphasizes his admiration for the architects of the Meiji government for managing to overthrow the shogunate in the midst of external threats (September 5, 1942, 485).

When Nakao was still at Fukuoka Higher School, he read the *History of American and British Colonial Expansion in Asia* (*Bei-Ei Tōa Shinryaku-shi*) by Ōkawa Shūmei (1886–1957), an ultra-right military and political leader who was sentenced as a class A war criminal at the International Military Tribunal for the Far East in 1946. Ōkawa suffered or pretended to suffer a nervous breakdown during the trial and was removed from the courtroom; he was released in 1948 and died in 1957. His book convinces Nakao that, as the strongest nation in Asia, Japan must liberate Asia from Western colonial encroachment. Nakao believes this to be the reason for Japan's entry into World War II (February 25, July 23, and October 4, 1942; 440, 474–76, 497–98). After watching the film *A Victory Song for Asia*, which depicts and offers a rationale for Japan's invasion of Bataan and Corregidor, he describes how Japan made the Filipinos, who had been influenced by American culture, aware of the power of Asia (December 27, 1942, 523–24). Nakao discusses his reading of the *History of Chinese Revolution* (*Shina Kakumei Gaishi*) by Kita Ikki, another well-known ul-tra-rightist, in relation to the need for mutual understanding between the Chinese and the Japanese for the defense of Asia against the West (October 10, 1942, 605–6). In 1938 the government initiated the policy known as the Greater East Asia Co-Prosperity Sphere (formally announced in 1940), which encouraged nationalism in other Asian countries and promoted eco-nomic cooperation among them, although the policy ultimately benefited Japan more than other members and prompted resistance to Japanese imperialism from other Asians. When Japan became an aggressor, its gov-ernment continued to use the rhetorical strategy of defending Asia against the threat of Western imperialism to cover up its own imperial ambitions. Nakao's case shows how easy it was for the state to mobilize young men's idealism—their dedication to a cause greater than themselves—by appeal-ing to the rationale of opposition to Western imperialism and transforming it into loyalty to the emperor *qua* Japan.

Japanese Cultural Identity

Nakao responded to the government's promotion of cultural nationalism as much as—or even more than—he responded to its political nationalism. Cultural nationalism had been a strong force among the people well before the Meiji period, especially among intellectuals. Nakao repeatedly speaks of Nishida Kitarō, a Japanese philosopher who established the Kyoto school of philosophy, as discussed earlier. Nakao reflects on Nishida's notion of "nothingness" in reference to various propositions by Dōgen, a Buddhist philosopher. Nakao feels that he has gained a new insight into "nothingness" in the light of Nishida's philosophy and by giving it a far more active agency. This nothingness constitutes a self that is cleared of "stubborn prejudices" and opens up a world by active engagement in it, thereby achieving the true inner life (553, 564). According to Nakao, this notion is a synthesis of Nishida and Dōgen (see March 15, April 20, and May 13, 1943, 552–53, 565–71). Nishida, like Tanabe, attempted to transcend Western philosophical traditions and to establish a distinctly Japanese tradition. Similarly, in his discussion of Chinese philosophers, Nakao emphasizes Asian philosophical traditions collectively, as distinct from Western ones (September 8, 1943, 598–99).

Nakao remarks on other, less abstract elements of cultural nationalism. For example, in 1940 he decides not to use the Gregorian calendar but to follow the new Japanese calendar, which counts the years starting from the time when the legendary first emperor was enthroned. But he also finds it amusing to consider how they chose the precise year for the imperial enthronement (January 1, 1940, 208). He is willing to subscribe to the new calendar, which arose from nationalistic ideology, while knowing very well that there was no way to identify the precise date of the enthronement and that it was therefore a fiction made up by the government.

Cosmopolitan Humanism

Nakao's patriotism is coupled not with chauvinism but with a deep concern for social justice and a commitment to humanity at large. He declares that the works of Kawai Eijirō prompted him to question his thinking so far and encouraged him to cultivate his own life course (January 1, 1939, 9; August 8, 9, 10, 1939, 168; January 11, 1940, 214; May 26, 1943, 572). Kawai (1891–1944), a highly respected economic historian who taught at the Imperial University of Tokyo, was very influential among young intellectuals at the time. He espoused the idealism of Thomas Hill Green and openly criticized both Marxism and fascism.

Nakao was impressed by Mori Ōgai's *The Abe Clan* (*Abe Ichizoku*), a novel in which Abe struggles with the feudal code of loyalty to his master, Hosokawa Tadayoshi (February 23, 1940, 233). Natsume Sōseki's work echoes Nakao's own dilemma of whether to give his life for the nation or to live for himself as an individual. He reads Shimazaki Tōson's *Ie* (*The Household*) (July 22, 1939, 162), which focuses on the problem of the individual and his or her responsibility as a member of a household, which

Tōson considered a basic kinship unit that was undergoing profound changes with modernity. In his readings of these works, Nakao finds ways of thinking about the contradictions between individualism and devotion to a social group, be it a household or a nation.

Nakao's comments about literature attest to his concern for human equality and his acceptance of ethnic and religious differences. He is deeply moved by Shimazaki Tōson's novel *The Broken Commandment* (*Hakai*), whose protagonist, a *hisabetsu-burakumin*—a member of a minority group that was often treated as separate from and inferior to the dominant Japanese—agonizes about his identity. The central character has become a teacher, despite the fact that until 1871, when they were legally liberated, hisabetsu-burakumin were barred from the profession, and he conceals his background for a long time until his torment becomes too much to bear. Nakao exclaims: "We throw a person into a hell [of ostracism and prejudice] far more torturous than hellfire by hating him and discriminating against him just because he belongs to another social group or people" (July 20, 1939, 161). On hearing of the death of Henri Bergson, Nakao writes an emotionally charged commentary sympathizing with Bergson, whom he regards as the second greatest philosopher after Kant, for the discrimination he suffered because of his Jewish identity (January 7, 1941, 336).

After reading Osaragi Jirō's book about the Dreyfus Affair, he is indignant at the way Dreyfus was treated. The affair, which had reverberations in Japan, took place in 1894 when Alfred Dreyfus, a French army officer of Jewish Alsatian descent, was wrongly accused of treason and sent to prison, not to be cleared until 1906. The controversy divided the French into two partisan groups: the anti-Dreyfus group, consisting primarily of royalists, militarists, and Catholics, and those who believed in his innocence, primarily republicans, socialists, and anticlericalists. The dispute eventually became a watershed event for the separation of church and state in France. Émile Zola played a prominent role by publishing his famous letter "J'accuse" in 1898 in defense of Dreyfus, for which he was sentenced to prison but fled to England. After reading Osaragi's work, Nakao exclaims: "The life of an innocent should never be at stake. However, for the military only its honor is at stake." He further explains the basis of his opposition to the military view:

> To threaten the life of an innocent should never be allowed. However, from the perspective of the military, it does not matter, since the honor of the military is the only thing they care about, filling the air with lies, and not questioning what is true.

After praising the Clemenceau brothers, Émile Zola, and the judge at the final trial, he declares:

Am I to enter the world of chaos in which one's partisan interests obstruct justice? I should not like to be part of the world that accrues justice only to the bureaucrats and almighty power to the military. I prefer to be in the outer field and, like Zola, try to steer the nation toward justice and truth. (December 12, 1939, 204–5)

Ambivalence and Agony

Nakao's writings pose a formidable challenge for interpretation because of his subtle means of expression. Nakao makes many explicit statements in support of the wartime ideology. Yet he also holds values that are at variance with militarism and imperialism, and on closer reading we realize that his entire life is a continuous struggle between the state ideology, which he thinks he ought to espouse, and his own passionate desire to live. Ambivalence is at the center of his situation as he perceives it.

While still in higher school, he already anticipates his imminent death:

Everything in front of me is in gray. Desperation and gloom with no hope of lifting. I am not sure at all if I can bear the physical and mental exhaustion. Am I to simply die without any meaning to my life? . . . I feel everything will suddenly collapse. (May 9, 1940, 253)

In order to accept his fate as unavoidable, Nakao resorts to historical determinism:

Although Hitler and Napoleon fought to expand their national territory, from a historical point of view, they are nothing but the rise and fall of people. Human beings are born and die. It is just a historical cycle. History repeats itself. What is the real meaning of our universe? (August 30, 1939, 177)

Other student soldiers express similar sentiments, proclaiming their deaths to be predetermined by impersonal historical forces. When they realize that they can no longer escape death, they begin to rationalize it, removing themselves from the role of historical agent.

Nakao's reflections on Tanabe are fraught with tension. On the one hand, he tries very hard to convince himself to accept Tanabe's call to recognize the importance of the nation, rather than seeing the individual in reference only to humanity. Tanabe's urging that people must act as citizens of the nation on the stage of history mean individual involvement in fighting the war. Nakao is drawn to historic figures who dedicated themselves to Japan by active participation in politics. In his search for a cause greater than himself, he finds purity of spirit in the notion of devotion. On the other hand, when he translates Tanabe's logic into the terms of his own life at the time, he finds nothing but his own death. Again and again, he cries out for life. If these passages are read superficially, he appears to have been completely taken in by Tanabe and his philosophy; but, on a closer reading of his diary, his utter desperation and agony leap out from every page. What follow are but a few of many examples.

In 1941 Nakao reads Philipp Witkop's *German Students' War Letters* (*Kriegsbriefe gefallener Studenten*), a well-known collection of letters by German student soldiers in World War I that was published in 1928. He records his reaction at some length:

Combat between human against another human, blood against blood—what else but cruelty? In the battlefield, daily witnessing friends being killed, observing grotesque slaughter, and feeling the imminent approach of one's death. . . . Yet many of these students take their fate in stride, recognizing the need to fight even in the face of cruel slaughter, sacrificing their lives to the nation, and dying while sending their blessings to their mothers and siblings. It is indeed amazing. Perhaps it is this spirit that makes Germany victorious today. (April 4, 1941, 365)

He cannot reconcile the two attitudes and says simply that he finds their willingness to die for their country in the midst of wanton slaughter "amazing."

After reading Nishida Kitarō's *Nothingness and the Limits of Self-Consciousness* (*Mu no Jikakuteki Gentei*) and Tanabe's *The Logic of the Nation* (*Kokkateki Sonzai no Ronri*) (April 30 and May 1, 1943, 566–67), he reflects:

We are fighting for life against Britain, the great empire on the decline, and America, at its peak for its material culture. Although I am not physically in the battlefield yet, I am already in it. I myself, in pursuit of the infinite and in love with the absolute, too, must sacrifice myself for the nation. . . . Is the "absolute" to be located in our sacrifice for the nation? . . . I cannot help but agonize over the contradiction. . . . I, who have come to know the depth of life and live that life, must sacrifice my life for our country since my life is destined to be given for the nation? . . . I painfully struggle in pursuit of truth.

This expression of agony is interrupted by a radio blaring government propaganda. The entry continues: "My neighbor's radio is broadcasting some pronouncement from the Imperial Headquarters." The Imperial Headquarters held tight control over the news released during the war, often exaggerating Japan's military victories and fanning false hopes for ultimate victory. The ironic juxtaposition of this broadcast, which he reports sarcastically, and the seriousness of the reflections into which it intrudes is palpable.

As time goes by, Nakao becomes even more introspective, a shift of mood that is most apparent in the increasing number of poems and poetic expressions in his diary. When he matriculates at the University of Tokyo in April 1942, he writes that he will be drafted in September of the following year and that he is already psychologically prepared. He then muses on the fragility of human life—recognizing that one bullet will simply destroy the body, a human being—but rationalizes that the death of an individual should not matter when it is given to the nation (July 14, 1942, 490).

Nakao frequently mentions his feeling of loneliness, which goes well beyond a mere psychological state. It derives from choosing justice and truth, as opposed to hypocrisy and unethical conduct. This choice, while morally satisfying, nonetheless leaves one isolated, because other people may not flock to one. For Nakao, Socrates is a model:

> Socrates is strong. He kept going against hypocrites and upholding his sense of justice. I feel that I am not as strong as Socrates. (April 8, 1940, 246)

His musings about death take a critical turn when he begins to focus on rebirth and life after death, rather than on death itself. This preoccupation seems to me to indicate that he could no longer face death as the finale. The diary entry for November 23, 1942, begins with his admiration of Socrates for calmly and courageously drinking hemlock when he was put to death for an official charge of impiety. Nakao's deliberation focuses on Socrates' notion of the immortal soul:

> The problem of immortality is important. However, since I have been painfully going through my life, death and immortality take on meaning only in terms of life. . . . The last writing by Socrates, in which he praises the beauty of the world after death, makes me want to live rather than die. (511–13)

This statement is followed by a poem he composed:

> Praying to find meaning in life,
> Long and painful sleepless nights I spent.

Nakao confesses that he is unable to get rid of an overwhelming desire to live. Unlike Socrates, Nakao could not find solace in the notion of immortality.

Rather than romanticizing and aestheticizing the notion of death, Nakao articulates his desire to live. Even his comments about art are pervaded by this attachment to vitality. For example, he admires Rodin because his sculptures expressed the vigor of life, and he praises Rodin for having found stability and beauty in an age that exposed humanity's hubris (February 23, 1942, 437–38).

The diary entries for 1943 are replete with references to life and death. He discusses Dante Alighieri's *Divine Comedy* (*Commedia*) in relation to Christianity and to the *Shōhō Genzō,* a Zen Buddhist text by Dōgon, to which he refers repeatedly. Both the existence of God and the possible meanings of Christian faith become subjects of debate. Nakao expresses despair about his inability to find peace of mind (February 10, 11, 15, 21; 540–42, 545–46). He goes back to his hero, Saigō Takamori: "Saigō died because he lived. I have not even lived and thus should not be obsessed with death" (September 19, 1943, 601). Nakao states that he still does not have a firm conviction about his military duty even though the day for the physical examination is nearing. He recalls Montaigne's thesis that it is not death itself but fear of it that makes one feel its weight and discusses death in relation to the body and the soul. He writes that he will really face death only when he enters the military to sacrifice his life and that when he exposes himself to the rain of bullets he will face death even more immediately (October 8, 1943, 607–8).

The later diary entries suggest that Nakao's apparent eagerness to sacrifice his life for the emperor may be a way to convince himself of the meaningfulness of the death that he is facing because, once drafted, the chances of escaping death are very slim indeed. He tries to convince himself that by sacrificing himself for a greater cause—his nation's effort in the war—his life would have a promise of continuing through the life of his nation. He writes that one lives for eternity by sacrificing oneself for the emperor (September 5, 1943, 597). He continues his search for meaning in his death both by paying homage at the Yasukuni National Shrine and by reading Plato, Descartes, and St. Augustine (Aurelius Augustinus). Nakao compares Augustine's Christianity with Asian modes of thought. He concludes his philosophical debate with a poetic musing (October 13, 1943, 615):

> The moon is beautiful tonight. . . . Like falling rain, the sound of the insect in the overgrown bush. . . . As I look up at it again and again, the moon looks like Princess Kaguya quietly weeping.[3]

Many entries are, like this one, suffused with his sadness and longing for life and for a woman he never had. In 1942 and especially 1943, his philosophical musings included more frequent commentaries about the beauty of nature.

Nakao travels all the way from Tokyo to Kyoto to listen to a lecture by Tanabe Hajime that inspires him enormously, but on his way back to Tokyo he observes:

> At Kyoto station, and the next station and the next, remains of the soldiers were making the "victorious return" (*gaisen*). It was painful to look at the whiteness of the box. "We shall meet again at Yasukuni Shrine"—Do soldiers utter these words without hesitation when they are in combat? (November 10, 1943, 625)

The phrase "whiteness of the box" refers to the white cloth placed over wooden boxes that supposedly contained the ashes of cremated soldiers; in truth, these boxes usually contained only a white piece of paper with the deceased soldier's name and rank, as was the case for Sasaki Hachirō and Hayashi Tadao. That Nakao pens this passage just before going into the navy reveals the depth of his ambivalence about his sacrifice.

In a lengthy commentary on Yanagida Kenjūrō's *The Japanese Spirit and the World Spirit* (*Nihon Seishin to Sekai Seishin*), he finds it difficult to justify war on a logical ground:

> If evil is justified on the basis of its good result, must one accept the consequence when the justification of evil results in evil, rather than in intended good? It is justified to bring evil to good, but evil is evil and one must identify it as such. (January 3, 1941, 333–35)

Haunted by Loneliness and Death

Events that take place in Nakao's family in 1940 lead him to ponder death as well. His family received a telegram about the death of his aunt. His mother went to the aunt's home although she was in the midst of making breakfast. On the same day, while his grandmother was preparing lunch, a neighbor came to tell them that a neighbor's baby had died. Hearing of two deaths in one day, he writes:

> Human life is even less dependable than the preparation of a meal. I was stunned. It is hard to imagine that these are human deaths. It is death that is coming to me soon or later. Buddha was supposed to have realized the

ephemerality of life and transcended it by overcoming changes in life thereby making them less painful. Yet, death is sad. It is sad to send off the dead. "Those who gain the eyes of wisdom would no longer become chained to desire and attachment"—those eyes of wisdom. My new departure in life must start here. (August 25, 1939, 175)

He is apparently trying to find a way to ease the pain of death, which befalls everyone, including himself.

Nakao goes to see his grandfather on his deathbed. He finds the grandfather's departure an absolute break from this world. He writes:

Grandfather, who would live through my father and uncle, is no longer a grandfather who lives on in history but discarded "remains" in this world. . . . His life would soon disappear as our memory of him fades away. He used to say that he was always with Buddha and thus he would not regret when and wherever he dies. . . . As for me, I do not want to die until my own work [goal] is accomplished. I don't believe in its accomplishment in the next world. (August 3, 1940, 274)

These encounters with death and loss intensify the loneliness that he has already felt. Anticipating his own death, Nakao, like other young men, often feels lonely. He quotes from Tayama Katai's *Life* (*Sei*): "People cry for me, they feel sad, and they console me. But, after all, one dies all alone" (August 12, 1939, 170). He composes several poems in October 1941. Here are two examples (October 19, 1941, 301):

Still raining. How cold it is to sleep alone at night.

How pitiful—a mosquito still alive, but alone.

After reading Kant, Nakao remarks:

People say they are lonely. When I open the book, the word *lonely* jumps out at me. I try to rebuff it—why should I be lonely? Why should one be lonely? Those who say "lonely" are those who indulge in their own sentimentality. Look directly at the objectives. Then, the world is filled with joy and all beings bless you. . . . You are lonely when you struggle with the discrepancy between the ideal and reality? . . . We cannot compromise with reality. . . . Be strong, be strong. My soul adores a strong person. Only a strong person can lead me. . . . But my soul often falls into the depth of loneliness. (March 2, 1940, 237–38)

Above all, Nakao is lonely because he so acutely senses that his own death is rapidly approaching. His poem "Stillness" (September 20, 1942, 491–92) painfully expresses this awareness:

How lonely is the sound of the clock in the darkness of the night.
The sound of the clock brings back fond memories of my childhood
Remembering those sleepless nights
Unable to sleep for loneliness
Many thoughts come to my mind as rain falls outside.

The clock is a metaphor of his life, ticking away toward his death.

ENTERING THE MILITARY

On several occasions Nakao writes that he is not psychologically ready to enter the military. Some diary entries from the days just before he goes to the military base vividly express his thoughts and feelings at this difficult time.

His grandmother has told him to visit a temple and to obtain an amulet that is believed to protect a soldier from bullets. He describes his experience there in a poem. When he arrives at the temple, he is told that the monk has already been drafted and that his wife, alone with a puppy, is guarding the temple. He stands in the temple garden, which is quiet in the warm sun. On his way back from the temple, he pays a visit to the tomb of a friend who entered the military before he did. The white tomb marker, with the notation that he died on the southern front on March 2, 1942, has already weathered.

The tomb marker of my friend who died in the south
How painful it is to see his age at death, twenty-one.
I pulled out a few autumn weeds
To purify my friend's tomb.

He is deep in thought on his way back, gazing at the mountain in the beautiful sunshine, recalling the time the jūdō club climbed the mountain and the time he felt self-confident when looking at the mountain as he returned home after visiting his father at Kumamoto (November 5, 1943, 622).

On November 6, 1943, the jūdō club holds a farewell party for members leaving for the military. Of thirty young men who gathered, eight are soon to be drafted. They play a farewell match. At night they put up a tent and they enjoyed a feast while looking at the moon, partially hidden in the clouds, like the moon in the spring (622). On November 8, 1943, Nakao goes home to pack up to return to the University of Tokyo. He finds his grandmother in a prostrate position in front of the family alcove. She explains that she was praying to their ancestors for his safety because she no longer can walk to a shrine or temple to pray (623–34).

ON THE NAVAL AIR BASE, 1943–45

The diary Nakao kept after entering the military was burned when the Takuma Naval Air Base was bombed. The writings that survive from this period consist only of letters to his parents, other family members, and friends.

On October 9, 1943 (645–46), in a letter addressed to his best friend, Yanagiura Fumio, he asks Yanagiura if he is going to be a pilot, adding that although he himself has good eyesight and thus should be a candidate for a pilot's position, he has not been able to make up his mind about it. He writes to this same friend on December 7, 1943: "I have taken up my pen in order to write my last letter from this world (*shaba*); thousands of thoughts come to me and it is difficult to express them in words." As he predicts in this letter, he was placed in the navy at Sasebo.

Although Nakao confides his doubts to his friend, his letters to his parents contain the statements that were expected of a soldier at the time. His letter to them of January 1, 1944, reads:

> Today we welcome the first day of the beautiful 1944. The navy battleship flag against the blue sky indeed looks vigorous. This year I am finally able to plunge onto the American and British battleships. I will be even more determined and do my best as I think of the banks of the Nagara River. (660)

He is referring to the river running through Gifu, where his parents live. He starts a letter written in April 1944 (661) by praising the cherry blossoms in full bloom at the Tsuchiura Naval Air Base and then asks about various members of the family, including his elder brother, who has been drafted into the army.

In a letter to his parents dated May 1944, he details the regulations for visiting the base. This would have been his parents' last opportunity to see him. But on arriving at the base in August 1944, they found that their son had been transferred to the Tokushima Naval Air Base, where he was trained as a scout pilot. When his younger brother (who edited the diary and letters years later) was able to see him, he expressed concern because the tokkōtai operation had started. Nakao replied: "It is the end [for Japan] if a scout pilot has to plunge into an enemy vessel" (662). But on February 28, 1945, he was placed in the Kotohira Suishin Corps of Shinpū Tokkōtai (662) and became a tokkōtai pilot. A letter written in March 1945 to his parents begins: "At this extraordinary time when the homeland of Japan is being bombed, our spirit is ever higher and determined" (663). There was no way the family could have known that when he wrote this letter he was in the final stage of training to be a tokkōtai pilot. In April 1945 he writes his parents that he has sent them and others some money because he has not spent much of his stipend, and he asks them to give one hundred yen to his grandmother. He mentions that the cherry blossoms along the Nagara River must have fallen but remarks how beautiful the azalea blossoms are in the mountains near the base and comments on the beautiful spring scenery at the Inland Sea. He concludes his letter by saying that he is well and thus they should not worry and asking them to take care of themselves. In a postcard to his younger brother dated April 8, 1945, he asks for a *sen'ninbari,* a white sash with one thousand red knots, each tied by a different woman, which is supposed to protect the soldier from bullets (see chapter 4). Because the letters to his parents and postcard to his brother were written when he was already in training for the tokkōtai operation, we may conclude that it was in preparation for his final flight that he sent them money, for which he had no more use, and requested a *sen'ninbari.*

Nakao's last letter to his parents is dated April 28, 1945 (666–67). It reads:

> At the farewell party, people gave me encouragement. I did my best to encourage myself. I am truly a happy person. I can now meet my death with the belief that I have been treated with sincerity by people when I have not done anything for them. I have nothing to say at this time. I only hope for health for you all.
>
> My co-pilot is Uno Shigeru, a handsome boy, aged nineteen, a naval petty officer second class. His home is in Hyōgo Prefecture. . . . He thinks of me as his elder brother, and I think of him as my younger brother. Working as one heart, we will plunge into an enemy vessel. My photo, which I had taken when I visited the home of my colleague Ensign Maeda, should be ready shortly. They will send it to you. Please send one to Yanagiura [his best friend]. . . . The other day I paid my visit to Kotohira Shrine and had a picture taken. I told them to send the finished photo to you. Just in case, I enclose the receipt. . . . I imagine you would like to come visit me. But I

don't even regret that we did not meet. I am sure we share our feeling for our country. Please do not get discouraged, and fight to defeat America and Britain. Please say the same to grandmother. I will leave behind my diary. Although I did not do much in my life, I am content that I fulfilled my wish to live a pure life, leaving nothing ugly behind me.

If you have a chance, please show my diary to Yanagiura. I have other friends from my student days and got to know some colleagues in the navy. I am sure Japan's future will be fine, with these people working for the country. Yoshitaka—do your best. If the books you sent me arrive by tomorrow, I will carry them with me. I wish to say my thanks to my uncle and many other people. Please convey my thanks to them. Wishing you the best for your future.

This letter was signed simply with his given name, "Takenori." The details of his comrades' addresses and the direct allusions to his final flight alarmed his parents, prompting them to make the fruitless visit to the Takuma Naval Air Base mentioned at the beginning of this chapter.

Nakao Yoshitaka, the younger brother, explains that the day after Nakao wrote his last letter, he took off but was forced to return to the base because the plane malfunctioned. He visited his home and stayed there overnight, but his parents had gone to Gifu, so he did not see them. On May 3 he moved from the Takuma Naval Air Base, and on May 4 he took off from the Ibusuki Naval Air Base in Kagoshima on his final mission.

Kurata Yoshiharu, a comrade of Nakao's on the base, saw Nakao off on his final flight. He remembers him as having a faint smile on his face but taking off without a word, as was the custom for tokkōtai pilots on their final flights. He also reports that it was the custom not to report the pilots' deaths when their parents came to the base. He recalls the time when Nakao's parents came and the head of the corps begged someone to see them. Kurata left the scene to avoid involvement, because it was too painful for him to meet his comrade's parents, and he did not know who actually met them (670–72).

CONCLUSION

The Record of a Spiritual Quest documents Nakao's deliberations about life and death. Exceptional in intellect and character, Nakao earnestly searched for purity of spirit. These very qualities—his innocence and idealism—prevented him from recognizing the government's reckless strategies, in which the intellectual crème de la crème were brutally sacrificed for a war Japan was sure to lose. The *Record* is a painful chronicle of Nakao's determined effort to follow the state ideology, which he translated into an unselfish dedication to the collectivity but which came into an agonizing conflict with his burning desire to live for some higher end. If Nakao had been more certain about the value of sacrificing his life for the emperor, he would not have engaged in such painful soul-searching.

Nakao's arguments about subjects ranging from literature to philosophy are highly sophisticated and based on a thorough understanding of philosophical and social theory. The interpretation of Nakao's writings presented here represents a shift from my first impressions of his thinking. Initially, I noticed statements that appeared supportive of the state ideology and more or less concluded that Nakao was a conservative nationalist. After multiple rereadings, I began to understand the full complexity of his thought, which was expressed in his subtle philosophical deliberations. His ambivalence and agony are often disguised in entirely cerebral terms. His poems, giving voice to his deep sorrow and anguish regarding his fate, testify to the depth of his feeling. Agony never ceased to occupy his mind until the moment of his death.

Nakao's case is especially revealing of the complexities involved in the state's effort to propagate its militaristic ideology, illuminating both its successes and its limitations. The most powerful tool of the state was the use and abuse of the threat posed by Western colonial powers. Opposition to such external pressure was the central theme the Japanese had rallied around ever since the overthrow of the shogunate. The Greater East Asia Co-Prosperity Sphere was presented as a vision of all Asians uniting against the West. Nakao found parts of this appeal persuasive. Still, despite his leanings toward the state ideology with regard to some matters, his underlying thought processes were far from those embraced and advocated by ultranationalists such as Ōkawa Shūmei and Kita Ikki. Nakao's intellectual foundation was cosmopolitan humanism, which led him to abhor social discrimination and to hold Émile Zola as his spiritual hero.

PARTIAL LIST OF NAKAO TAKENORI'S READINGS

Philosophy, including economic and political philosophy and ethics. French: Henri Bergson, René Descartes, Blaise Pascal; *German:* Georg W. F. Hegel, Immanuel Kant, Karl Marx, Friedrich Nietzsche; *American:* William James, George Santayana; *Classical:* Aristotle, St. Augustine, Plato, Plutarch, Scipio, Socrates, Xenophon, Zeno; *Danish:* Kierkegaard; *Chinese:* Confucius, Mencius, Wang Yang-ming; *Japanese:* Kawai Eijirō, Motoori Nironaga, Nishida Kitarō, Suzuki Daisetsu, Tanabe Hajime, Watsuji Tetsurō.

Sociology and anthropology. French: Emile Durkheim, Lucien Lévy-Bruhl; *German:* Georg Simmel; *English:* Bronislaw Malinowski (Polish by birth).

Literature. French: Honoré de Balzac, Charles Baudelaire, Paul Bourget, Alexandre Dumas (père et fils), Gustave Flaubert, Anatole France, André Gide, Alphonse de Lamartine, Guy de Maupassant, Prosper Mérimée, Roger Martin du Gard, Michel de Montaigne, Romain Rolland, La Rochefoucauld, Stendhal; *German:* Hans Carossa, Johann Wolfgang von Goethe; *Swiss:* Hermann Hesse; *English:* William Shakespeare, Christopher Marlowe, George Bernard Shaw, Oscar Wilde; *Russian:* Anton Chekhov, Fyodor Dostoevsky, Nikolai Gogol, Aleksandr Pushkin, Leo Tolstoy, Ivan Turgenev; *Japanese:* Akutagawa Ryūnosuke, Hori Tatsuo, Izumi Kyōka, Kawabata Yasunari, Kunikida Doppo, Mori Ōgai, Mushakōji Saneatsu, Natsume Sōseki, Shiga Naoya, Shimazaki Tōson, Yamamoto Yūzō.

Notes

PREAMBLE

1. The terms used to refer to the series of wars in which Japan was involved during the late nineteenth and early twentieth centuries have been controversial, both in Japan and among historians of Japan elsewhere. I use the term *World War II* because it expresses the global nature of the conflict, in which Japan played a prominent role. Some scholars prefer the label *Pacific War*, which is intended to recognize Japan's role as an aggressor (Coox 1988, 381; Young 1998). However, I think that the term actually conceals Japanese aggression prior to 1941 in the parts of Asia that are located far from the Pacific. For discussion of these and other terms, see Coox (1988, 381) and Hosaka (2003).

2. According to Cumings (2001), Vlastos (2001), and others, U.S. leaders knew about the attack in advance. Cumings (2001) contrasts the attacks of September 11, 2001, which were "utterly unexpected and unprovoked, [and] had no rational military purpose," with the attack of December 7, 1941, which came "after several years of what Harvard professor Akira Iriye has called a U.S.-Japan Cold War, and after weeks of expecting Japan to strike at American interests." Persico (2004), however, argues that Roosevelt was aware of an imminent Japanese attack but was not informed of its exact location.

3. Iwo Jima is the main island of the Volcano Islands, which were annexed by Japan in 1887 and held by Japan until the American occupation (not recapture) in 1945. James Bradley (2000), the son of John Henry Bradley, one of the six flag-raisers in Associated Press photographer Joe Rosenthal's Pulitzer Prize–winning photo, has revealed that the flag shown in the photo was not the original small flag hoisted on Mt. Suribachi on Iwo Jima (see also Blumenthal 2000; Marling and Wetenhall 1991) while the battle was still raging. Rosenthal's photo, which immediately appeared across front pages nationwide, nonetheless established the myth of the American recapture of Iwo Jima and the heroism and patriotism of these marines. The photo and the myth were resurrected at the time of the 9/11 incident and placed alongside Thomas E. Franklin's photograph of the spontaneous flag-raising by the Brooklyn-based firefighters at the site of the Twin Towers.

The pair of photos repeatedly appeared in many American newspapers and magazines. A number of articles in the *New York Times* juxtaposed the two. "It's the same, but not" was the headline of an article by Greg Ryan on December 2, 2001 (Week in Review, Section 4, p. 5), accompanied by two photos, captioned "December 7, 1941: Pearl Harbor" (left) and "Sept. 11, 2001: World Trade Center" (right). The article begins by pointing out the differences between the two events: "recognizable enemies in the form of nation-states (Japan, then Germany and Italy)" versus "a faceless, borderless fanaticism that extends from the Middle East to middle America." Nevertheless, the overall impression of the article to the reader, with the two photos juxtaposed, is that Pearl Harbor and the 9/11 were the same. (I am grateful to Kenji Tierney for sending me this article.) Five days later, "Pearl Harbor's old men find new limelight since September 11" (*New York Times*, December 7, 2001) describes how Pearl Harbor survivors, who had been ignored, were suddenly called to make speeches and became heroes after 9/11.

Other newspapers followed the lead. Most of the following examples are confined to a few articles published in *the Wisconsin State Journal*. A two-full-page article, headed "America's darkest days" (Souvenir Section, December 7, 2001), has a cover photo spreading over both pages. The left side of the photo is marked "1941," and the right side "September 11, 2001." The photo on the left is captioned "The USS Arizona goes down in flames and smoke as a result of the surprise attack on Pearl Harbor on December 7, 1941." Pages A2 and A3 are exclusively on Pearl Harbor, as remembered by the veterans. A guest column by Raymond G. Boland, "Today, as in 1941, freedom is not free," appeared in the same newspaper one year later (December 7, 2002). "We're in pain, but our resolve is strong," wrote Leonard Pitts Jr. on September 14, 2001. The accompanying photos show, on the left, the Iwo Jima flag hoisting and, on the right, the firefighters hoisting the flag after 9/11, captioned "Iwo Jima—1945" and "New York City—2001."

An article by David Foster of the Associate Press is headed "Attack of Pearl Harbor proportions? Greater?" Foster begins, "In lives lost, death toll could easily top the 2,400 in Japanese assault," and goes on, "The attack drew immediate comparisons to the 1941 attack on Pearl Harbor, but even that event pales next to this week's attack. In lives lost, authorities say this week's death toll may easily outstrip that in the Pearl Harbor attack, which killed more than 2,400. And in psychological impact, this week's attack struck deeper, wider and closer home. The Pearl Harbor attack killed mostly military personnel, it struck at a time when the world was already girding for war, and it occurred on a remote Pacific island that wasn't even a state yet" (*Wisconsin State Journal*, September 13, 2001).

The analogy was fueled by the Bush administration. On December 8, 2001, the *New York Times* printed four photos on its front page: (1) dropping a memorial wreath from the Intrepid in New York; (2) President Bush in Norfolk, Virginia (on USS Enterprise); (3) Former President George Bush at the National D-Day Museum in New Orleans; (4) a Pearl Harbor survivor at the graves of comrades in Honolulu. In "Remembering Pearl Harbor; Bush ties it to the current campaign" (pp. B1 and B7), Elizabeth Bumiller explains how President Bush drew strong comparisons between the two: "Pearl Harbor, he said, was the start of a 'long and terrible' war for America, . . . 'a steadfast resolve' to defend freedom. . . . Among the 10,000 people aboard the Enterprise . . . were 25 survivors of the Pearl Harbor Attack" (p. B1). A photo showing Bush greeting saluting sailors is captioned "Remembering Pearl Harbor, Bush ties it to current war" (p. B7). Also on December 8, 2001, a report in the *Wisconsin State Journal*, with the headline "President praises crew of USS Enterprise," carries a photo showing Bush shaking hands with sailors after his speech aboard the USS Enterprise in Norfolk. The caption reads: "On the 60th anniversary of the attack on Pearl Harbor, the president compared that day of infamy to the September 11 suicide hijackings." The analogy has been repeated ever since. For example, in "Pearl Harbor Day, 2002" (*New York Times*, Op-Ed section, December 7, 2002), Frank Rich writes, "History will eventually tell us whether Pearl Harbor Day 2002 is the gateway to a war as necessary as World War II or to a tragedy of unintended consequences redolent of World War I."

INTRODUCTION

1. For the importance of writing as the primary mode of communication, see Ohnuki-Tierney (1984, 65). On the importance of diaries, see Hashimoto (1990); Keene (1984a, 10–14). Keene's interest in the genre of diary literature (Keene 1984a, 1984b) originated during World War II, when he was assigned to translate the diaries that Japanese soldiers left on the battlefield. Some soldiers even wrote messages in English addressed to American soldiers who, they hoped, would find their diaries after their death (Keene 1984a, 14–18).

2. *Fascism, totalitarianism,* and *authoritarianism* are notoriously difficult to define. I use the term *fascism* to refer to a political ideology that combines nationalism with the totalitarian goal of deploying the ideology to penetrate the quotidian lives of every subject of the nation.

3. Although the higher schools and imperial universities were national institutions, they were residential, and the students' parents had to pay the cost. Two other national institutions were completely free: the Teachers' School, whose establishment was decreed in 1886, and the army and navy schools, most of which were established in the early Meiji period. There were two levels of military schools: one for officer training and the other for noncommissioned or petty officers. Given the primogeniture system in use at the time, first-born males were spared the draft and inherited the property, while the other sons were drafted owing to universal conscription. Landowners in rural Japan sent their first-born sons to middle school, but they had to stay at home to inherit the land. Other sons were sent off to higher schools, the military schools for officers, and other institutions of higher education in lieu of inheritance. The oldest son of tenant farmers inherited the tenancy while others were drafted, and many went to the military schools for noncommissioned officers. Some of them rose through the ranks to be in charge of student soldiers. This situation created some reversals of class hierarchy and resultant conflicts in the military.

4. Ebina 1983, 142–43, 189, 272, 275–82; Kaigun Hikō Yobigakusei Dai-14-kikai 1966a, 13–17, 115–25, 1966b, 225; Mainichi Shirīzu Shuppan Henshū 1981, 108; Morioka 1995, 59–60, 67–73, 81, 85; Nihon Senbotsu Gakusei Kinenkai 1988, 241–44 (for an English translation of this volume, see Yamanouchi and Quinn 2000). Ebina (1983, 275) lists Ichijima's rank as second lieutenant.

5. According to the Meiji constitution, male members of the imperial family must serve in the military, with the first-born serving in the army, the next serving in the navy, and so on in alternation.

6. This perceptive phrase was offered by Pierre Bourdieu after listening to my description of the tokkōtai pilots' position.

7. In this key chapter of *Capital,* Marx develops his well-known model of the transformation of money into capital and the embodiment of capital in commodities

(Marx 1867 [1967]: 145–53). On socialism, liberalism, and Marxism during the first three decades of the twentieth century in Japan, see Duus and Scheiner (1998).

8. For example, this vision was articulated by Okabe Heiichi, who was born in February 1923, graduated from Taihoku University, a Japanese university in occupied Taiwan, and died as a tokkōtai pilot in 1945. Ebina 1983, 137, 169–70, 173–74; Inoguchi and Nakajima 1963, 180; 1975: 235–37; Kaigun Hikō Yobigakusei Dai-14-kikai 1966a, 128–29; 1966b, 195; Morioka 1995, 110–14, 125, 137–38, 142, 153, 154–55, 160–61, 172.

9. These remarks concerning the forms that Romanticism took in various European countries are very broad, pointing out only the characteristics most relevant to this discussion. For *Die Romantik,* see Mosse (1988, 29–64, 237–49) and Garland and Garland (1977); for *Le Romantisme,* see Crossly (1995); for Russian Romanticism, see Leighton (1985) and Malia (1999). See also Garland and Garland (1977), France (1995), and Terras (1985) for discussion of major figures. When the Romantic movement reached Japan, it gave rise to the *Nihon Romanha* (Japanese Romantic movement), a curious combination of Romanticism with the ultra-right. The student soldiers' diaries do not show the direct influence of this reactionary version of Romantic thought. For details of this movement in Japan, see Doak (1994); Ohnuki-Tierney (2002).

10. Most Japanese Christians, including prominent Meiji Christians and Hayashi Ichizō's parents, became Christians through personal conversion. Christians were known for their strong moral convictions and disciplined life; for example, they abstained from alcohol.

11. Although some of the pilots were aware of the atrocities the Japanese Army was inflicting on other peoples, Sakharov closed his eyes for a long time: "The revolutionaries and the poets both hated arrogant capitalism and a rotten social order that needed to be swept away by elementary forces. . . . The elementary catastrophe that both poets and revolutionaries assumed would cleanse the world was not long in coming" (Lourie 2002, 12). Sakharov at the time held "the belief that historical upheavals are impossible without suffering, which was the message of Soviet propaganda" (138–39). Likewise, Dimitri Svyatopolk-Mirsky (D. S. Mirsky) was a believer in Soviet self-glorification, which tried to justify Lenin and retained a nostalgia for Mother Russia (Smith 2003). Intellectuals sometimes become actively involved in politics with what Lilla calls "reckless mind," without fully realizing the impact of their activities, which often are utilized by the regime (Lilla 2001; see also Aron 1957; Milosz 1953; Sartre 1972).

CHAPTER 1

1. In his eagerness to enroll Sasaki in school, his father registered his birth date as March 7 instead of July 7, when he was actually born. This enabled Sasaki to enter the school, which begins its term in April, one year earlier. In other references (Nihon Senbotsu Gakusei Shuki Henshū Iinkai 1952 [1949]), Sasaki is sometimes listed as having died at the age of twenty-three, although he died in February, before his twenty-third birthday. Some differences in reckoning the age of these young men derive from the parallel systems the Japanese had until recently: one system, called *man,* calculates the actual years and months between birth and death, while the other, called *kazoe,* more commonly used at the time, treats the child as one year old at the time of birth and adds a year at every New Year (which used to be based on the lunar calendar). In the latter system, then, a child who is born at the end of one annual cycle becomes two years old at the beginning of the next.

2. The title of the 1981 volume of Sasaki Hachirō's collected works in Japanese is *Seishun no Isho: Seimei ni Kaete, Kono Nikki, Ai.* Sasaki is introduced in Ohnuki-Tierney 2002, 193–211, and also briefly in Mainichi Shirīzu Shuppan Henshū 1981, 108; Ebina 1983, 138, 184–86, 272, 295–97; Tōkyō Daigaku Gakusei Jichikai and Senbotsu Gakusei Shuki Henshū Iinkai 1951 [1947], 13–17; Nihon Senbotsu Gakusei Shuki Henshū Iinkai 1952 [1949], 113–22; Kaigun Hikō Yobi Gakusei Dai-14-kikai 1966a, 20–23, 137; 1966b, 225; and Morioka 1995, 59–67, 72–73, 81, 85. In the collections edited by Fujishiro, Sasaki's lengthy essay on Miyazawa Kenji is mentioned only briefly, and his last poem, composed on April 11, 1945, is not included, but they are reproduced in Nihon Senbotsu Gakusei Shuki Henshū Iinkai 1952 [1949] and in Ebina 1983, respectively. Ebina also includes some excerpts from the diary Sasaki kept while on the base. I have heard that the final volume of Sasaki's diary remains with his sister.

3. This sort of relationship between mother and son is not unusual in Japan: a mother takes a nonauthoritarian and at times subordinate position in relation to her male child when he achieves adulthood, which starts around the time he enters a higher school.

4. While some scholars, such as Augustin Berque, William LaFleur, and Michael Marra, evaluate the work of the Kyoto school of philosophy favorably, others, such as Kevin Doak, Harry Harootunian, and Naoki Sakai, are critical of its political implications. For a detailed discussion of the school, see Barshay 1988.

5. See the diary entries for October 14, 15, 18, 19, 1943. The government's construction of Yamamoto Isoroku as the model for the Japanese soldier was questioned by his own men, who saw him otherwise (Umezawa Shōzō, pers. comm.).

CHAPTER 2

1. Selected entries from Hayashi Tadao's diaries have been published in Ebina 1983, 42–43, 46–47, 87–89, 272, 298–303; Kaigun Hikō Yobigakusei Dai-14-kikai 1966a, 48–56, 86–92, 174–76, 194–97, 205–7; 1966b, 149, 206; Mainichi Shirīzu Shuppan Henshū 1981, 26–27, 108, 114–15, 157; Ohnuki-Tierney 2002, 211–18; Hayashi Tadao 1967.

2. See the entries for May 5, November 26, and December 13, 1940 (10, 26–28, 29–30) and for February 27, April 20 and 30, May 4, October 15, 25, and 29, and November 3, 1941 (35, 39, 41–42, 43–45, 64, 66, 66–67, 68–69).

3. This is a reference to "Purgatory" in Dante's *Divine Comedy.*

4. These are all prose poems in *Paris Spleen.*

CHAPTER 4

1. Because the brothers served in the army, rather than in the navy, into which most of the tokkōtai pilots were drafted, their writings do not appear as often as those of the others do but are quoted in length in Nihon Senbotsu Gakusei Kinenkai (1988, Matsunaga Shigeo 8–9, 40–45, 88–111, 174–221), in which "A Beautiful Illusion" is quoted at the very beginning in its entirety. It also appears in Izumi (1968, 77).

2. *Handwritten Notes of a Student Soldier (Gakutohei no Shuki)* was edited and published privately in May 1940 (Nihon Senbotsu Gakusei Kinenkai 1988, 90). It was published as volume 1 of *Shirachidori Sōsho* (the White Plover series) and was to be followed by the publication of other writings by Matsunaga Shigeo, but Matsunaga Tatsuki could not do so (Izumi 1968, 41).

3. Matsunaga quotes these poems without identifying where they appeared. I am most grateful to Mack Horton of the University of California, Berkeley, who found the poems in the original collections and provided me with their identification numbers. All the translations are his, and the line breaks follow those in the originals. His explanation of the first poem, expressing Teika's mourning for his mother, was helpful in understanding Matsunaga's identification of himself with Teika.

CHAPTER 5

1. The title in Japanese is *Hi nari Tate nari: Nikki, Haha e no Tegami, Hayashi Ichizō Ikōshū*. Selections from his diary and letters were first published in Nihon Senbotsu Gakusei Shuki Henshū Iinkai (1949). More extensive selections were published by Ebina (1977, 227; 1983, 137, 173–74, 224–28, 272, 303–12) and Morioka (1995, 114–17, 128, 140–42, 154–59, 163–69, 172). Ohnuki-Tierney (2002, 232–39) introduces Hayashi. The following sources also include briefer coverage of Hayashi: Inoguchi and Nakajima (1963, 177–80); Inoguchi, Nakajima, and Pineau (1975, 231–35); Kaigun Hikō Yobigakusei Dai-14-kikai (1966a, 171–74; 1966b, 66–69, 136–37); Mainichi Shirīzu Shuppan Henshū (1981, 138–41); and Nihon Senbotsu Gakusei Shuki Henshū Iinkai (1949, 215–18). Itō Kazuyoshi (1995: 161) points out that Hayashi's letter to his mother is the only one by a Japanese included in *Letters to Mother*, edited by C. V. Doren and published in 1959, and that a letter by Hayashi is also included among the letters by tokkōtai pilots in *Sturm der Götter*, published in Germany (no date cited).

2. The English text is published by the National Council of Churches of Christ in the United States of America (1962: 84–85).

3. The government proclaimed that there were a million Japanese people at that time.

4. The *Chūshingura* (*The Treasury of Loyal Retainers*), originally a puppet play with an anti-Shogunate theme, was transformed into a pro-emperor story to inculcate loyalty; see Ohnuki-Tierney 2002, 142–51.

5. The second quotation in English also appears in his letter to Tsuchii Kentarō (Hayashi 1995, 111).

CHAPTER 6

1. Short passages about Nakao Takenori also appear in Ebina (1983, 145); Tōkyō Daigaku Gakusei Jichikai and Senbotsu Gakusei Shuki Henshū Iinkai (1947, 165–66); Nihon Senbotsu Gakusei Shuki Henshū Iinkai (1949, 129–30); and Kaigun Hikō Yobigakusei Dai-14-kikai (1966a, 83, 166).

2. In 1870 the Meiji government turned the mythical origin of Japan, accession to the throne by the legendary emperor Jinmu, into a "historical fact" and established the Japanese calendar beginning in that year.

3. Princess Kaguya (*Kaguyahime*) is a protagonist in a Japanese fairy tale of the Heian period who was born of a bamboo and raised by a kind old man. Although she was exceptionally beautiful and was courted by many noble men, including the emperor, she rejected them all and went up to the moon on August 15.

References

The place of publication for works in Japanese is Tokyo, unless specified otherwise.

Appiah, K. Anthony. 2004. *The ethics of identity.* Princeton: Princeton University Press.

Aron, Raymond. [1955] 1957. *The opium of the intellectuals.* New York: Doubleday.

Barshay, Andrew E. 1988. *State and intellectual in imperial Japan.* Berkeley and Los Angeles: University of California Press.

Benjamin, Walter. [1958] 1968. *Illuminations.* New York: Schocken.

Berlin, Isaiah. [1959] 1992. *The crooked timber of humanity.* New York: Random House.

———. 2003. *Freedom and its betrayal: Six enemies of human liberty.* Edited by Henry Hardy. Princeton: Princeton University Press.

Bitō, Masahide. [1986] 1994. Junshi (Suicide following one's master). *Kokushi Daijiten* (Encyclopedia of national history), ed. Kokushi Daijiten Henshū Iinkai, 7:416–17. Yoshikawa Kōbunkan.

———. [1993] 1996. Yōmeigaku (Wang Yang-ming). In *Kokushi Daijiten* (Encyclopedia of national history), ed. Kokushi Daijiten Henshū Iinkai, 14:351. Yoshikawa Kōbunkan.

Blumenthal, Ralph. 2000. A son pierces the long silence of a flag-raiser. *New York Times,* May 17, 2000.

Bradley, James. 2000. *Flags of our fathers.* New York: Bantam.

Brent, T. David. 1977. *Jung's debt to Kant: Kant's transcendental method and the structure of Jung's psychology.* Ph.D. diss., University of Chicago.

Burke, Edmund. [1757] 1998. A philosophical enquiry into the origin of our ideas of the sublime and beautiful. In *A philosophical enquiry into the origin of our ideas of the sublime and beautiful and other pre-revolutionary writings,* 49–199, ed. David Womersley. London: Penguin.

Buruma, Ian. 2004. The destruction of Germany. *New York Review of Books,* October 21, 8–12.

Buruma, Ian, and Avishai Margalit. 2004. *Occidentalism: The West in the eyes of its enemies.* New York: Penguin.

Caryl, Christian. 2005. Why they do it. *New York Review of Books,* September 22, 28–32.

Coox, Alvin. 1988. The Pacific War. In *The Cambridge history of Japan,* ed. P. Duus, 6:315–82. Cambridge: Cambridge University Press.

Crossley, C. 1995. Romanticism. In France 1995, 714–16.

Cumings, Bruce. 2001. Point of view: Pearl Harbor a bad analogy for Sept. 11 attacks. *The Asahi Shimbun Asia Network.* December 7, 2001.

Doak, Kevin Michael. 1994. *Dreams of difference: The Japan Romantic School and the crisis of modernity.* Berkeley: University of California Press.

Dumont, Louis. [1966] 1970. *Homo hierarchicus.* Chicago: University of Chicago Press.

———. 1994. *German ideology: From France to Germany and back.* Chicago: University of Chicago Press.

Duus, Peter. 1988. Socialism, liberalism, and marxism, 1901–1931. In *The Cambridge history of Japan,* ed. P. Duus, 6:654–710. Cambridge: Cambridge University Press.

Duus, Peter, and Irwin Scheiner. 1998. Socialism, liberalism, and marxism, 1901–31. In *Modern Japanese thought,* ed. B. T. Wakabayashi, 147–206. Cambridge: Cambridge University Press.

Dyson, Freeman. 2005. The bitter end. *New York Review of Books,* April 28, 4–6.

Ebina Kenzō. 1977. *Kaigun Yobi-Gakusei* (The navy reserve student soldiers). Tosho Shuppansha.

———. 1983. Taiheiyō Sensō ni Shisu—Kaigun Hikō Yobi Shōkō no Sei to Shi (To die in the Pacific War—Life and death of the Navy Aviation Reserve Officers). Nishida Shoten.

Edelman, Bernard, ed. 1985. *Dear America: Letters home from Vietnam.* New York: Norton.

Ferguson, Niall. 2001. 2011: Ten years from now, historians will look back and see the events of Sept. 11 as mere ripples in a tidal wave of terrorism and political fragmentation. *New York Times Magazine,* December 2, 76–79.

France, Peter, ed. 1995. *The new Oxford companion to literature in French.* Oxford: Clarendon.

Fujishiro Hajime. 1981. Kaisetsu Sasaki Hachirō no Shōgai (Commentary: The life of Sasaki Hachirō). In Sasaki 1981, 421–66.

Fussell, Paul. [1975] 2000. *The Great War and modern memory.* Oxford: Oxford University Press.

Garland, Henry, and Mary Garland, eds. 1977. *The Oxford companion to German Literature.* Oxford: Oxford University Press.

Golomb, Jacob, and Robert Wistrich, eds. 2002. *Nietzsche, godfather of fascism? On the uses and abuses of a philosophy.* Princeton: Princeton University Press.

Gray, John. 1995 *Enlightenment's wake: Politics and culture at the close of the modern age.* London: Routledge.

———. 2003 *Al Qaeda and what it means to be modern.* New York: New Press.

Hanada Chiyo. 1995. Kokoro ni Kizamikomu Wadatsumi no Ko'e (The Voice of the Sea God Engraved in our Heart). In Hayashi Ichizō 1995, 123–25.

Hashimoto Yoshihiko. 1990. Nikki (Diaries). In *Kokushi Daijiten* (Encyclopedia of national history), ed. Kokushi Daijiten Henshū Iinkai, 11:39–41. Yoshikawa Kōbunkan.

Hattori Shōgo. 1996. Kamikaze. *Air Power History* 43(1): 14–27.

Hayashi Ichizō. 1995. *Hi nari Tate nari: Nikki, Haha eno Tegami, Hayashi Ichizō Ikōshū* ([The Lord is] a sun and shield: Diary, letters to mother, writings left by Hayashi Ichizō). Edited by Kaga Hiroko. Fukuoka: Tōka Shobō.

Hayashi Katsuya. 1967. Kaisōni Ikiru Hayashi Tadao (Hayashi Tadao in my memory). In Hayashi Tadao 1967, 217–30.

Hayashi Tadao. 1967. *Waga Inochi Getsumei ni Moyu: Ichi Senbotsugakuto no Shuki* (My Life Burning in Moonlight: Handwritten record of a fallen student soldier). Edited by Hayashi Katsuya. Chikuma Shobō.

Horace [Quintus Horatius Flaccus]. 1997. *The Odes of Horace.* Bilingual ed. New York: Noonday.

Horiuchi Keizō and Inoue Takeshi, eds. 1958. *Nihon Shōkashū* (Collection of Japanese songs). Iwanami Shoten.

Horkheimer, Max, and Theodor W. Adorno. [1944] 2002. *Dialectic of enlightenment: Philosophical fragments.* Stanford: Stanford University Press.

Horton, H. Mack. Forthcoming. *Tra/versing the frontier: The Silla envoy in Manyōshū.* Cambridge, MA: Harvard University Press.

Hosaka Masayasu. 2003. Sensō no Koshō (Labels for the war). *Mainichi Shinbun,* June 30.

Ikuta Makoto. 1977. *Rikugun Kōkū Tokubetsu Kōgekitaishi* (History of the special attack forces of the Army Air Division). Bijinesusha.

Inoguchi Rikihei and Nakajima Tadashi. 1963. *Shinpū Tokkōtai no Kiroku* (Record of the Shinpū special attack forces). Sekkasha.

———. 1975. *Taiheiyō Senki (4): Shinpū Tokubetsu Kōgekitai* (The Pacific war chronicle, no. 4: *Shinpū* special attack force). Kawade Shobō Shinsha.

Inoguchi Rikihei and Nakajima Tadashi with Roger Pineau. 1953. *The divine wind: Japan's kamikaze force in World War II.* Annapolis: United States Naval Institute; reprint, New York: Ballantine, 1958.

Irokawa Daikichi. 1993. *Wadatsumi no Tomo e* (To my friends perished in the sea). Iwanami Shoten.

———. 2003. Tokkōtai'in Shutsujin Gakutono Shiseikan wo Mitsumete (Concepts of death and life of student soldiers). Dialogue with Emiko Ohnuki. *Sekai* no. 718 (September): 157–65.

Itō Kazuyoshi. 1995. Kumo no Hate no Hayashi Ichizō (Hayashi Ichizō beyond the clouds) In Hayashi Ichizō 1995, 157–63.

Izumi Aki. 1968. About Matsunaga Shigeo and Matsunaga Tatsuki. In Matsunaga Shigeo and Matsunaga Tatsuki 1968, 1–12.

Kaga Hiroko. 1995a. Omoide no Naka no Nakano'o Yoshitake Mura (Nakano'o Yoshitake Village in memory). In Hayashi Ichizō 1995, 175–99.

———. 1995b. Atogaki (Postscript). In Hayashi Ichizō 1995, 201–12.

Kaigun Hikō Yobigakusei Dai-14-kikai, ed. 1966a. *Aa Dōki no Sakura* (The cherry blossoms of the same class). *Honhen* (vol. 1). Mainichi Shinbunsha.

———. 1966b. *Aa Dōki no Sakura* (The cherry blossoms of the same class). *Bessatsu* (vol. 2). Mainichi Shinbunsha.

Kamo Momoki, Kaigun Daijin Kanbō, and Rikugun Daijin Kanbō, eds. 1933–35. *Yasukuni Jinja Chūkonshi* (History of the loyal souls at the Yasukuni Shrine). 5 vols. Yasukuni Jinja Shamusho.

Kant, Immanuel. [1790] 2000. *The critique of judgment.* Translated by J. H. Bernard. New York: Prometheus.

Keene, Donald. 1984a. *Hyakudai no Kakyaku* (Travelers of a hundred ages). *Jō* (vol. 1). Asahi Shinbunsha.

———. 1984b. *Hyakudai no Kakyaku* (Travelers of a hundred ages). *Ge* (vol. 2). Asahi Shinbunsha.

Kelly, John D. 1998. Time and the global. *Development and Change* 29(4): 839–71.

———. 2003 U.S. power, after 9/11 and before it: If not an empire, then what? *Public Culture* 15(2): 347–69.

Kermani, Navid. 2002. A dynamite of the spirit: Why Nietzsche, not the Koran, is the key to understanding the suicide bombers. *Times Literary Supplement,* March 29, 13–15.

Khosrokhavar, Farhad, in collaboration with Paul Vieille. 1990. *Le discourse populaire de la révolution Iranienne.* 2 vols. Paris: Éditions Contemporanéité.

———. 1997. *Anthropologie de la révolution Iranienne, le rêve impossible.* Paris: L'Harmatten.

———. 2001. Neo-conservative intellectuals in Iran. *Critique* no. 19:5–30.

———. 2002. *Les nouveaux martyrs d'Allah.* Paris: Flammarion. Translated as *Suicide bombers: Allah's new martyrs* (London: Pluto Press, 2005).

Kōdansha Sōgō Hensankyoku, ed. 1997. *Nichiroku Nijūseiki* (The daily record of the twentieth century). Vol. 1, no. 22. Kōdansha.

Koshar, Rudy. 1998. *Germany's transient past.* Chapel Hill: University of North Carolina Press.

Leighton, Lauren G. 1985. Romanticism. In Terras 1985, 372–76. New Haven: Yale University Press.

Lilla, Mark. 2001. The reckless mind. New York: New York Review of Books.

Lourie, Richard. 2002. *Sakharov: A biography.* Hanover, N.H.: University Press of New England.

Mainichi Shirīzu Shuppan Henshū, ed. 1981. *Gakuto Shutsujin* (Drafting of the student soldiers). Mainichi Shinbunsha.

Malia, Martin. 1999. *Russia under Western eyes.* Cambridge: Harvard University Press.

Marling, Karal Ann, and John Wetenhall. 1991. *Iwo Jima: Monuments, memories, and the American hero.* Cambridge: Harvard University Press.

Marx, Karl and Friedrich Engels. [1867] 1967. *Capital.* Edited by Friedrich Engels New York: International.

Matsunaga Shigeo and Matsunaga Tatsuki. 1968. *Sensō, Bungaku, Ai: Gakutohei Kyōdai no Ikō* (War, literature, and love: Writings left behind by two brothers who were student soldiers). Edited by Izumi Aki. Sanseidō.

Milosz, Czeslaw. 1953. *The captive mind.* New York: Knopf.

Misa Tokikazu. n.d. Misa Shiryō (no. 4): Ichi Yobi Shikan no Mita Kaigun (no. 2) (Records left by Misa, no. 4: A view of the navy seen by a student officer, no. 2). Handwritten ms.

Miura Hitoshi. 1996. Miyazawa Kenji. In *Kokushi Daijiten* (Encyclopedia of national history), ed. Kokushi Daijiten Henshū Iinkai, 13:840–44. Yoshikawa Kōbunkan.

Morioka Kiyomi. 1995. *Wakaki Tokkōtai'in to Taiheiyō Sensō* (Young pilots of the special attack forces and the Pacific war). Yoshikawa Kōbunkan.

Mosse, George L. [1964] 1981. *The crisis of German ideology*. New York: Schocken.

———. 1975. *The nationalization of the masses*. Ithaca: Cornell University Press.

———. 1988. *The culture of Western Europe*. Boulder: Westview.

Nakao Takenori. 1997. *Tankyūroku* (Record of a spiritual quest: Handwritten diary left by Nakao Takenori, a student who perished in the war). Edited by Nakao Yoshitaka. Fukuoka: Tōka Shobō.

National Council of Churches of Christ in the United States of America. 1962. *The Holy Bible*. San Francisco: Cokesbury (Published by The World Publishing Company).

Nihon Senbotsu Gakusei Kinenkai, ed. [1988] 1995. *Kike Wadatsumi no Koe* (Listen to the voices of the sea gods). Iwanami Shoten.

Nihon Senbotsu Gakusei Shuki Henshū Iinkai, ed. [1949] 1952, 1981. *Kike Wadatsumi no Koe* (Listen to the voices of Wadatsumi). Tōkyō Daigaku Kyōdō Kumiai Shup-panbu. Republished in 1952 by Tōkyō Daigaku Shuppankai.

Ninagawa Jukei. 1998. *Gakuto Shutsujin* (Drafting of student soldiers). Yoshikawa Kōbunkan.

Oguma Eiichi. 2002. *Minshu to Aikoku: Sengo Nihon no nashionarizumu to kōkyōsei* (Democracy and patriotism: Nationalism and the public sphere in postwar Japan). Shinyōsha.

Ohnuki-Tierney, Emiko. 1984. *Illness and culture in contemporary Japan*. Cambridge: Cambridge University Press.

———. 1993a. *Rice as self*. Princeton: Princeton University Press.

———. 1993b. Nature, pureté et soi primordial. *Géographie et Cultures* 7:75–92.

———. 2002. *Kamikaze, cherry blossoms, and nationalisms: The militarization of aesthetics in Japanese history*. Chicago: University of Chicago Press. Translated as *La vera storia dei kamikaze giapponesi: La militarizzazione dell'estetica nell'Impero del Sol Levant* (Rome: Paravia Bruno Mondadori Editori, 2004).

Okano Tayao. [1979] 1995. Iwanami Bunko (The Iwanami series). In *Kokushi Daijiten* (Encyclopedia of national history), ed. Kokushi Daijiten Henshū Iinkai, 1:863–64. Yoshikawa Kōbunkan.

Pape, Robert A. 2005. *Dying to win: The strategic logic of suicide terrorism*. New York: Random House.

Persico, Joseph. 2004. Early warnings: What did he know, and when? *New York Times*, April 18.

Remarque, Erich Maria. [1928] 1996. *All Quiet on the Western Front*. New York: Ballantine.

Sartre, Jean-Paul. 1972. *Plaidoyer pour les intellectuels*. Paris: Gallimard.

Sasaki Hachirō. 1981. *Seishun no Isho: Seimei ni Kaete, Kono Nikki, Ai* (A testament of the youth: Diary and love, in the absence of life). Edited by Fujishiro Hajime. Shōwa Shuppan.

Sasaki, Taizō. 1995. Sasaki Hachirō Tsuioku (Reminiscence of Sasaki Hachirō). *Kōryō* 37 (1): 66-79.

Satō Takumi. 2004. *Genron Tōsei* (Speech control). Chūōkōronshinsha.

Schama, Simon. [1995] 1996. *Landscape and memory*. New York: Vintage.

Smith, G. S. 2003. *D. S. Mirsky: A Russian-English life, 1890–1939*. New York: Oxford University Press.

Takushima Norimitsu. [1961] 1967. *Ikō Kuchinashi-no-Hana: Aisuru Sokoku no Hito-e*

(The writings left behind: The flower without a voice [Cape jasmine])—for the beloved people of my homeland). Edited by Takushima Norijirō. Daikōsha.

Terras, Victor, ed. 1985. *Handbook of Russian literature.* New Haven: Yale University Press.

Tōkyō Daigaku Gakusei Jichikai and Senbotsu Gakusei Shuki Henshū Iinkai, eds. [1947] 1951, 1980. *Harukanaru Sanga ni* (Far-off mountains and rivers). Tokyo Daigaku Shuppankai.

Ugaki Matome. 1991. *Fading victory.* Pittsburgh: University of Pittsburgh Press.

Umezawa Shōzō. 1997. Umezawa Kazuyo. Essay on his late brother. Posted in the exhibition case for his brother at the Yasukuni Shrine in 1997.

Vlastos, Stephen. 2001. Recalling Roosevelt's day of infamy. *Cedar Rapids Gazette,* September 14.

Wada Minoru. 1972. *Wadatsumi no Koe Kieru Koto Naku* (The voices of the sea deity shall not be silenced). Kadokawa Shoten.

Wada Tan. 1972. Ani Minoru no Koto (My elder brother Minoru). In Wada Minoru 1972, 311–21.

Witkop, Philipp. 1929. *German students' war letters.* New York: E.P. Dutton. Originally published in German in 1916.

Wolf, Eric. 1999. *Envisioning power.* Berkeley: University of California Press.

Yamada Ryū. 1997. *Watakushi no Anabaputizumu tono Deai* (An essay on Anabaptism: My encounter with Anabaptism), no. 3.

Yamanouchi Midori and Joseph L. Quinn, trans. 2000. *Listen to the voices from the sea* (*Kike Wadatsumi no Koe*). Scranton: University of Scranton Press.

Yasuda Takeshi. 1967. Kaisetsu "Ikō Kuchinashino Hana" ni tsuite (On the testament "The flower without a voice"). In Takushima Norimitsu 1967, 267–78.

Young, Louise. 1998. *Japan's total empire.* Berkeley: University of California Press.

Yui Masaomi, Fujiwara Akira, and Yoshida Yutaka, eds. [1996] 1989. *Guntai Heishi* (Armies and soldiers). *Nihon Kindai Shisō Taikei,* vol. 4. Iwanami Shoten.

Index

9/11 and Pearl Harbor, xv–xvii, 36, 213n2,
    213–15n4

aesthetic
    beauty, sublimity, and, 18, 20, 30,
        31–33, 75, 99, 110, 143
    of cherry blossoms, xvii–xviii, 22,
        26–30, 37, 49–51, 68–69, 99–100,
        128–29, 193
    of death, 6–11, 22, 50–51, 81, 163,
        169–70, 178–80
    deployed by the military, xvii–xviii, 22,
        26–37, 193
    nationalism and, 22, 26, 28, 30–33, 67,
        116
    nature and, 26–27, 30, 31, 47, 49–51,
        68–69, 86, 99, 109
    patriotism and, 26, 30, 37, 97, 114–15
    purity and, 62, 99–100, 186, 192–93
    study of (aesthetics), 16, 26, 47–51, 105,
        110–11
    tokkōtai and, xvii–xviii

cherry blossoms, xvii–xviii, 39, 91, 122
    aesthetic of, xvii–xviii, 22, 26–30, 37,
        49–51, 68–69, 99–100, 128–29, 193
    emperor and, 69, 181
    nationalism and, 26–33, 181–82
    symbolism of, 20, 87
        personal, 49–51, 68–69, 99–100,
            128–29, 131, 181–82, 192–93
        and the state, xvii, 26–29, 167,
            181–82

Yasukuni National Shrine and, 22,
    28–29, 35, 51, 69, 183
Christianity, 20–21, 136, 146, 154, 164,
    173, 174, 175, 176, 183, 216n10
    belief in, 51, 170, 203
    opposition to war and militarism, 54–57,
        165–68
    patriotism and, 7, 168, 178–79
    "shield" in, 165, 177, 180
    suicide and, 182

death, 4, 87, 158–59, 200–206
    aesthetic of, 6–11, 22, 50–51, 81, 163,
        169–70, 178–80
    agony of, xiv, 22–23, 62–67, 71, 77–78,
        83, 95–96, 132–33, 170, 182, 187,
        210
    inevitability of, xiii–xiv, xvii, 14–15, 17,
        25, 36, 66–68, 77–79, 131–32, 163,
        170, 178
    as meaningless, 1–2, 21, 63, 166–67,
        170–71, 187
defeat, prospect of, 8, 20, 59–60, 88, 92,
    95, 97, 98–99

emperor, 179–80, 194, 196
    cherry blossoms and, 69, 181
    divinity of, 189
    eternal line of, 189, 218n2
    sacrifice for, 6, 27–28, 33–35, 58, 65,
        169–72, 175, 210
        resisted, 51, 61, 68, 163, 170,
            180–81

emperor (*continued*)
  soldiers as shield for, 61, 177, 179–80
  Yasukuni National Shrine and, 28, 69

Fascism
  defined, 215n2
  Liberalism and, 18, 115, 192

higher school (*kōtōgakkō*), 11–15, 215n3
homeland, xv, xvi, 1, 31, 79
  invasion of, xv, xvi, 25, 36, 132, 208
  love for, 6, 20, 22, 30, 56, 97, 101, 131, 157, 186

imperial aggression, opposition to, 56, 59–60, 101, 136, 139–40, 157

kamikaze (*shinpū*). See tokkōtai

Liberalism, 45–47, 76, 138, 139
  Fascism and, 18, 115, 192

Marxism, 16, 17–19, 51, 53–56, 60, 84, 98–99, 215–16n7
  rejection of, 186, 191–93
  Romanticism and, 23–24, 53, 67
militarism
  opposition to, 50, 68, 74, 82, 97, 101, 114–15, 129, 144, 148–49, 157, 161–62
  Christianity and, 54–57, 167–68
  Yasukuni National Shrine and, 28–29
military
  brutality of training in, 3, 4–11, 20, 21, 41, 89, 90–91, 136, 178
  students in, 2–11
  tokkōtai operations, 1, 9–11, 25
  use of aesthetic, xvii, 22, 26–37, 193
misrecognition (*méconnaissance*), 29–30, 31, 67, 139
  nationalism and, 31–33
  patriotism and, 37, 57, 124
  symbolism and, 29–30
  totalitarianism and, 31–32

nationalism, xvii, 57–62
  aesthetic of, 22, 26, 28, 30–33, 67, 116
  cherry blossoms and, 26–33, 181–82

cultural, 30–33, 197–98
  misrecognition of, 31–33
  myths of, xvii, 179–81
  patriotism and, xvii, 18, 30, 55–56, 103, 114–15, 138, 180
  Romanticism and, 30–33, 103, 113, 129–31
  state, 22, 25, 57–59, 157, 188–91, 193–98
nature, aesthetic of, 26–27, 30, 31, 47, 49–51, 68–69, 86, 99, 109
Nazi Germany, 29, 31, 32, 57, 72–73, 115, 123, 139

patriotism, xv, 6–7, 17, 25, 67, 157–58, 198
  aesthetic of, 26, 30, 37, 97, 114–15
  Christianity and, 7, 168, 178–79
  misrecognition in, 37, 57, 124
  nationalism and, xvii, 18, 30, 55–56, 103, 114–15, 138, 180
  Pearl Harbor, 9/11 and, xv–xvii, 36, 213n2, 213–15n4
purity, 51, 210
  aesthetic of, 62, 99–100, 186, 192–93

Romanticism, 15, 19–20, 32, 99, 105–8, 111–13, 161, 216n9
  French, 19, 30, 115–16
  German, 19, 23–24, 30–31, 47, 52, 111, 112, 129–30
  Japanese, 15, 47, 48–49, 63, 99, 137, 148
  Marxism and, 23–24, 53, 67
  nationalism and, 30–33, 103, 113, 129, 130–31

sacrifice, 129, 155, 161
  for loved ones, 57, 58, 61–62, 66, 124, 131, 139, 171
  for one's country, 7, 58, 61, 83, 92, 103, 131, 202
  for the emperor, 6, 27–28, 33–35, 58, 65, 169–72, 175, 210
    resisted, 51, 61, 68, 163, 170, 180–81
self-cultivation (*Bildung*), 16, 100–101
"shield," 60–61, 66
  in Christianity, 165, 177, 180
  for the emperor, 61, 177, 179–80

Shintō, 136, 173–74, 194, 206, 208
  Buddhism and, 35, 166
  Yasukuni National Shrine, 35
soldiers
  brutality in training of, 3–11, 41, 89,
    90–91, 136, 178
  students as, 2–11
suicide, 4, 33–34, 42, 58, 62, 73, 126, 145,
  168, 171
  Christianity and, 182
  contemporary "suicide bombers", xv,
    xvi–xvii, 23–24, 34, 35, 37
  symbolism, xvii. *See also* cherry blossoms;
    misrecognition

tokkōtai, xiv–xviii, 1–2, 4–11
  aesthetic of, xvii–xviii
  coercion and, xvi, 6–9
  contrasted with "suicide bombers," xv,
    xvi–xviii, 33–37
  operations, 1, 9–11, 25

wars, opposition to, 55, 56, 59, 66, 79, 144,
  157–58, 165–68
women
  desire for, 76
  ideal of, 186

  as mothers, 61, 136
  love for, 93, 96, 101, 117–19, 121–24,
    126–27, 132–33, 148, 152–54,
    172–76, 179, 183
  love shown by, 74–75, 104, 112–13,
    116, 129
  support for sons, 164–67, 169–70,
    217n3
  romantic symbolism of, 22, 50, 71,
    94–95, 99, 105–11
  sacrifice for, 61–62, 101
  support for soldiers, 29, 138, 208
  as sweethearts, 61
  intelligence valued in, 101, 114, 142
  love for, 94, 119–21, 124, 127,
    128–29, 141–42, 145–48, 154–55,
    158–60

Yasukuni National Shrine, 22, 28–29, 35,
  51, 166, 183, 203, 204
  cherry blossoms and, 22, 28–29, 35, 51,
    69, 183
  emperor and, 28, 69
  militarism and, 28–29
  Shintō and, 35